ENCOUNTERS
BETWEEN
Judaism
AND
MODERN
PHILOSOPHY

ENCOUNTERS
BETWEEN
Judaism
AND
MODERN
PHILOSOPHY

❁ ❁ ❁ ❁ ❁ ❁ ❁ ❁ ❁

A PREFACE TO FUTURE
JEWISH THOUGHT
BY
Emil L. Fackenheim

BASIC BOOKS, INC., *Publishers*

NEW YORK

© 1973 by Basic Books, Inc.
Library of Congress Catalog Card Number: 72-89177
SBN 465-01969-2
Manufactured in the United States of America
DESIGNED BY VINCENT TORRE
73 74 75 76   10 9 8 7 6 5 4 3 2 1

TO THE ISRAELIS

After darkness, light

רבי טרפון אומר היום קצר והמלאכה מרבה והפועלים
עצלים והשכר הרבה ובעל הבית דוחק.

Rabbi Tarphon said: *The day is short, and the work is great, and the laborers are sluggish, and the wages are high, and the Householder is urgent.*

(Written some time after 70 C.E., the greatest catastrophe in Jewish history prior to the Nazi Holocaust)

ACKNOWLEDGMENTS

Thanks are due to the following for permission to quote from their material:

Random House, Inc., New York and George Weidenfeld and Nicolson, London for the selections from *One Generation After* by Elie Wiesel. © 1965, 1967, 1970 by Elie Wiesel.

New Outlook (May 1967) for the selections from the press conference with J. P. Sartre. *New Outlook*, a Middle East monthly, published at Karl Netter Street 8, Tel Aviv, is devoted to problems of the Middle East and Israeli-Arab relations.

Schocken Books, New York, for the selections from *Anti-Semite and Jew* by Jean-Paul Sartre. © 1948 by Schocken Books, Inc.

Manès Sperber for the selections from "Hourban ou l'inconcevable certitude," *Preuves* (March 1964), Paris. The English version from which the selection was taken appeared with . . . *Than a Tear in the Sea* (New York: Bergen Belsen Memorial Press, 1967).

Several parts of this book have previously been published in somewhat different form. Chapters 1 and 4 have appeared, respectively, in *The Religious Situation 1969* and *The Religious Situation 1968*, D. R. Cutler, ed. (Boston: Beacon Press, 1969, 1968.) Thanks are due to Indiana University Press for permission to incorporate in chapter 2 of this book large sections of chapter 14 of my *Quest for Past and Future* (Bloomington: Indiana University Press, 1968). If these bibliographical data cause the impression that this book is a mere collection of essays, I urge the reader not to overlook the systematic impulse which animates it. That impulse, in a word, is to join together two disciplines—philosophy and Jewish thought—which, for a variety of reasons (mostly good, I still hope) I had found myself forced to hold apart for nearly three decades. Obeying that impulse I consider a demand at this hour in Jewish history.

I have received help from many people. Understanding my purpose, my friends Professors Shlomo Avineri and Michael Meyer have supplied me with relevant recondite material. The members of the I. Meier Segals Institute, meeting for several summer sessions in the Quebec mountains, gave me inspiration, courage and insight. (While

I cannot name individuals, I must single out David Hartman, the guiding spirit of the Institute, and I. Meier Segals, whose generosity made our meetings possible.) Every gathering of the World Federation of Bergen Belsen Associations has increased my strength. Finally, I thank my wife Rose who, I suspect, knew before anyone else that the thinker, no more than the man, can remain neatly compartmentalized forever.

CONTENTS

Contents

Contents

ENCOUNTERS
BETWEEN
Judaism
AND
MODERN
PHILOSOPHY

INTRODUCTION

At high school in pre-Nazi Germany I had a music teacher who loved Johann Sebastian Bach. He taught us Bach chorals. Sometimes he would ask us to sing the words and then, being a meticulous man, he would rarely fail to state that Jews, if so instructed by their consciences, had the right to abstain. On other occasions he would just make us hum the tunes, and then he would let no one abstain. The music, it was his custom to declare, was neither Jewish nor Christian. It was impartial. It was universal. And I, then as now fond of Bach, would gladly join in.

However, my old music teacher was wrong.

Is modern philosophy "universal"? Is it "impartial"? Is it "neither Jewish nor Christian"? One would not wish to question that all great philosophy (like all great music) is somehow universal, nor deny the fact that modern philosophy has striven mightily for impartiality ever since Descartes and Bacon first waged war on the idols of presupposition and prejudice. But has, in this case, general virtue always manifested itself in particular justice? Has modern philosophy been true to itself in being neither Jewish nor Christian?

This common assumption is challenged in the present work. Two disciplines are concerned. One is modern philosophy itself. The other is what, for want of a more accurate term, may be called modern Jewish thought, that is, the critical inquiry into the modern destiny of the Jewish people and its faith.

For modern philosophy, more is involved than the possible need to remove unconscious but accidental prejudice from some limited area such as the philosophy of religion. In a Christian world, uneven justice to Judaism and Christianity would prove modern philosophy guilty of an unconscious parochialism contrary to its own conscious aspirations. What is more, the stake in overcoming this particular parochialism might well be higher than at first sight appears. The foundations of our civilization are Athens and Jeru-

[3]

salem, and philosophy is the critical self-consciousness of a civilization. If one assents to these two propositions one must also charge
modern philosophy with the task of doing to Jerusalem no less a
justice than to Athens. To be sure, ancient philosophy could not
know of Jerusalem, while medieval Western philosophy could only
see an "old" Jerusalem through the eyes of a "new." However,
since modern philosophy transcends these ancient and medieval
limitations, it cannot escape the task of seeing Jerusalem through
her own (as well as through other) eyes. And the persistent failure
to do so would be tantamount to having somehow failed our
civilization as a whole. Thus the maximal stake of modern philosophy in the subject of this book may well be considerable. Even the
minimum stake, however, is simple philosophical integrity.

The stake for modern Jewish thought is nothing less than survival. In premodern times Jewish thought showed a certain
stubbornness to Greek philosophical universalism, which it knew
to be pagan, and to Christian and Muslim religious universalism if
only because they pushed Jewish existence into the limbo of "has
been" or "never was." No comparable stubbornness was shown
when in modern times philosophy (and all its offspring from
physics to psychology and sociology) appeared on the scene. Was
not here, at last, a radically critical and hence truly universal judge
of what *any* man could believe—and hence of what a Jew could
believe? What, however, if this judge too had suffered from parochial bias? In that case, modern Jewish thought erred naively but
gravely when (except for some recent thinkers) it handed Judaism
over to the unilateral criticism of modern philosophy. Indeed,
unless there were a modern recovery of the premodern Jewish
stubbornness, this error would be irreparable and fatal.

The questions raised thus far must remain hypothetical until
they are examined. One question, at least, has already been
answered by historical events. When the men of the French
Revolution emancipated the Jewish people they proposed to give
to Jews "as men" everything, and to Jews "as Jews" nothing. This
proposal had two hidden assumptions. One was that Jews were an
anachronism as Jews, and on trial as men. The other was that the
faith of Jews could fairly be judged, and their humanity properly
be put on trial, by a civilization that had oppressed them for nearly
two millennia.

Modern philosophy, rather than question these two assumptions,
simply accepted them. Kant looked forward to the "euthanasia" of
Jews and Judaism in modern civilization. Marx declared that the
"social emancipation of the Jew" was the "emancipation of society

Introduction

from Judaism." And while all such expressions have become taboo since the Nazi holocaust, the term "Judeo-Christian," as currently used by the Anglo-Saxon philosophical establishment, signifies, not a serious examination of things Jewish, but a mere alteration in the vocabulary.

If modern philosophy failed to question the two assumptions of the Emancipation era, modern Jewry, until quite recently, failed as well. The people failed whenever it took upon itself the arduous but false and fruitless task of being "men abroad," and "Jews," if anywhere, only "at home." Its thinkers failed whenever they appeared before the judgment of modern philosophy without examining the credentials of the judge.

Today, the once hidden assumptions are hidden no longer but visible for all who do not shut their eyes. Moreover, they have proved to be unacceptable. Ever since the Nazi holocaust it is Western civilization that is on trial. And ever since the rebirth of the Jewish people in its ancient land the age-old image of this people as a dead people or a nonpeople has become as absurd factually as, morally and spiritually, it always was.

The people has perceived this absurdity and testifies against it, in Moscow no less than in Jerusalem. For how long can the courage of life put the courage of thought to shame? Modern philosophy must reject the false assumptions of the Emancipation era if it is to preserve its integrity. Modern Jewish thought must reject them if it is to find its way to a modern liberty. To be sure, critical modernity requires it to continue to expose Judaism to modern philosophy. But the same criterion requires it also to begin to expose modern philosophy to Judaism. There may be many paths to future Jewish thought. Not the least of them consists of encounters between Judaism and modern philosophy.

At the time I was humming Bach I also had a rabbi, a good Jewish scholar who loved modern philosophy. Many bar mitzvah lessons were devoted to Spinoza and Kant. He was fond of quoting the biblical promise that Japheth would dwell in the tents of his brother Shem (Gen. 9:27). The Midrash explains that many things Greek (deriving from Japheth) are welcome within Judaism (deriving from Shem). As I heard him, my rabbi went considerably further. Let all modern culture be welcome within Judaism! In particular, let modern philosophy be welcome! Judaism cannot be endangered or destroyed by such hospitality but only enriched.

It was a beautiful vision. One thing, however, was wrong with

[5]

it: to this day, the welcome has not been mutual. Ever since he was given emancipation, Shem has shown unlimited hospitality to his brother. Ever since he gave emancipation, Japheth has acted as though to free a brother were to bury him. For Japheth's as well as his own sake, Shem must recognize and cease to tolerate this fault in his brother. For his own sake as well as that of Shem, Japheth must at long last recognize that his brother is and always has been alive, and must prepare a place of honor for him in his own tent as well.

Chapter 1

ELIJAH AND THE EMPIRICISTS

THE POSSIBILITY OF DIVINE PRESENCE

INTRODUCTION

In the Jewish religious and theological imagination, there is no one to compare to the prophet Elijah. It is Elijah who did not die but rode to heaven in a fiery chariot. It is he who still wanders about on earth, and is the invisible guest during the Passover Seder in every Jewish home. And in the end of days he will become universally visible as no less than the precursor of the Messiah himself.

Doubtless Elijah has this prominent place in large measure because of his celebrated action at Mount Carmel, for this makes him at once universal and unique. Every religious Jew identifies with Elijah's situation at Mount Carmel, for it is the crisis-situation of all Jewish religious existence. Yet no one can identify with his response to that situation, the very thought of which causes fear and trembling.

Elijah confronts the age-old choice between faithfulness to, and betrayal of, the ancient covenant, and he is alone during that confrontation. This is the crisis-situation of every prophet in Israel. It is, moreover, the situation of every Jew in extremis, when, looking around for allies in his desperate struggle for survival in faithfulness, he finds, like Elijah, none but the God of the covenant Himself.

Elijah's situation was universal but his action was altogether unique. In their solitary survival in faithfulness Jews have been forced a thousand times to question their one remaining Ally. But through the more than three millennia of the Jewish faith no other Jew has ever had the staggering recklessness of putting, for the sake of the covenant, the God of the covenant to a single, decisive, win-all-or-lose-all test. The Jewish reader trembles at the thought of Divinity failing the test. His imagination boggles at the fact that Elijah risked the possibility that the heavenly fire would devour the sacrifice of the four hundred and fifty priests of Baal, rather than his own. No wonder no one else ever ran such a risk. Yet to this day the Jewish faith celebrates the one man who

[9]

did. Not accidentally it is Elijah who is expected to return when the final, eschatological choice between faithfulness and betrayal will be made.

Thus does the Jewish religious imagination celebrate Elijah. But if contemporary empiricist philosophers of religion are to be believed, all such celebrating should forthwith be ended by any Jew claiming to be modern, enlightened, and scientifically minded. Ever since John Wisdom's *Gods*[1] began the fashion, these philosophers have mentioned the account of Elijah's action at Mount Carmel as epitomizing what is dated, unscientific, and, indeed, superstitious in mankind's religious heritage. They invoke the story because they view Elijah's action as "an experiment to test the hypothesis that Jehovah and not Baal control[s] the physical world."[2] They dismiss it then without any further thought because, of course, in these scientifically minded days everyone knows that this sort of "experiment" does not work—and never did. Religion in general may or may not have contemporary significance and validity. Elijah's "experiment," at any rate, has none. To these empiricists it is a primitive, magical, superstitious legend from a prescientific, long dead past.

Elijah's "experiment" is hardly buried, and his "God-hypothesis" dies as well. For one critic, if qualified in the light of mature experience, it suffers "death by a thousand qualifications,"[3] and Elijah must be instructed that he risked all for nothing. For another critic, *Adonai*[4] becomes a mere *blik*, a way of viewing the universe,[5] and since presumably Baal is another *blik*, the quarrel at Mount Carmel should have been amicably settled—say, by a majority vote. For yet a third critic, at issue was a policy of behavior only, and Elijah was deficient in logical acumen when he ascribed to *Adonai* an objective reference.[6] Even the most sensitive and sympathetic of the empiricist critics, John Wisdom, cannot save the Elijah at Mount Carmel but only the Elijah of the "still, small voice," and of him he gives an interpretation that bears no resemblance either to the biblical account or to any possible Jewish understanding of it. For Elijah himself, the still, small voice belongs to the God of the covenant, and Elijah calls upon Him to save both the covenant and his own life (I Kings 19:9–14). As Wisdom interprets it, however, it is the voice of the Christian kingdom of heaven[7]—a kingdom that, as here understood, can save neither covenants nor human lives, for it is within the soul alone and nowhere elese. Nor does it seem that there is any need for covenants to be saved. As Elijah understands it, the voice speaking to him is that of the true God sternly opposed to all false gods.

But as Wisdom appears to understand it, the voice dissolves all distinctions between true and false gods. Not accidentally his essay is entitled, not *God*, but *Gods*.

JUDAISM AND EMPIRICISM

Some believers may scorn the lowly empiricist concern with what can be seen, heard, and touched. No Jewish believer can follow so lofty a course. His God does not, like that of some philosophers, dwell in sheer transcendence above the empirical, nor, like that of mystics, in an ineffable inwardness empirically inaccessible. The God of Israel rules neither solely over thoughts nor simply over souls but rather over complete, empirical man, and He can do so only if He is empirically manifest in the world. Moreover, this characteristic, while shared by Judaism with Christianity, is far more inescapable in Judaism. Since Divinity already has manifested itself decisively to him, the Christian can always deny the need for further empirical manifestations: when pressed by embarrassing philosophical critics, he can seek refuge either in the soul within or in heaven beyond. No Jew can escape so easily, if only because for him, unlike for the Christian, the decisive empirical manifestation of Divinity has not yet occurred. For a Jew a divine Presence in the empirical world would lose all substance were it confined to a conveniently remote historical past: divine manifestations must continue to occur, if not in the present, then certainly in the future. It must thus be said that Judaism is vulnerable both to empirical reality and to empiricist philosophy. Indeed, among all religions still extant, quite possibly its vulnerability is unique.

A Jewish thinker is thus unable to evade empiricist criticism. At the same time, he may well wonder whether the need for criticism is all on one side. In encounters between religious faith and philosophical thought it is in any case a thought-provoking question who is to be the judge and who the judged, and a rash enthronement of philosophy is as likely to be uncritical as a rash enthronement of faith. In the present, specific case, there are additional reasons for caution, indeed, for wariness. Even Christians, whose faith is given much attention in recent empiricist thought, have cause to wonder whether the critics have understood what they criticize. A Jew must ask why not a single recent empiricist ever treats Judaism—even biblical Judaism—in its own terms, but only in terms of what the academic establishment refers to as the "Judeo-Christian tradition." He must also ask why, concerning postbiblical Judaism, there is total and universal silence. If it is true that Judaism has a unique empirical vulnerability, is it not conceivable that it may also have found unique ways of responding to this vulnerability? And might empiricist philosophers not have shown an interest in Judaism, for this if no other reason?

It is of course possible that Judaism deserves no philosophic interest in its own right by empiricists. This cannot, however, be taken for granted. For it is also possible that an encounter between Judaism and empiricism would reveal that Judaism has a logic of its own. In that case, the failure of empiricists to confront Judaism, with a view to disclosing its logic, would reflect nothing more than an age-old prejudice, philosophically disguised. Such a result would not overly surprise a Jewish thinker. In the history of Western thought, prejudice against Judaism, sailing under the banner of an objective discipline, is nothing new.

VERIFICATION

One may discount anti-Judaic prejudice when philosophies engage, not in specific examinations of selected religious beliefs, but rather in a universal examination of all such beliefs. This is true of logical positivism, which claims to be, and is, an a priori criticism of religious beliefs without distinction.

Logical positivism is now generally considered untenable in academic philosophic circles. Its fundamental principle is arbitrary, and its fundamental goal unattainable. Except for logical propositions, only verifiable propositions are meaningful within this philosophy, all others—metaphysical, moral, religious—being merely pseudopropositions, i.e., projected feelings. But this principle is itself neither logical nor empirically verifiable, and hence is not a proposition but merely an arbitrary "proposal." Moreover, the main purpose to which this principle is put is to classify all scientific propositions as meaningful, and all metaphysical, moral, and religious propositions as meaningless. But despite great pains no way has been found of both saving all of the first and destroying all of the second.[8]

Such are the troubles of logical positivism. A religious thinker ought not to respond to them with a premature triumphalism. The verifiability proposal may be arbitrary, but still it is widely proposed by scientifically minded secularists. No tenable dichotomy can be established between genuine scientific and spurious religious propositions. The fact still is that many—perhaps most—among the modern-minded are quite sure *that* (if not *how*) the first class of propositions is genuine, and they are at a loss about how to give meaning to the second. For either statements such as "God created the world" are taken as explanations of observable phenomena; but then they are outmoded, mythological, prescientific explanations. Or else they are taken not as statements of fact but as expressions of feeling; but then it is illegitimate to project the feelings upon facts. In short, logical positivism, however dubious philosophically, still powerfully articulates a modern way of life and thought, and it is perhaps as such, rather than as a philosophic argument, that it has always had its power.

Insofar as it articulates one form of modern, scientifically inspired secularism, logical positivism makes two points vis-à-vis all religious faith that would appear to be totally conclusive. One is that the Divine is not among the data of the scientific consciousness, the psychical no more than the physical, for the former include at most *feelings* of a divine Presence, not the Presence itself. The other point is that the Divine cannot be inferred from either group of data as an hypothesis necessary to explain them. "Supernatural" causes of natural effects may have been tolerated in prescientific times. But in modern times they are—even in the case of "miracles" without and "revelations" within—cut off, with the help of Ockham's razor.

These two points bring to light one insight that religious thought cannot henceforth ignore: if (as Jewish and Christian faiths both insist) a divine Presence can and does manifest itself in the empirical world, that Presence is not, in any case, a publicly verifiable phenomenon.

Perhaps this insight is of no serious consequence for religious faith.[9] It is, however, of serious consequence for theological thought. Throughout the Middle Ages it was possible for Jewish (like Christian) theologians to regard revelations as historical facts exactly like any other and, like these, as acceptable on reliable authority. Thus the events at Mount Sinai were accepted on the authority of the six hundred thousand witnesses (too many to be mistaken), while the fact of their presence as witnesses was accepted on the authority of a tradition both unbroken and reliable.[10] No modern Jewish thinker can persist in this line of argument. The modern critical historian will accept even "natural" facts, not on the basis of past authorities but only on the basis of a present, critical reconstruction.[11] As for the modern critical philosopher, he would not accept "supernatural"—but supposedly publicly verifiable—facts even if the troublesome mediation of authorities could be avoided, i.e., if he could project himself backward and be present at the events.

Even the author of the celebrated *Of Miracles* would refuse to accept past miracles, on the grounds that the criterion of their acceptability would have to be not past authority but present experience.[12] The author of *Language, Truth and Logic*[13] quite rightly goes a decisive step further. Were he himself projected into the past, to stand with Moses before the burning bush, he would observe nothing more than an unexplained chemical phenomenon. Were he present at Mount Sinai, he would view the six hundred thousand as prey to a mass-delusion. And if per absurdum he were himself to hear the voice of God he would anxiously repair to the nearest psychiatrist. No conceivable experienced datum— no "miraculous" physical datum without and no "revelatory" psychical datum within—would force him to alter in the slightest these words:

> The theist . . . may believe that his experiences are cognitive experiences, but, unless he can formulate his "knowledge" in propositions that are empirically verifiable, we may be sure that he is deceiving himself. . . . Those philosophers who fill their books with assertions that they immediately "know" this or that moral or religious truth are merely providing material for the psychoanalyst.[14]

Could *any* empirical evidence verify any theistic "knowledge"? Elijah's remains unmentioned in *Language, Truth and Logic*, for to mention him was quite superfluous. Not only did Elijah's "experiment" never happen; it would fail to confirm any God-hypothesis even if per impossibile it *had* happened. To a prescientific mind, to be sure, the descent of a heavenly fire in response to prayer might prove that the prayer had been heard—that "Jehovah and not Baal control[s] the physical world."[15] To a modern scientific mind (and to logical positivism acting as its spokesman), the event in question would be either a coincidence or a case of magic. But magic, as Francis Bacon saw, is the prescientific precursor of technology.[16]

And yet, *did* Elijah at Mount Carmel conduct an "experiment"? And did *any* Jewish believer, however innocent of mature experience (not to speak of modern scientific enlightenment), ever think of Elijah in these terms—and of *Adonai* as a confirmed hypothesis? The empiricists might have asked these questions had they been less predisposed to consider "Old Testament" stories as already superseded religiously by Christianity before modern criticism comes on the scene. Had they taken the drastic step of consulting postbiblical Jewish interpreters, they would have found them inescapable. As the rabbinic Midrash embellishes the story—and Midrash, for all its deceptively simple story form, is profound and sophisticated theology—*Adonai* at Mount Carmel did not perform the miracle of the fire only. First, the bullock intended for Baal refused to move. Next, when the priests of Baal prayed, the whole universe fell silent, lest any sound be mistaken for an answering voice. Third, when Elijah stepped forward, water began to flow from his fingers, filling the trench of his sacrifice. And when the final, climactic event of the fire occurred, it was an unmistakably authentic miracle that no skeptic could pass off as a magical trick. These miracles all occurred, so absolutely conclusive was Elijah's test: yet, according to the Midrash the people nevertheless refused to believe and to turn from their idolatrous ways.[17] So utterly clear, so totally unambiguous is Jewish tradition on two fundamental points—that Elijah's actions at Mount Carmel were not an experiment, and that *Adonai* is not a God-hypothesis.

The empiricists might have reached this conclusion even if they had done no more than ask a simple question about the biblical Elijah himself. What if the heavenly fire had devoured the sacrifice of the priests of Baal rather than his own? We cannot yet ask what Elijah *would* have done. It is, however, already quite clear what he would *not* have done. As the Bible tells the story, Elijah had been zealous on behalf of *Adonai* when the consensus had accepted the evidence favoring Baal. He had been forced to defy the surrounding nations, his own king, his own people, and now stood alone against four hundred and fifty priests of Baal. It is ludicrous to think of Elijah—of all prophets—as joining these priests of Baal on the grounds that their "hypothesis" had been verified.

Sophisticated philosophers have overlooked this fact. No Jewish believer, however unsophisticated, was ever able to do likewise. For whereas the Christian majority may view consensus as a sort of confirmation—at least if its Christianity is innocuous enough to find easy consensus—this particular confusion is one by which Jews are not tempted. If consensus ipso facto confirms a religious faith, then the Jewish faith is always ipso facto falsified. If *Adonai* had ever been a God-hypothesis there would be no Jews.

FALSIFICATION

For all their hasty dismissal of Elijah the empiricists do recognize that, whether or not originating as some simple God-hypothesis, religious faith could not survive as such in mature experience. The facts too obviously indicate that evidence mounts against religious beliefs, yet faith persists. By itself, this fact by no means suffices to lend to faith modern philosophical respectability, and the author of *Language, Truth and Logic* will not waver in his view that it is mere projected feeling. But once a priori disposals of faith are replaced by more open-minded a posteriori investigations, even empirically inclined philosophers are encouraged to consider specific religious affirmations, prepared to accept the possibility that they may have a logic and meaning in their own right.

A group of philosophers sharing this viewpoint was some time ago asked a challenging question. The questioner recognized that faith, if originally falsifiable, in due course resists actual falsification, and that, whereas it still takes good fortune to verify a loving God, it refuses to concede that ill fortune does or can refute it. The divine Father is praised when a child is born; if he dies and the divine Father (unlike the human father) "reveals no obvious signs of concern," His love is not denied but merely considered inscrutable. The questioner asks: "Just what would have to happen, not merely (morally and wrongly) to tempt us but also (logically and rightly) to entitle us to say 'God does not love us' or even 'God does not exist'?" His own answer is that religious faith, originally falsifiable, responds to the threat of actual falsification with a strategy of qualification until, in the end, it becomes in principle unfalsifiable—at the price of loss of all content. The God-hypothesis has died "death by a thousand qualifications."[18]

From the standpoint of Jewish belief, the question is, as it were, admirably crude, in that it blocks any all-too-quick recourse from empirical realities, either to the soul within or to heaven beyond. It is also admirably disturbing. What if more than three thousand years of Jewish stubbornness had indeed remained unrefuted but, unknown to the believers, *Adonai* had become indistinguishable from Baal and, indeed, from nothingness?

But a Jewish thinker must anticipate the philosophers' answers with caution as well as expectancy. Since he is now dealing with selective examinations of specific beliefs, no longer with a priori

[16]

doctrines concerning all religious beliefs, the possibility already mentioned must be reckoned with—that philosophical answers offered, so far as Judaism is concerned, reflects unconscious prejudice.

At least the first of the respondents[19] confirms this fear. One is led by him to expect a religiously impartial philosophical conception of religion, for he will not "defend Christianity in particular, but religion in general [because] . . . you cannot understand what Christianity is until you have understood what religion is."[20] The conception of religion offered, however, has flaws that would have prevented any Jew, or any philosopher ecumenical enough to include Judaism among the religions worthy of serious attention from ever offering it.

What is religion? In the view of the respondent it is a *blik*, a *Weltanschauung*, a way of looking at the world. As such it is empirically both unverifiable and unfalsifiable, and yet not without logical justification. For whereas the insane man has one *blik*, the sane man differs, not by having no *blik*, but rather by having another. To have a *blik*-less reality is impossible, and the religious believer is no more and no less "dogmatic" than the unbeliever.

That this conception is not without merit has been recognized ever since it originated among the post-Kantian German philosophers, and it is, incidentally, puzzling that it is now again offered as though it had not been subject of much discussion. Attention must be focused, however, not on its merits but rather on its difficulties, and on the fact that, unlike the post-Kantians, the present respondent seems unaware of them. Schleiermacher noticed the problem of how to choose between *Weltanschauungen*, and that the choice was not only between a religious and a nonreligious *Weltanschauung*, but also, more seriously, between different religious *Weltanschauungen*. He was not, however, able to solve the problem, for, glory though he did in the plurality of religions, he could escape a thorough-going relativism only through a conscious religious imperialism that made Christianity the "religion of religions."[21] Is an unconscious imperialism at work when the present respondent, far from solving the problem, as much as fails to notice it? Is it being unconsciously assumed that among the properly enlightened there are only two serious options—secularism and a broad-minded Christianity?

But the imperialism, if any, is after all unconscious. In all likelihood the respondent, had he noticed the problem, would accept Schleiermacher's pluralism but reject his imperialism. The basic question is whether religion can be understood as a *blik* at all, or rather, which religions can be thus understood, and on what grounds others are ruled out.

Here a difference between Judaism and Christianity comes to light. Both religions affirm a divine-human covenant in which God as well as man is actively involved. Both affirm a scandal of particularity in the respective divine actions. But whereas the Christian scandal is an incarnate God who died for believers among all peoples—or for all peoples regardless of belief or unbelief—the Jewish scandal includes a relation between the God of all peoples and one particular people. How do the two faiths fare when understood as *bliks?*

The question of whether orthodox Christianity can be rescued by such an understanding we may here leave open. Liberal Christianity, at any rate, can be rescued, for it can be understood as a universally possible *blik*. To understand Judaism as such, however, is quite impossible, for it would then fall apart into two elements that must remain inseparable—a universally possible *blik* of Judaism only accidentally related to the Jewish people, and a Jewish people only accidentally related to the *blik* of Judaism. That this split, which is tantamount to the destruction of the religious significance of Jewish existence, is unavoidable has often been argued both on religious and on philosophical grounds, and a Jewish thinker must confront all serious arguments. But he will not consent to the burial of his people on the strength of a mere definition that would hardly have been advanced if the unconscious model of "what religion is" had not been a liberal Christianity.

A welcome note of biblical realism is struck when the second respondent[22] replies to the question of falsifiability as follows:

The theologian does recognize the fact of pain as counting against Christian doctrine. But . . . he will not allow it—or anything—to count decisively against it; for he is committed by his faith to trust in God.[23]

Early biblical man cries out to God in the immediacy of his pain, even as he praises Him in the immediacy of his salvation. To be sure, even in biblical times Jewish believers, faced as they were with ambiguous and negative evidence, lost this naive immediacy. But no Jewish believer, however defiant about the evidence, can ever be indifferent to it. As for philosophers capable of viewing the Christian "God is Love" as an analytical proposition,[24] these express, if any sort of Christianity, one so unworldly as to be wholly cut off from its Jewish origins.[25]

In striking his note of biblical realism, the second respondent is led to conclusions as applicable to Judaism as to Christianity. Because pain does count against God, faith is not dissipated into "vacuous formulae to which experience makes no difference and which make no difference to life." Because pain does not count decisively against God, faith is not a "provisional hypothesis to be discarded if experience counts against [it]." We are left, the second respondent concludes, with a third possibility—"significant articles of faith."[26]

But just what *are* significant articles of faith that are vulnerable to no experience whatever? This question is answered by a third respondent,[27] who writes as follows:

Does anything count against the assertion that God is merciful? Yes, suffering. Does anything count decisively against it? No, we reply, because it is true. Could anything count decisively against it? Yes, suffering which was utterly, eternally and irremediably pointless. Can we design the crucial experiment? No, because we can never see the whole picture. Two things at least are hidden from us, what goes on in the recesses of the personality of the sufferer, and what shall happen hereafter.[28]

Here at last is a statement that gives content to the insight that biblical faith (whether Jewish or Christian) is neither hypothetical nor indifferent to experience. Indeed, insofar as the statement articulates Christian faith, a Jew can have no quarrel with it, but only ask whether it does not seek refuge from history too speedily, in the soul within or heaven beyond. And even this question a Jew can only ask, for Christians themselves must answer it.

What is not for Christians alone to answer, however, are the philosophical implications of the statement, at least if the impression is given that Jewish faith, insofar as it differs from the Christian, might not lead into a different but philosophically no less legitimate direction. In the "University Discussion" commented on in the previous pages, this impression is given by omission. In other contemporary treatments of the same topic, it is given by well-meant but altogether dubious denials of significant Jewish-Christian differences. Is it really proper to speak of a "Judaic-Christian theism" that is in *total* agreement about "an ultimate, unambiguous *in patria* as well as our present, ambiguous *in via?*"[29] Eschatological empirical verification has become a subject of some interest among recent empiricist philosophers of religion. Might it not have been worth inquiring whether Jewish eschatology, insofar as it differs from the Christian, commands philosophical interest in its own right?

Let us return to portions of the already cited statement:

Could anything count decisively against . . . [the assertion that God is merciful?] Yes, suffering which is utterly, eternally and irremediably pointless. Can we design the crucial experiment? No, because we can never see the whole picture.

It is unlikely that any biblically inspired thought about the suffering of individuals *qua individuals* could take a different turn than is indicated in this passage. Judaism, like Christianity, embraced the belief in a hereafter the moment it focused on individual, as well as collective, human destiny. At the same time, it is of the greatest significance that in Judaism the later eschatological hope for eternity never replaced the earlier hope for future history. The two hopes coexisted. Had Judaism, like Christianity (or a major strain within Christianity) become a religion of the salvation of individual souls, it would have ceased to be the religion of a people. The "point" of this people in history lies in future history, and had future history been replaced by eternity, the Jews, if they survived at all, would have become a community of individuals.

This gives rise to a new dimension to the problem of suffering. Like other men, the Jews suffer apparently pointless pain. Like Christian martyrs, Jewish martyrs suffer because of their faith. But the Jew also exposes himself, his children, and his children's children to suffering, by his mere insistence on Jewish survival. The ultimate "point" of *this* suffering—and a Jew's right and/or duty to expose his children's children to it—can lie only in future history.

How must a philosopher confront this suffering? He must rewrite the previously cited statement, along these lines:

Does pre-Messianic suffering, risked for the sake of a Messianic future, count against the assertion that God is merciful? Either against His mercy or against His power. Does it count decisively against at least one of these? No, and pious Jews both work and wait for the Messiah, even though he hesitates. Can we design the crucial experiment? *Not yet, but circumstances are conceivable which might design it for us. Unlike the Christian eschatological expectation, the Jewish is at least in part falsifiable by future history.*

Sophisticated philosophers have overlooked this possibility at a time when even ordinary Jewish believers are unable to overlook it. After Auschwitz, it is a major question whether the Messianic faith is not *already* falsified—whether a Messiah who could come, and yet at Auschwitz did not come, has not become a religious impossibility.[30]

Falsification is not, in any case, unimaginable. Imagine a small band of Jewish believers as the sole survivors of a nuclear holocaust. Imagine them to be totally certain that no human beings have survived anywhere else, and that they themselves and their children are inexorably doomed. They are not faced with a repetition of Noah's flood but rather with the end of history. Of the destiny of individual souls, the whole picture is not yet in sight. But the whole picture of history is already seen, and it refutes the Jewish eschatological hope concerning it. The suffering of individuals as such may still be given its point. But the suffering to which Jews have exposed themselves by remaining a people is already seen to have been pointless. (This is true at least of suffering radical enough to have remained pointless in pre-Messianic history.) Precisely insofar as it holds fast to history, Jewish faith risks falsification by history.

Is Jewish faith, then, insofar as it is falsifiable, a mere hypothesis, special only in that before the nuclear age actual falsification seemed virtually impossible and in that even now it cannot be anticipated? If so, Judaism would be in this respect, like Pascal's Christianity, a kind of wager, with the bet being on future generations rather than on one's own place in heaven. Yet how is this possible when, unlike Pascal's Christian, no present Jewish generation can expect a personal gain, and when it loses much in such periods as the Crusades and the Inquisition, not to speak of the Nazi holocaust?

Let us return to the example of the survivors of the nuclear catastrophe. Exactly what part of their faith is refuted? That God exists? No. That He loves us? To the extent to which it holds fast to actual history, Jewish faith has in any case long qualified any such sweeping and simplistic affirmation. Some evils in history may be only apparent, such as deserved punishment. Not all historical evils are apparent—history is unredeemed. Jewish faith cannot say why history is unredeemed, why God "hides His face," or is, as it were, temporarily without power, and in any case restrains the Messiah from coming. This does not, however, either refute Jewish faith nor deprive it of content, so long as the promised coming of the Messiah can still be expected. It is this promise, and it alone, that would be falsified by a catastrophic end of human history.

How would a Jewish believer respond to this falsification? He could of course at long last surrender his age-old stubbornness, and accept his faith as having been, all along, a mere hypothesis, now falsified. But then he should have let go of his stubbornness long ago, for the hypothesis had, after all, always been most improbable. The authentic Jewish believer would take a different course. He has in any case spent his life *working* for the coming of the divine kingdom, as well as waiting for it. He would now cite the divine commandment to do this work against God Himself, would refuse to abandon what God either chose to abandon or could not help abandoning, and spend his last hours on earth beating swords into plowshares.

It is a telling proof of anti-Judaic bias that contemporary empiricists treating the subject of the falsifiability of religious faith have wholly overlooked the possibility of citing God against God Himself. This possibility appears even in the New Testament, for Jesus asks why God has forsaken him. In the Jewish Bible the theme is everywhere. Abraham cites God against God. So does Job. So do most of the prophets. Elijah at Mount Carmel would have done likewise had the necessity arisen. What if the heavenly fire had devoured the sacrifice of the priests of Baal, rather than his own? We have already seen what Elijah would *not* have done— accept the "hypothesis" that Baal "control[s] the physical world."[31] It has now emerged what he *would* have done. He would have lamented that, already forsaken by men, he was now forsaken by *Adonai* as well—and continued to do His work, alone.

FAITH AND THE LIMITS OF EMPIRICISM

If the Jewish Messianic hope is in principle falsifiable is it verifiable as well? Not according to the author of *Language, Truth and Logic*. We have guessed his reaction to the Sinaitic revelation. It would be the same to the Messianic redemption. He would observe men beat their swords into plowshares. He would watch them unite in the worship of God. But however he might explain this remarkable change in human affairs—in the ordinary terms of the social sciences, in those of some extraordinary mutation, or even as the long-delayed effect of ancient prophecies that had thus turned out to be remarkably self-fulfilling—he would in no event have recourse to a God-hypothesis. And if per absurdum he should catch himself participating in worship, he would once again repair to the psychiatrist, though this time not so anxiously. In the Messianic age, who could control his feelings of exuberance?

[22]

This behavior suggests that the discourse just completed has lacked in sufficient analysis. Must not the Jewish eschatological expectation be separated into two elements—a hope for future history, and a connection of God with that future? And is not the first of these elements both verifiable and falsifiable, while the second is neither, thus being, by the standards set by empiricism, still meaningless?

This consequence may not hold when "empirical eschatological verification" is geared to the hereafter (not to future history), for we may well then perceive Divinity itself in a transfigured world. But it is mistaken to think that resort to the hereafter can bridge the gulf between faith (whether Jewish or Christian) and empiricism. Not even the most otherworldly Christian can confine the meaning of "God loves man" *wholly* to a realm beyond all present experience. And no empiricist could take the statement at face value even if it were admittedly falsifiable. If no child ever died of cancer, and if "God loves man" were admittedly falsified should this happen, the empiricist would still translate "God loves man" into "I feel secure about certain matters, and the universe justifies this feeling."

Our above discussion concerning the falsifiability of faith, then, does have the merit of disclosing that faith (if biblically inspired) cannot consist of "vacuous formulae to which experience makes no difference and which makes no difference to life,"[32] but this is its limit. As for the central issue between faith and empiricism, so far from disposed of, it is not even touched.

What is that issue? Believer and unbeliever inhabit the same empirical world; but for the believer a divine Presence is manifest—however obscurely and intermittently—in and through that world. The unbeliever (and his empiricist spokesman) recognizes the *feeling* of such a Presence in the believer, and on occasion may even share it; but he denies an *actual* divine Presence. The believer on his part makes the actual divine Presence—not the mere feeling of it—his central affirmation, without which statements such as "God loves man" lose the core of their meaning. For a believer to abandon or suspend this core for the sake of a meeting ground with empiricism is *already* to have entered into alien territory and to have endangered if not destroyed the substance of his faith.

The believer, to be sure, must venture into *some* alien territory, unless he rules out all impartial philosophical criticism. However, the question is whether this can or should be the territory inhabited by the empiricist. One thing, at any rate, is clear. The believer who enters into the empiricist's territory executes, so far as his core commitment is concerned, immediate and total surrender. Consider the case of a prophet addressed by the divine Presence. In the empiricist view, the prophet has *immediately* only a *feeling* of being addressed, and an *actual* divine address is an inference on his part. But, first, since the prophet is aware of no such inference, it must be unconscious, and the modern empiricist is superior to the ancient prophet in making the unconscious conscious. Second, having performed this task he must restate the prophet's message from "Thus saith the Lord," to "I have a feeling of the Lord speaking, and hence make the probable inferences that there is an actual divine speech, and that *Adonai* and not Baal is the speaker." (Having been thus redirected, how long would Elijah hold out against the priests of Baal?) Also, if he is truly radical, the empiricist will cut off the inference altogether, for who in these psychological days requires or tolerates the outlandish hypothesis of an *actual* divine address to account for the *feeling* of being divinely addressed?

The believer does well to hesitate before surrendering so swiftly and totally the core of his faith. The empiricist criticism is, after all, very obvious, and it would be strange if it had never occurred to believers. However, it may well owe its destructive powers to a concealed presupposition, in which case the situation calls not for unilateral criticism but rather for mutual, and mutually critical, exposure. This latter is possible, however, only if, before understanding the biblical faith in alien categories, an attempt is made to spell out the categories in which it understands itself.

Such an attempt was made in recent times by the doctrine of a divine-human encounter, and this, for the present purpose, may be stated with utmost brevity.[33] In a *genuine* divine-human encounter—if and when it occurs—Divinity is *immediately* present to the believer; feelings of such a Presence are a "mere accompaniment to the metaphysical and metaphysical fact of the relation which is fulfilled not in the soul but *between* the I and Thou."[34] When the immediate is feeling *only* (and a divine Presence is merely inferred), there already has been a prior "withdrawal"[35] from the encounter into self-enclosed subjectivity; and when the inference is cut off, the withdrawal is complete.

Empiricism will of course criticize the doctrine of encounter; already disposing of biblical faith as an unconscious and illegitimate inference, it will dispose of the doctrine articulating that faith as merely articulating its vices. But empiricism may in turn be criticized in terms of the doctrine of encounter, as articulating the vice of withdrawal from the present Divinity into mere feeling. The two doctrines, in short, confront each other as articulations of two ways of life and experience, one of which may be called *believing openness*, and the other, *subjectivist reductionism*. The clash between them results in a stalemate.[36]

In this situation, the philosopher, to be sure, will wish to "step outside" both the biblical faith and the doctrine articulating its categories, demanding that a theological "embargo on philosophizing" if any, "be lifted."[37] But he must surely seek equally to step outside subjectivist reductionism (and the kind of empiricism that acts as its spokesman)—unless, that is, he is to cease to be an impartial philosopher and become a mere partisan. What territory, then, may he *step into*, as being, in the situation, adequately philosophical?

This question may momentarily be suspended, for at least one claim made in behalf of divine-human encounters is untenable by *any* philosophical standard. One recent philosopher makes the believer say, "You couldn't have these experiences and at the same time sincerely deny God's existence."[38] Another invokes certain Protestants' claims to a *"self-authenticating* direct awareness of God."[39] If to assert an immediate divine Presence is ipso facto to assert an infallible human experience of such a Presence, then the doctrine is, in toto, untenable.

This may be shown by merely pointing to the fact of serious but conflicting religious claims, or to the more exotic varieties of religious enthusiasm, not to speak of madness taking itself for prophecy. In the present context, which is geared to the conflict between faith and empiricism, we do better to remain with the example to which we deliberately keep returning—that (to put it more cautiously than hitherto) the author of *Language, Truth and Logic could* regard the Sinaitic experience as a mere subjective feeling, even if he himself had shared in it. Far from *unable* "sincerely [to] deny God's existence"—or, perhaps more appropriately, His Presence—he would be lacking in philosophical integrity if he did not at least question it. All religious claims to self-authenticating experiences are at best lacking in sufficient analysis.

The question is, however, whether to assert the possibility of an immediate divine Presence is ipso facto to claim infallibility for a human experience of such a Presence. Here the empirically minded philosophical critic would do well to turn to the Jewish author of the doctrine of encounter, rather than to the use made of that doctrine by Protestant theologians.[40] A self-authenticating religious experience could escape the aforementioned difficulties, if at all, only if it were the comprehensive experience, such as the Easter that conquers all discord; and even then it will hardly be claimed except by such Protestants as find all believing individuals equidistant to the Christ. For a Jew, however, the divine Presence is not (or not yet) comprehensive, but rather bound up with the fragmentariness of history; nor are all believers equidistant to it, for not all are prophets—and prophecy has ceased.[41]

Even about prophets the Jewish author of the doctrine of encounter writes as follows: "The false prophets make their subconscious a god, whereas for the true prophet their subconscious is subdued by the God of truth."[42] This remarkable statement has three important implications for the present purpose. First, the false prophet, no mere charlatan, is as sincere as the true; hence since he is sincere and yet false, the prophetic experience is not self-authenticating. Second, the true prophet, while recognizing the sincerity of the false, yet bears witness to his falsehood; hence he *knows* that the prophetic experience is not self-authenticating— that he himself runs the risk of being false. Third, the modern doctrine of encounter (if not the prophet whose faith it articulates) knows that all prophets might in principle be false—that, if sufficiently psychoanalyzed, the subconscious *might* emerge as the source of all gods. (And is the prophet himself, however innocent of modern subjectivist reductionism, *totally* unaware of this possibility? Jeremiah staked more on the heart than any other prophet, yet knew that "the heart is deceitful above all things, and exceeding weak." [Jer. 17:9])

These implications are of great moment in two respects. First, if even prophetic experiences may be false, a faith permeated with this knowledge will hardly stake all on piecemeal experiences accessible to ordinary individuals. Rather than wait for philosophers to point out "the immense possibilities of misreading the experience,"[43] to cope with at least some of these will be part of its own life, and in so coping it will structure piecemeal experiences and affirmations into a whole. (Thus even biblical Judaism searches, however inconclusively, for criteria for distinguishing between true and false prophecies. In postbiblical Judaism it is held that there are no more prophets in the pre-Messianic age, and that until then it is hazardous to affirm divine voices wholly unconnected with the past.)

Second, if the subconscious *may* be the source of *all* gods, the modern doctrine of encounter cannot dispose of this possibility by merely pointing to *some* (prophetic or modern) experiences, for these would then have to be, after all, self-authenticating. It must, rather, make an absolutely vital distinction between experience and faith. This distinction is hardly absent in biblical faith itself, for the psalmist does not lose faith when he fails to "see" and "hear" (when God "hides His face"), and the idolater (or rebellious Israel) may hear and see and yet refuse to believe. As for the doctrine of encounter, it is unintelligible without this distinction. There is no faith when there is actual hearing but no listening, when "withdrawal" dissipates what is heard into subjective feeling. And there already *is* faith when there is listening openness while yet no voice is heard; and when a voice once heard has fallen silent faith can remain faith, waiting in an "eclipse of God"[44] for a divine voice to be heard.

For the philosopher confronted only with this much of faith (and of the doctrine of encounter articulating it), the question arises of how he may "step outside" both, with a view to a critical appraisal. It is a most difficult question. If he takes faith (or the doctrine of encounter) as it takes itself he does not step outside it and can furnish no philosophical appraisal. If he takes it in any terms other than its own, he may well a priori interpose alien criteria between the divine Presence and the believer, thus ruling out the divine Presence by an arbitrary fiat. The question, in fact, is difficult (and complex) enough to transcend wholly the context of the present discourse.[45] Within that context, however, one is led at least to a negative conclusion—that in order to appraise impartially either biblical faith or the doctrine of encounter a philosopher must shed every trace of empiricism.

Consider the following example. The recent work already cited (which is sufficiently critical of subjectivist reductionism to give the doctrine of encounter a serious examination) outlines this program for philosophically coping with "the immense possibilities of misreading the experience."[46] The philosopher must

. . . step outside the felt experiences themselves and consider reflectively the pros and cons of each. . . . The sort of reflection necessary . . . is not speculation in the grand sense. It is the clarifying, sharpening and testing of the analogies used by people in speaking of their experiences, the examining of the logic of words like "self-authenticating" in their various contexts . . . , and not least the honest and *imaginative* consideration of views like that of Freud and the Freudians.[47]

Whatever else such reflection may achieve, it will apparently be competent wholly to settle "the preliminary but important question, 'Am I or am I not in personal contact with someone'?"[48]

[27]

The statement bristles with misunderstandings, all traceable to empiricist prejudice. To affirm even the possibility of an immediate divine Presence is already to stand within the circle of faith; to begin with mere felt experiences is already to have stepped outside that circle and to rule out by initial fiat any possible immediate divine Presence. To do justice to the claim of faith (and of the doctrine of encounter), the philosopher must step outside its circle to appraise it impartially; yet of such an appraisal empiricism (at least the kind dealt with in this chapter) is in principle incapable.[49] We have seen that it is Protestant bias that induces certain theologians to affirm self-authenticating experiences. We now see that it is empiricist bias that makes certain proreligious philosophers fasten on to this claim, for it is with the help of such claims alone that the antireligious, reductionist empiricist can become a proreligious empiricist. This strategy, however, is futile. For it is quite safe to predict before this proreligious empiricism has performed its "clarifying, sharpening and testing" activities, that no experience will ever be found that might not be preyed on by some Freudian or other reductionists.

The true datum furnished to philosophy by biblical faith (and the doctrine of encounter) is not self-authenticating experiences but rather a faith open to an immediate divine Presence. (On its part, unbelief is capable of treating all experiences so as systematically to deny any such Presence.) To cope with this datum (insofar as philosophy turns out to be capable of doing so), requires not the "piecemeal examination" either of experiences or of their linguistic expression, but rather a far "grander" metaphysical speculation than is possible for empiricism. Is an immediate divine Presence compatible with experience as modern thought understands it? If compatible, on what grounds is it claimed, and what is its content? Any one of these questions exceeds the grasp of empiricism.

Yet such is the naive trust of the empiricist in his empiricism (and in the logical analysis that has become his highly prized tool) that he shows no awareness of its limitations. "Am I or am I not in personal contact with someone?" It is by no means certain that *any kind* of philosophy can answer this question, and philosophy may well have to content itself with the task, difficult enough, of merely stating the question in all its ramifications. It is quite certain that it is no mere "preliminary" question, and that no simple semantic inspection of analogies and the like can hope to settle it. The question, in fact, is ultimate for faith itself and is answered by it only in fear and trembling. This must surely have been so even in ancient times, at least in periods when God "hid His face." For modern faith (and the doctrine of encounter, which articulates faith, both modern and ancient), the fear and trembling are inescapable. No modern believer could affirm an immediate divine Presence except in total awareness of the subjectivist reductionism that surrounds him on every side; and when he affirms an "eclipse of God" he knows the risk implied in the rejected alternative—the possibility that his present failure to experience a divine Presence evidences, not an obstacle interposed between man and God, but rather the final end of a millennial illusion.

Is then no bridge discoverable between the two circles emerging from the present discourse: a subjectivist reductionism articulated by empiricism and a believing openness to a divine Presence, articulated by the doctrine of encounter? The believer, all along aware of subjectivist reductionism, embraces that position not when he ceases to hear but when he turns away from listening. The unbeliever, too, may turn. Such a turn may or may not require an experience; if it does, it will be a *turning* experience. For the author of *Language, Truth and Logic* to *accept* the voice heard at Mount Sinai—or his urge to worship in the Messianic age—he would have to be converted. But conversion is both a turning and a being turned.

According to Jewish legend Elijah will come before the Messiah and perform a number of necessary tasks. Of these, the first is most necessary. It is to turn all men to the one God.[50]

EPILOGUE

The Day of Atonement is the holiest day in the Jewish liturgical year. Its theme is turning—turning away from false ancient gods without and false modern gods within to the direct presence of *Adonai*, the Lord of the covenant.

The holiest moment of the holy day is the last. In that moment, the congregation reaffirms an ancient affirmation, first made by their ancestors in response to Elijah's test: "Adonai, He is Lord." (1 Kings 18:39)

Chapter 2

ABRAHAM AND THE KANTIANS

MORAL DUTIES AND DIVINE COMMANDMENTS

INTRODUCTION

To this day Jews call on the God of Abraham, and with good reason, for great was the faith of the ancient patriarch. It was great when he obeyed the divine call to leave his country, saying, "I am ready to go whithersoever Thou sendest me."[1] It was greater when, while Sarah laughed, he trusted in the divine promise of a son for his old age. His faith was greatest of all during the *Akedah*[2]—the sacrifice of Isaac. In obeying the divine command he repressed parental love, suspended all he knew of divine justice and mercy, and even renounced all reliance on the divine promise: the nations would not, after all, be blessed in his seed. Thus, in the pure love of God, he set out for Mount Moriah, on the longest journey of his life. No wonder Abraham is the father of all sons of the divine-Jewish covenant. No wonder that covenant was given, and will be sustained to the end, on account of his merit. For, as the Midrash has it, of the horns of the ram Abraham sacrificed in place of Isaac, one was blown by God at Mount Sinai, and the other, somewhat larger, will be blown to usher in the Messianic days.[3]

Such is traditional Jewish reverence for Abraham. But if Immanuel Kant is right, there must be an end to this reverence. In a minor but significant treatise on faith and reason, Kant deals with the *Akedah*, and he briefly but uncompromisingly condemns Abraham. Unlike some empiricists treated earlier in these pages,[4] Kant does not hold that divine voices are all illusory, nor that no man should ever obey them, and this despite his view (contrasting with that of other empiricists[5]) that they must always be objectively uncertain. Kant's charge is that the particular voice that sent Abraham to Mount Moriah must necessarily have been false.

According to the Midrash, it is Satan who warns Abraham against trusting the supposedly divine voice, saying, "The Lord would not do unto man such an evil, to command him, 'Go and slaughter thy son,' and Abraham displays firmness and faith when he resists the temptation.[6] According to Kant, however, it is moral conscience that speaks in this vein, and Abraham shows moral obtuseness which he fails to obey or even hear it.

Abraham should have replied to this putative divine voice: "That I may not kill my good son is absolutely certain. But that you who appear to me are God is not certain and cannot become certain, even though the voice were to sound from the very heavens." . . . [For] that a voice which one seems to hear *cannot* be divine one can be certain of . . . in case what is commanded is contrary to moral law. However majestic or supernatural it may appear to be, one must regard it as a deception.⁷

Who could disagree with Kant? Who at this late date could conceivably side with the Midrash against him? What modern Jew could possibly fancy himself hear what Abraham heard and *not* reject it? But alas, if one takes this view it seems that Abraham is a blind idolater—if not a murderer.

One may protest that this does not follow; that, after all, Abraham "rose to ethical monotheism" in the end, and that the story of his struggle symbolizes a stage in the evolution of the religious consciousness. The case, however, is not so simple. For to accept the evolutionary view is, first, to dismiss Abraham (who learned only after a harrowing experience a nowadays altogether banal truth). Second, it is to dismiss Jewish tradition when it exalts the *Akedah;* and third and crucially, it is to remain totally perplexed by the fact that the same tradition that exalts the *Akedah* as manifesting the pure love of the true God unequivocally condemns human sacrifice as an abomination to this same God.

If Kant's attack on Abraham confounds the modern Jew, Kierkegaard's defense does little to reassure him. Kierkegaard's general position is anti-Hegelian. His *Fear and Trembling,*⁸ however, is best understood as a sort of anti-Kantian Kantianism, for the Abraham pictured in that work is as if designed to meet the Kantian criticism. Both thinkers place Abraham above history, for the one assumes that the patriarch knows "the ethical," and the other criticizes him as though he *should* have known it. Moreover, in both cases Abraham is pictured as understanding the ethical in terms of its universality, and this lends it what Kant calls "absolute certainty." Finally, both thinkers make Abraham recognize that, in Kierkegaard's language, an "individual" (or in Kant's language, an "empirical") divine voice must always remain "objectively uncertain." Yet against this common background, Kierkegaard's Abraham opposes the Kantian criticism. And what makes him do so is his realization that the divine voice speaks *immediately* to him, or rather, *claims* to, and that he is forced to

[34]

face up to this claim even if he should eventually be obliged to reject it.

How can Abraham face up to this claimed immediate address? Not, as Kant would have him do, by testing the putative divine voice in the light of universal, ethical standards, for this involves the prior rejection of its claim to immediacy. He can respond to the claim *to* immediacy only *in* immediacy, that is, through a commitment wholly bereft of the mediation of universal, ethical standards. No wonder Kierkegaard's Abraham is lonely; and the loneliness is terrifying because the command is not merely extra-ethical but contrary to the ethical—not to speak of parental love.

Kierkegaard's Abraham faces an ultimate religious dilemma. Is ethical universality absolute? But then God a priori can *never* immediately speak to a man, the ethical is itself divine, and any other God becomes unnecessary and impossible. Or can God single out an individual for an immediate relation? But then He may now demand Isaac's sacrifice, thus teleologically suspending the ethical. Abraham cannot escape from this dilemma into some third alternative but must make an existential decision, and this will make him either a murderer or what Kierkegaard calls the "knight of faith." "Either there is a paradox, that the individual as individual stands in an absolute relation to God, or Abraham is lost."[9]

Can a Jew find comfort in Kierkegaard's Abraham? If this first of all knights of faith is radically lonely so is every other knight after him, for the ethical, in fact teleologically suspended in Abraham's case, is potentially suspended in every other. But a Jew dare not ignore that the Torah relates men to each other even as it relates them to God—and that the same tradition that exalts the *Akedah* abhors human sacrifice. Nor can a Jew accept Kierkegaard's original knight of faith, i.e., his Abraham himself. This latter's "absolute relation to the Absolute"[10] has isolated him from every human contact, and he must be silent of his purpose even to Isaac. The Midrashic Abraham, in contrast, communicates with Isaac, and Isaac shares his father's purpose. The two are at one in the love of God.

Let us for the present renounce Abraham. Traditionally the *Akedah* may initiate the divine-Jewish covenant, yet far more central is the covenant itself, and there is no prima facie reason why it might not satisfy both the Kierkegaardian demand for an immediate divine-human relation and the Kantian demand for conformity with moral law. (Incidentally, the same might be said of the Noahidic covenant,[11] which precedes that at Sinai.) Why might not God single out individuals or groups for purposes in no way contrary to moral law? If this were possible, our loss even of Abraham would not be total. In bidding the patriarch to leave his country, or giving him a promise concerning his descendants, God assuredly singled him out. Yet no teleological suspension of the ethical was involved. Only the *Akedah* would be lost.

Yet neither Kant nor Kierkegaard permits this avenue of escape. Kierkegaard grants that moral duty may be referred to God, and indeed holds that it *becomes* duty by being so referred. He denies, however, that what is thus constituted is a relation to God.

It is a duty to love one's neighbor, but in performing this duty I do not come into relation with God but with the neighbor whom I love. If I say then in this connection that it is my duty to love God, I am really only uttering a tautology, inasmuch as "God" is in this instance used in an entirely abstract sense as the Divine, i.e., the universal, i. e., duty. . . . God becomes an invisible vanishing point, a powerless thought, His power being only in the ethical which is the content of existence.[12]

The individual stands in an *actual* relation to God only if it is an *absolute* relation, and in this the ethical is potentially, if not actually, suspended. Hence every genuine believer shares "absolute isolation"[13] with Abraham. Hence any knight of faith "in the solitude of the universe never hears any human voice but walks alone in his dreadful responsibility."[14]

Kierkegaard's uncompromising individualism clearly contrasts with the Christian as well as the Jewish faith, at least whenever authentic communal existence is achieved by it. Why then should Kierkegaard have embraced it? Religiously, one may have to look to his personality and to the conditions of his time. Philosophically and theologically, one must once again look to Kant and view Kierkegaard as a response to Kant. We have stressed that in his treatise Kant does not deny outright the possibility of "empirical" divine voices. We must now add that the main body of his moral and religious doctrine makes it clear that this is after all no serious concession. The source of moral commandment consists not of divine voices without but rather of self-legislating reason within, and one is obliged not to regard laws as moral because God has given them, but rather to attribute them to God because they are intrinsically moral, i.e., apart from all God-givenness. But if this is the case, does one, in performing one's duty—including that of loving God—"come into relation with God?"

It thus emerges that it is Kant and not Kierkegaard who poses the essential challenge. He forces a modern Jewish thinker to ask: can a law be at once moral and the direct and immediate will of God? Can one accept it at the same time as a moral duty and divinely revealed? Or is, perhaps, radically considered, a revealed morality nothing less than a contradiction in terms?

ON THE REVEALED MORALITY OF JUDAISM[15]

At one time, the foregoing questions would have seemed preposterous to uncritical religious believers, and even critically minded philosophers would have seen no need to ask them. Today, they have become part of the fabric even of popular religious thought. Most popular moral and religious tracts do not so much as mention Kant's name. Indeed, even present-day academic moral philosophy pays little attention to him. Nevertheless, on the question of the possibility of a revealed morality, it is Kant who breaks new ground, and all subsequent modern thought stands consciously or unconsciously under his shadow.

A modern Jewish thinker concerned with the revealed morality of Judaism does not therefore engage in a mere antiquarian exercise if he brings about a confrontation between Kant and Judaism. He asks vital and inescapable questions, and in asking these questions he does far better to confront Kant himself than any of the epigones.

The question we ask is: taking Judaism as our example of a revealed morality and Kant as our guide in moral philosophy, must the moral characteristics of a religious law or commandment clash with the manner in which it is revealed? We say "must clash." For that a clash is possible must be taken for granted, and one need not be either modern or a philosopher to recognize this possibility. Kant teaches that human behavior falls short of true morality if it is motivated solely by fear of heavenly punishment or the hope of divine reward. An ancient rabbi said: "Be not like servants who serve their Master for the sake of reward, but be like servants who serve their Master without thought of reward, and let the awe of God be upon you."[16]

Pre-Kantian Philosophy and the Revealed Morality of Judaism

Philosophy has always questioned revelation in general and revealed morality in particular. But no philosopher prior to Kant found it necessary to ask whether all revealed morality might be less than moral simply by virtue of its being revealed. The question of whether all revealed morality, strictly considered, might be a contradiction in terms is a question that was not asked.

This may be shown by a brief review of the most radical objection to revealed morality made by pre-Kantian philosophy on grounds of morality alone. Theologians often claim that revelation is the sole source of our knowledge of moral law. Philosophy has almost always been forced to reject this claim. For to be obligated to any law, a man must be able to know that law; and to qualify as moral, a law must be universally obligatory. But on the admission of theologians themselves, revealed moral law is accessible only to those who possess the revealed Scriptures. It will be noted that this objection by no means amounts to a rejection of revealed morality. It is merely a threat of rejection, unless a certain demand is met. The demand is for an independent, universally human access to moral law, in addition to revelation.

Can Judaism meet this philosophical demand? One's first resort would be to the general Noahidic revelation, which, unlike the revelation at Mount Sinai, is given to all men. But this can satisfy the philosopher only if he can exact a further concession. The Noahidic revelation—if one chooses to retain this term—must be accessible without a scripture, for the Noahides have none. It must be a universal human capacity—just what the philosopher has called reason all along.

Traditional Judaism may have misgivings about this concession. If pressed, however, it will concede. For it must then, itself, distinguish between moral revealed laws that "had they not been written by God, would have had to be written by men," and nonmoral revealed laws, "to which Satan and the Gentiles object."[17] But if, except for divine action, men would have *had* to write moral law, they must be *able* to write it. And if the Gentiles—who object to nonmoral revealed law—do not object to moral revealed law, they must have written or be able to write at least some of it.

This clarifies sufficiently for the present purpose the relation between Jewish revealed morality and philosophical morality, as set forth prior to Kant. However loudly and lengthily the two moralities may quarrel about the content of morality, they have

[38]

no necessary quarrel concerning its foundations. The philosopher has no moral reason for objecting in principle to a morality resting on revelation. And the Jewish thinker has no religious reason for objecting in principle to a morality resting on reason. What is more, this mutual tolerance concerning the foundations of morality produces opportunities for settling conflicts concerning its content as well. This is attested to by a long line of Jewish rationalists who believed that, since the same God was the creator of human reason and the giver of the Sinaitic revelation, the discoveries of reason and the teachings of Judaism could be in no genuine conflict.

The Revolutionary Kantian Thesis of Moral Self-Legislation

This peaceful coexistence was upset by a thesis advanced by Kant, first prominently stated in his *Groundwork of the Metaphysics of Morals* (1785). Kant himself recognized that his thesis was both crucial and revolutionary; he held that previous moral philosophy did not contain it, and that, because of this failure, it had failed as a whole. Kant also recognized the revolutionary implications of his thesis for revealed morality. Indeed, this is a theme to which he kept returning, as if unable to leave it alone. In a passage exemplary for our purpose Kant writes that if the will is moral, then:

[the will is] ... not merely subject to the law, but is so subject that it must be considered as also *making the law* for itself and precisely on this account as first of all subject to the law (of which it can regard itself as the author). ... We need not wonder, when we look back upon all previous efforts made to discover the principle of morality, why they have one and all been bound to fail. Their authors saw man as tied to laws by his duty, but it never occurred to them that he is subject only to *laws which are made by himself* and yet are *universal,* and that he is bound only to act in conformity with a will which is his own but has as nature's purpose for it the function of making universal law. For when they thought of man as merely subject to a law (whatever it might be), the law had to carry with it some interest in order to attract and compel, because it did not spring from *his own* will: in order to conform with the law his will had to be necessitated by *something else* to act in a certain way. This absolutely inevitable conclusion meant that all the labor spent in trying to find a supreme principle of morality was lost beyond recall; for what they discovered was never duty, but only the necessity of acting from a certain interest.[18]

But this, Kant concludes, is at best only an impure morality. An externally compelling or cajoling law must necessarily be heteronomous or impure so far as moral motivation is concerned. To be pure, a moral law must be autonomous, or self-imposed.

We must be sure to grasp the essence of the Kantian thesis. It is by no means the mere assertion—which, as we have seen, is far from new—that in order to be morally obligatory, a law must have a universality enabling all men to know it. Kant would have thought this condition satisfied by those ancient moralists who identified the moral law with the law of the universe, or by their present-day heirs who identify it with the laws of mental health. The essence of the Kantian thesis is that neither of these laws, however universal, can by itself obligate a man to obedience; they can do no more than promise happiness or mental health as the reward of obedience, and threaten unhappiness or neurosis as the punishment of defiance. This is because both laws confront man only from without. They are not imposed by man himself. A law that cannot unconditionally obligate may be prudent, wise, or beneficial, but it cannot be moral. According to Kant, then, there may be much that can induce us or force us to obey. But no law in heaven or on earth can obligate us to obey unless we accept ourselves as obligated to obey. And unless we can *accept ourselves* as obligated we cannot *be* obligated. Once clearly identified, the Kantian thesis seems very nearly irresistible.

It poses, however, an unprecedented challenge to every revealed morality, regardless of content, and simply by virtue of its being revealed. If in order to be moral a law must be self-imposed, not imposed from without, then how can a law given or imposed by God have genuine moral qualities? Pre-Kantian moral philosophy, as was seen, could accept revealed morality conditionally. Kant's moral philosophy threatens it radically. It does so at least if revelation is either a gift from without—the gift of a God *other* than man—or not revelation at all.

Kant's Moral Theology

According to one popular interpretation of Kant's thesis, the will, in imposing moral law on itself, *creates* that law. Moral law is the collective creation of Spirit in man; and only because it is such a creation is it moral at all. In rising to the life of morality, man actively transforms his own being in the light of ideals that are themselves a creative product of Spirit in man. All true morality is creative simply by virtue of being truly moral. And all passive submission, no matter to whom or what, is less than truly moral simply *because* it is passive submission.

Philosophers who accept this version of the Kantian thesis must reject in principle all revealed morality radically, unequivocally, and immediately. To them, such a morality must be at worst a mere passive submission to the whims of an alien Deity. Even at best, it is just a creative morality that fails to recognize itself for what it is, for it mistakes its own creation for a passively received gift. And by virtue of this mistake it still falls short in some measure of the ideal morality.

But it is a matter of great importance that this version of the Kantian thesis is decidedly not Kant's own.[19] Kant does not assert that Spirit in man—and certainly not the *human* spirit—creates moral law; he emphatically denies it. And his denial dramatizes his conviction, often stated by Kant himself but frequently overlooked by his interpreters, that in order to impose moral law on himself, man need be neither its individual nor its collective creator. He need be capable only of appropriating a law, which he has not created, as though he *had* created it. The attacks of "creative morality" on revealed morality are doubtless not without merit and deserve to be considered in an appropriate place.[20] In the present context, however, they are best ignored.

Unlike these attacks, Kant's own doctrine does not rule out revealed morality from the start. For if the moral will need only appropriate, and not create, moral law, why might it not be prima facie possible for it to appropriate a law given by God? This, however, seems possible only prima facie. While not ruling out revealed morality from the start, Kant's doctrine deeply threatens it in the end. Indeed, this threat is in one respect more dangerous than that of the "creative morality" philosophies. These philosophies, which reject revealed morality on the basis of criteria external to it, invite a similar treatment from the defenders of revealed morality. This is not true of Kant, who takes revealed morality in its own right with a considerable degree of seriousness before he questions it radically.

Kant does not rule out revealed morality from the start: his moral will does not create moral law. Yet he threatens that morality in the end, for his moral will must act as though it were the creator of moral law. This Kantian assertion confronts the believer in a revealed morality with a grave dilemma. Either he concedes that the will can and must impose the God-given law upon itself (but then its God-givenness becomes irrelevant in the process of self-imposition and appropriation) or he insists that the God-givenness of the law does not and cannot become at any point irrelevant (but then the will cannot impose the law on itself; it can only submit to it for such nonmoral reasons as trust in divine promises or fear of divine threats).[21]

Kant himself perceives this dilemma with the utmost clarity, but for him it is not a dilemma. In his view, the religious man must choose between what Kant terms, respectively, "theological morality" and "moral theology." But to choose moral theology is to gain everything and to lose nothing.

The religious man chooses theological morality when he accepts laws as moral because they are the will of God. In so doing he not only submits to an alien law, but he submits to it because it is alien. Hence he cannot impose that law upon himself; he can obey it—if obey it he must—because of its external sanctions alone.[22] Theological morality is, and must be, heteronomous morality.

The religious man can rise above such heteronomy only if he embraces moral theology. He then does not accept laws as moral because they are the will of God, but rather ascribes laws to God because they are intrinsically moral, and known to be so, quite apart from the will of God. It is because the human will is capable of recognizing their intrinsic morality that it can impose laws upon itself and thus achieve moral autonomy. This achievement, however, is bought at a price. In imposing moral laws on itself, the will need not and, indeed, cannot pay heed to their God-givenness. The same act that appropriates the God-given moral law reduces its God-givenness to irrelevance.

One might therefore well ask why Kant's religious man, when achieving moral autonomy, should still *be* a religious man. Why should he end up with moral theology rather than with morality pure and simple? What necessity is there for ascribing the moral law to divine authorship, and what is the function of this ascription?

In view of the fact that Kant defines religion as the "recognition of our moral duties as divine commandments"[23] this is a question of considerable importance. It is, however, too complex to be treated in the present limited context, for on some occasions Kant sounds as if he wishes to identify the voice of moral duty with the voice of God, thus dissolving the distinction between morality and religion,[24] while on others he seems to say that the ascription of moral law to divine authorship is a mere fiction, albeit useful or even inevitable;[25] and on yet other occasions—and these would seem most adequately to reflect his considered doctrine—he views religion as both an extension of morality and a truth in its own right.[26] Even on this last-named view, however, the God-givenness of a moral commandment becomes inessential in the act of human appropriation, and this is why, with Kant—not Hegel—in mind, Kierkegaard quite rightly asserts that "in performing . . . [the duty to love my neighbor] I do not come into relation with God but with the neighbor whom I love. . . . 'God' is in this instance used in an entirely abstract sense as the divine, i.e., the universal, i.e., duty."[27] On his part, Kant leaves the question of the authorship of moral law open so long as he moves in a moral context, and he might well have left it open altogether had he seen no reason to ask questions beyond moral law and its obligatoriness. He writes:

The veiled goddess before whom we bend our knees is the moral law within us. . . . To be sure, we hear her voice and clearly understand her commandments, but are, in hearing them, in doubt as to who is speaking: whether man, in the self-sufficient power of his own reason, or Another, whose nature is unknown, and who speaks to man through the medium of his reason. Perhaps we would do better to refrain even from inquiring. For such a question is merely speculative, and our duty remains the same, whatever the source from which it issues.[28]

Judaism between Autonomy and Heteronomy

Such, then, is the challenge of Kant to the revealed morality of Judaism, and indeed to all revealed morality. The Jewish thinker who considers in its light the classical sources of Judaism makes two extraordinary discoveries. One is that the morality reflected in these traditional sources cannot be classified as either autonomous or heteronomous in the Kantian sense. The other is that, in the nearly two hundred years since the Kantian doctrine first appeared to challenge them, Jewish religious thinkers have noticed this fact but rarely, and then only dimly.

Apologetic tendencies have marred all the standard Jewish responses to the Kantian challenge. Thus, orthodox thinkers can certainly never have forgotten that, according to a central traditional Jewish doctrine, the commandments are not truly performed until they are performed for their own sake. Yet when faced with the Kantian challenge these thinkers have tended to behave as though they had indeed forgotten that Jewish doctrine. Rightly concerned to rescue the divine Law-giver from irrelevance, they have been prone to argue that, but for divine sanction, the commandments would remain universally and necessarily unperformed. They should have insisted that the revealed morality of Judaism is not heteronomous. What all too often they did insist on was that all human morality must be so. But thereby they not only put forward a false doctrine but pleaded Judaism guilty to a mistaken charge.

Liberal responses to Kant have suffered even more gravely from apologetic bias. While orthodox thinkers argued that the morality of Judaism is revealed but heteronomous, their liberal colleagues have often acted as though it were autonomous but not revealed. They would have prophets and rabbis speak with the Kantian voice of self-legislating reason.

This can be done in one of two ways; but both are foredoomed to failure. One can say that prophets and rabbis taught an autonomous morality, as it were, unconsciously, for they still gave conscious fealty to a revealing God. But then their morality stood, after all, still in need of liberal purification, which finally eliminated the revealing God. Or one can picture prophets and rabbis teaching an autonomous morality for what it is. This picture, however, is a scandalous distortion of historical fact.

Because of the haste with which they resorted to apologetics, both of these standard reactions to Kant failed to bring to light the authentic revealed morality of Judaism, particularly as reflected in the rabbinic sources—the fact that it is outside the realm of both autonomous and heteronomous morality. One group of apologists saw that the revealed morality of Judaism is not autonomous, because it stands in an essential relation to a commanding God. The other saw that it is not heteronomous because, bidding man to perform commandments both for their own sake and for the sake of God, it rises above all blandishments and threats. But neither group was able to perceive the essential togetherness of these two elements. Yet the source and life of the revealed morality of Judaism lies precisely in the togetherness of a divine commanding Presence that never dissipates itself into irrelevance, and a human response that freely appropriates what it receives.

The Jewish thinker does not respond adequately to the Kantian challenge until he brings this togetherness to philosophical consciousness in order to ask a question that Kant literally forces upon him: How can man appropriate a God-given law or commandment, accepting and performing it as though it were his own, while yet remaining, in the very act of appropriation, essentially and receptively related to its divine Giver? How can a man *morally* obey a law that is, and never ceased to be, *essentially* revealed? According to Kant, this is clearly impossible. Puzzlement and wonder arise for the Jewish philosopher because—if he is to believe the testimony of both Jewish life and thought—what Kant thought impossible is real.

The Pristine Commanding Presence in Judaism

We must make sure that what is essential in this remarkable togetherness does not slip from notice. This would happen if one were to attend, now to the divine commanding Presence in its otherness, and then to the human response in its power of free appropriation, but not to the two together. This togetherness is essential. In displaying it, we shall find that it exists in Judaism from its beginnings and throughout its history. Only in periods of spiritual decay can the one element seem capable of existence without the other. And this *is* the decay. With the exception of such periods, there is no age in the history of Judaism so "primitive" as to manifest—in the style of "theological morality"—only a divine commanding Presence but "not yet" an act of human appropriation. Nor is there an age "advanced" enough to manifest—in the style of "moral theology"—only a free human appropriation but "no longer" a commanding God who can be present in all His otherness.

At no moment in the history of Judaism is the otherness of the divine commanding Presence so starkly disclosed as in that pristine one in which the Divine, first reaching out to the human, calls him to its service. For in that moment there are as yet no specified commandments but only a still unspecified divine commanding Presence. Abraham is commanded to go to another country without being told of the country or of the purpose his migration is to serve. Prophets are called as messengers, without as yet being given a specific message. Israel as a whole is challenged, knowing as yet no more of the challenge than that it is divine. In the pristine moment, the divine commanding Presence does not communicate a finite content that the human recipient might appraise and appropriate in the light of familiar standards. On the contrary, it calls into question all familiar content, and, indeed, all standards. Whatever may be true of subsequent history, there can be no mistaking this initial voice for one already familiar, such as conscience, reason or "spiritual creativity."[29]

It may therefore seem that, whatever the nature of the human response to this pristine challenge, it cannot, at any rate, be free appropriation. There can certainly be no appropriation of specific commandments in the light of commensurate human standards, for there are as yet no such commandments. And how could there be an appropriation of the unspecified divine commanding Presence itself, when in the pristine moment it discloses itself as wholly other than human? It may thus seem that if there is human freedom at all in the pristine moment, it can at most be only heteronomous freedom—that is, the kind that is conditioned by fear or hope.

Yet just a freedom of this sort could not survive the touch of the divine Presence. Such freedom might survive, perhaps, in moments of divine distance, which, giving rise only to finite fear or hope, could leave room, as it were, for a freedom conditioned by them. But a fear or hope produced by the touch of the divine Presence would of necessity be absolute fear or hope, and as such would of necessity overwhelm the freedom conditioned by them. If in relation to God man is capable of heteronomous freedom only, then the event of divine Presence would reduce him, while that event lasts, to a will-less tool of a blind fate.

Such a reduction is indeed the primordial experience of some religions, but not of Judaism. For here the Divine manifests itself as *commanding*, and in order to do so it requires real human freedom. And since the Divine is *presence* as well as commanding, the required human freedom cannot be merely conditional—it must be unconditional and absolute. Finally, this unconditional and absolute freedom must be more even than the freedom to accept or reject specific commandments for their own sake, for there are as yet no such commandments. The freedom required in the pristine moment of the divine commanding Presence, then, is nothing less than the freedom to accept or reject the divine commanding Presence as a whole, and for its own sake—that is, for no other reason than that it is that Presence. It is such freedom that the prophet displays when he responds, "Here I am, send me"; or that the people as a whole display when they respond, "We shall do and hearken."[30]

This pristine human freedom of choice is not autonomous. Without the Other, man might have the self-sufficient power for all kinds of choice, but the power of choice to accept or reject the divine commanding Presence he would not have. How could he accept God, unless God had become present for him to accept? How could he reject Him, unless He had become present for him to reject? The divine commanding Presence, then, may be said to give man this choosing power. It may even be said to force the actual choice upon him. For in being present, it singles out; and thus rules out every escape from the choice as some spurious third alternative.

Yet this pristine choice most decidedly *is* a choice. The divine

[46]

commanding Presence may force the choice on singled-out man. It does not force him to choose God, and the choice itself (as was seen) is not heteronomous; for it accepts or rejects the divine commanding Presence for no other reason than that it *is* that Presence. But this entails the momentous consequence that, if and when a man chooses to accept the divine commanding Presence, he does nothing less than accept the divine Will as his own.

How is this humanly possible? We have already asked this question, in a general form. But it may now be given a sharper form, which states with full clarity what is at stake: How can man, at the very moment that starkly discloses the gulf between God and him, presume to bridge that gulf—by accepting God's will simply because it is God's, thus making it his own? How can man presume to act out of love for the sake of God? It is perhaps no wonder that a philosopher, when first coming upon this decisive question, should shrink from it in thought. Even prophets shrank from it when first confronted with it in life.[31]

The Torah as Bridge between Divine Giver and Human Recipient

It may therefore seem prudent for a philosopher to suspend that question for a while, by turning from the pristine moment that initiates the revealed morality of Judaism to the developed life of that morality itself. Here revelation has become a system of specified laws and commandments, and at least insofar as these are moral in nature they possess in Judaism undoubted permanence and intrinsic value.[32] A Jeremiah may believe that in one situation God demands resistance to the enemy and in another, submission.[33] But one cannot conceive of his believing this about justice or love and injustice or hatred. Just how moral law can assume permanence and intrinsic value within the framework of a revealed morality is a deep and weighty question, involving issues between philosophical and revealed morality that it would be premature at this point to raise.[34] The fact that moral law does assume permanence and intrinsic value within Judaism can be in no serious doubt.

This may suggest to the philosopher that, once permanent law of intrinsic value has made its appearance in Judaism, the divine commanding Presence of the pristine moment has vanished into the irrelevant past. What could be the function of this Presence? If it contradicted moral standards already in human possession, its voice would surely have to be rejected, as the voice of temptation. And if it confirmed these standards, it would only tell what is already known. In short, once revelation has become specified as a system of laws, new and revealing immediacy is either false or superfluous.

If this were the full truth of the matter, then revealed moral law in Judaism would allow only two human responses. One may obey it for its own sake, by recognizing and appropriating its intrinsic value. Then, however, one obeys it for its own sake *only*, and the divine Giver of the law becomes irrelevant in the process of appropriation, and so does the revealed quality of the law itself. Or one may obey it *because* it is revealed. But then one could not obey it either for God's sake or for its own—not the former because the Divine, having lost commanding presence, i.e., immediacy, after the rise of law, would have reduced itself to the mere external sanction behind the law; not the latter because the law would then need such sanction. In short, one would be driven back to the Kantian alternative between a moral theology essentially unrevealed, and a theological morality that is less than fully moral.

But must the divine Presence pass into irrelevance once revealed moral law has appeared? To ask this question is to recognize that the Kantian alternative contains a hidden premise. This premise, to be sure, is hard to reject, but Judaism implicitly rejects it. According to the testimony of Jewish life and teaching, the divine commanding Presence does *not* pass into irrelevance once moral law has assumed permanence and intrinsic value. The Torah is given whenever men are ready to receive it,[35] and the act of receiving Torah culminates in the confrontation with its Giver. The prophet, to be sure, has a specific message; yet the words "thus saith the Lord" are not an empty preamble but an essential part of the message. Kant holds that, mediating between man and God, moral law rules out or renders irrelevant an immediate divine commanding Presence. Judaism affirms that, despite the mediating function of the revealed moral law, the Divine is still present in commanding immediacy. The Kantian premise is that moral law is a bar between man and its divine Giver. The premise of Judaism is that it is a bridge.

How can the law be a bridge? Only by making a most startling demand. For Kant, all morality, including religious morality, demands a two-term relationship between man and his human neighbor. The revealed morality of Judaism demands a three-term relationship—nothing less than a relationship involving man, his human neighbor, and God Himself. If it demanded a human relationship only, then the God in whose name it was demanded would indeed reduce Himself to a mere external sanction behind the demand.

(And Kierkegaard would be quite right to say, of biblical faith as well as of Kantian morality, that in performing one's duty to love one's neighbor, one comes into a relation with one's human neighbor only, and not with God.) The startling claim of the revealed morality of Judaism is, however, that God Himself enters into the relationship. He confronts man with the demand to turn to his human neighbor, and in doing so, turn back to God Himself. Micah's celebrated summary of the commandments does more than list three commandments that exist side by side. For there is no humble walking before God unless it manifests itself in justice and mercy to the human neighbor. And there can be only fragmentary justice and mercy unless they culminate in humility before God. Here lies the heart and core of Jewish morality.[86]

What human response is adequate to this divine demand? The response remains fragmentary until the commandments are performed, on the one hand, for their own sake, and, on the other, for God's sake. And each of these must point to the other.

Moral commandments, to be moral, must be performed for their own sake. For unless so performed they do not realize the three-term relation that takes the human neighbor in his own right seriously; they function merely within an attempted two-term relation between man and God. We say "attempted." For such a relationship is rejected by God Himself, at least once the pristine commanding Presence has specified itself in moral commandments. It is God Himself who bids man take his neighbor in his own right seriously. To obey God, man both accepts his neighbor, and the commandment concerning him, as possessing intrinsic value. He performs the commandment for its own sake.

Yet the commandment remains fragmentary if performed for its sake only. For if such performance discloses the human neighbor, as well as him who performs the commandment, as being of intrinsic value, it is ultimately because the divine commanding Presence so discloses them. (This is true whether or not this disclosure, or something resembling it, is accessible independent of the divine commanding Presence as well. This would supply welcome but not indispensable support, for the revealed morality of Judaism develops by its own inner dynamic.) This is why, even if beginning with the acceptance of the disclosure only, a man is finally led to confront the divine Discloser; why performance of the commandment for its own sake points to its performance for God's sake. Both are certainly part of Jewish teaching. And they exist not contingently side by side, but in an internal and necessary relation. God is not barred from direct human access by the intrinsic value of man, or by the intrinsic value of the command-ment that relates man to man. On the contrary, He disclosed Him-self through all intrinsic value, as its ultimate Source. And the man who accepts this disclosure acts for the sake of God. In the hour of his martyrdom, Rabbi Akiba knew that the love of God is not one commandment side by side with others. It is the life of all.[37]

Thus the territory in which we have sought philosophic refuge from the decisive but bewildering question raised by the pristine moment of divine commanding Presence, while no doubt safer, is by no means absolutely safe, if by "safety" is meant the com-fortable distance, and hence irrelevance, of the Divine. We first saw that in the pristine moment of divine commanding Presence there is already the possibility of free human appropriation, and we have now seen that, once human freedom can appropriate specific laws and commandments endowed with permanence and intrinsic value, the divine commanding Presence will still confront it. Divine commanding Presence and appropriating human freedom still point to each other. And the philosophical question raised by their togetherness can no longer be suspended or avoided. In the light of the foregoing, we may reformulate that question, to read as follows: How can man presume to participate in a three-term relationship that involves not only his human neighbor but God Himself? How can he—as he must, in order to participate in such a relationship—act out of love for the sake of God, when God is God while man is only man? In Kantian language, what is the condition of the possibility of such an action?

The Parting of Ways between Kant and Judaism

It is a testimony to Kant's genius as a religious thinker that he should not have wholly ignored this question. He even supplied it with an answer. But Kant's answer is not and cannot be the Jewish answer. Instead, we have come to a final parting of ways. Kant writes:

The virtuous man fears God without being afraid of Him. This is be-cause he is not worried lest he himself might wish to resist Him or His commandments. God is awe-inspiring because such resistance, while unthinkable in his own case, is not in itself impossible.[38]

For Kant's virtuous man, it is unthinkable that he might not will the will of God. For a prophet when first singled out, it is unthinkable how he *could* will it. To fear God at all, Kant's vir-tuous man must imagine himself as willing what he is in fact incap-able of willing. The rabbis need no such strategy in order to stand in fear of God. Their impossible possibility is not the fear but rather the love of God.[39] For Kant, the oneness of the human with the divine will is automatic once virtue is achieved. For prophets and rabbis, such oneness is very far from automatic even for the virtuous man, and, in a sense, for him least of all. For prophets and rabbis, there is a radical gulf between God, who is God, and man, who is only human. How then is a oneness of wills possible at all?

It is possible if God Himself has made it possible. Man can appropriate divine commandments if they are handed over for human appropriation. He can live by the Torah in the love and for the sake of God, if the Torah itself is a gift of divine love, making such a life a human possibility. He can participate in a three-term relationship that involves God Himself if God, who in His power does not need man, in His love nevertheless chooses to need him.

The belief in the reality of such a divine love is as pervasive in Judaism as is the belief in revealed law itself. For here divine commandments and divine love are not only coeval; they are inseparable. The Torah manifests love in the very act of manifesting commandment; for in commanding humans rather than angels, it accepts these humans in their humanity.[40] Hence in accepting the Torah, man can at the same time accept himself as accepted by God in his humanity. This is why to attempt to perform the commandments, and to do so both for their sake and for the sake of God, is not to attempt the humanly impossible. At least in principle, the commandments can be performed in joy.[41]

This belief in a divine love manifest in the divine commandment is present in Judaism from its pristine beginnings and throughout its history. From its beginnings: having first shrunk from the divine commanding Presence, the prophet ends up accepting it because he has experienced the divine love that makes acceptance possible.[42] Throughout its history: a daily prayer renders thanks for the divine love in which God has given the commandments.

If this faith permeates Jewish life so universally and so obviously, one may well ask why Jewish thought, when confronted with the Kantian challenge, should have failed to bring it clearly to philosophical consciousness. Had it done so, it would not have accepted so meekly the terms of the Kantian dilemma, between a morality that, because it is genuinely moral, cannot be essentially revealed, and a morality that, because it is essentially revealed, must be less than truly moral. It would have repudiated this dilemma, recognizing and clearly stating that if divine love is manifest in the revealed commandments, the dilemma does not arise.

Perhaps it is not far-fetched to identify as the cause of failure, in the case of non-Jewish philosophers such as Kant (or, for that matter, Kierkegaard when he accepts the Kantian scheme) an ancient prejudice against Judaism bolstered by ignorance of it; and, in the case of Jewish philosophers, uncritically assimilated reliance on non-Jewish modes of philosophical thought.

An ancient prejudice contrasts Jewish law with Christian love, and this is only slightly modified by the concession that love "evolves" in later stages of Judaism as well. Against this prejudice, it is by no means enough to insist that divine love is as ancient in Judaism as divine commandment. For such a love might be confined, in Pelagian style, to the remission of sins that strict justice would condemn; and this would still leave law itself prior to love, and in itself loveless. In Judaism the primordial manifestation of divine love is not subsequent to but *in* the commandments; primordial human joy is not in a future subsequent to the life of the commandment but in that life itself.

Now it is precisely this teaching that Paul either could not comprehend or could not accept. Paul did not merely assert that the commandments cannot be performed wholly, which to his Jewish contemporaries was not new. He asserted that they cannot be performed at all. This was because he accepted one aspect of Jewish teaching but not the other. He saw man commanded to act for God's sake, by a God incommensurate with all things human. But he did not see, or was personally unable to experience, the divine love that, handing the commandments over for human appropriation, makes their performance a human possibility. Hence he thought that man was obligated to do the humanly impossible.

Kant's moral philosophy may be regarded, among many other things, as a protest against this Pauline conclusion. It rightly insists that man can be morally obligated to do only what he is able to do, and hence that, if an unbridged gap exists between the human and the Divine, divine commandments cannot be moral commandments. It also properly refuses to divorce the Divine from the moral. But this compels his philosophy to deny the gap between the Divine and the human. The result is that the divine will becomes a moral redundancy.[43] In all this, Kant's anti-Pauline protest shares one assumption with Paul's own position: the denial of a divine love manifest in the God-given commandment. From the standpoint of the revealed morality of Judaism, Kant may therefore be viewed as the nemesis of a tradition that begins with Paul.

Conclusion

Does God in moral duty become an invisible vanishing point? Or is all duty, absolutely considered, duty to God, so as forever to threaten the ethical with teleological suspension? In the three-term morality of Judaism this dilemma does not arise. It is true that times occur in which that morality is threatened with fragmentation, into a two-term divine-human and a two term interhuman relationship. But for those who in such times continue to cleave to the Torah the promise is held out that this fragmentation is not final. In the Midrash God speaks: "Would that they had deserted Me and kept My Torah; for if they had occupied themselves with the Torah the leaven which is in it would have brought them back to Me."[44]

ON THE AKEDAH, OR SACRIFICE AND MARTYRDOM

Introduction

We must now recall that the conclusions just arrived at required of us the prior, at least temporary, renunciation of the Abraham of Mount Moriah. The question now arises whether this renunciation has not resulted in a display of philosophical complacency. Could it be that the *Akedah*, if reintroduced, might threaten the constructive results arrived at? Might it cast us into turmoil once more?

In their respective ways, Kant, Kierkegaard, and the Midrash all treat the biblical incident as being somehow of momentous import. In every case, it is the touchstone of revealed morality as a whole. It is by condemning Abraham that Kant makes every divine-human relation one that is essentially an interhuman moral relation. It is by praising him that Kierkegaard exposes every moral relation to the threat of a teleological suspension religious in nature. And if it has thus far appeared that the Midrash avoids this fatal alternative by means of the Torah—a three-term relation in which God, man, and fellowman are all immediately involved—we must now face the rabbinic view that the Torah itself was given on account of the merit of Abraham's act at Mount Moriah.

What lends this pivotal position to the *Akedah?* Unquestionably, it is its radicalism. If any human-divine relation is purely religious, it is that of sacrifice. If any sacrifice is total, it is that of life itself. And if any such sacrifice ever runs counter to morality under all circumstances, it is when the life in question is not one's own, or even that of another (possibly consenting) adult, but rather the life of an innocent, helpless, choiceless child. Moreover—if one can speak of "better" and "worse" where only horror seems appropriate—the case is, in at least one sense, worse when the child is one's own, that is, when one acts as though to be a parent is to be an owner.

Only horror is appropriate, humanly and morally. Yet religiously we cannot cut off further questioning, lest we shun prematurely dark possibilities to which openness is a philosophical requirement. If religion is taken seriously in its own right, can one fail to entertain the idea of sacrifice? If it is taken radically, can one simply exclude the notion of total sacrifice? Yet with respect to totality every other sacrifice real or imaginable—one's possessions, one's life, and even spiritual self-abnegation of a seemingly radical and unsurpassable character—is dwarfed by what Abraham would have offered at Mount Moriah had not the divine word stayed his hand.

It is no wonder, then, that the *Akedah* becomes the touchstone of all religious morality: if sacrifice is ruled out, religiosity is not serious in its own right; and if sacrifice is admitted, the possibility of a radical sacrifice that destroys morality is not excluded. Nor is it surprising that Kant and Kierkegaard view the *Akedah* as illustrating the most radical possible clash between the religious and the ethical. What must baffle us is not that these thinkers arrive at antithetical conclusions but rather how Judaism can hope to avoid them. How, except by dint of a monumental inconsistency, can Jewish tradition be unanimous both in revering Abraham for his intention to offer a child sacrifice, *and* in condemning such as Mesha, the king of Moab, for actually offering it?[45] In the account just completed we have found ourselves able to affirm the three-term morality of Judaism against the challenge of Kant's moral philosophy. Now the possibility comes into view that the radical case of the *Akedah* retroactively causes ruin. We have therefore no choice but to reexamine, in the light of the *Akedah*, the concepts that have thus far seemed satisfactory, prepared to see them destroyed.

In order to do justice, less to specific hallowed texts than to the inner dynamic of the morality of Judaism as a whole, we have distinguished between pristine moments of a divine commanding Presence (in which every familiar content and all standards are called into question), and the developed life of the revealed morality of Judaism (in which revelation has become a system of specific commandments endowed with intrinsic value). Except for the pristine moments and the possibility of their continued appropriation, how could the human will make the divine will unconditionally its own, and perform specific commandments for *God's* sake as well as for their own? And unless the commandments acquired intrinsic value, how could they be performed for *their* sake as well as God's? To dissolve the intrinsic value of the moral commandments into the immediately commanding divine Presence would be to arrive at a two-term, divine-human, religious relationship; to permit the intrinsic value of the moral commandments to cut off all pristine moments of a divine commanding Presence would be to arrive at a two-term, interhuman, moral relationship. In either case the three-term revealed morality of Judaism would be lost.

Our distinction, then, was necessary. The *Akedah*, however, now endangers it radically. In every respect except one it is a case of a pristine commanding divine Presence as thus far described; this one difference, however, threatens to be fatal. First, every familiar content and all standards are called into question. Second, the human will, singled out by the divine, must decide for or against this "putative" divine will, without choice of a third alternative. Third, in deciding for the divine will, it must be one with it, that is, be motivated not by extraneous expectations such as fear or hope but rather by the pure love of God. Only one difference emerges. While in all other instances hitherto cited—prophets when first called, Israel at Sinai, and, for that matter, Abraham himself in every other situation—it is an as yet unspecified divine commanding Presence that calls every familiar content and all standards into question, this occurs, in the case of the *Akedah*, through a Presence that issues a commandment that is all too specific. Every other case may be understood as *premoral*. The commandment that initiates the *Akedah* cannot be understood, try though we may, except as *antimoral*. And therein lies its scandal.

Kant and Kierkegaard recognize this scandal. Jewish religious thought cannot evade it. (We have already criticized the evolutionary interpretation of the tale, and may now add that in any such account we can take seriously at best its outcome, and not Abraham's intention at the beginning, for while this may be premoral by Abraham's own standards it is antimoral by our own.) To recognize the scandal, however, is to be faced with a dilemma. If every pristine moment of a divine commanding Presence calls every familiar content and all standards into question, is not any such moment potentially antimoral, instead of being merely premoral? And if specified moral commandments do and must have intrinsic value, must there not be some familiar contents and standards that no commanding divine Presence can call into question—a premoral no more than an antimoral Presence? (Is our distinction concerning Jeremiah[46] without substance?) In short, the distinction we found it necessary to make is now threatened with destruction.

Let the dilemma be spelled out. Are there authentic pristine moments of a divine commanding Presence, and do these remain foundational to the revealed morality of Judaism? If so, they then dissipate the intrinsic value of all subsequent commandments into arbitrary divine whim, making them subject to potential if not actual teleological suspension. Or are there moral commandments that possess authentic intrinsic value and rule out abrogation or suspension even from a divine source? If so, they then retroactively destroy every truly *pristine* moment of divine commanding Presence, that is, one in which *all* familiar content and *every* standard is called into question. But in the first case the commandments can be performed for God's sake and not for theirs, and are not truly moral; and in the second case they can be performed for their sake and not for God's, and are not truly religious. (God is a mere sanction behind the commandments, the need for which, moreover, disappears once theological morality is transcended and moral theology is achieved.) In short, the three-term morality of Judaism has suffered collapse, and the radical case of the *Akedah* has served to disclose the collapse.

Jewish tradition does not, of course, know of Kant, or of Kierkegaard, or of the dilemma uncovered by their thought. It would, however, be rash to assume that this tradition lacks the resources that might enable a Jewish thinker to cope with this dilemma once he brings what is implicit in Judaism to philosophical consciousness. We have cited Micah's statement concerning justice, mercy, and humility as a summary of the three-term morality of Judaism. The Midrash makes use of the fact that the prophet prefaces his summary with a condemnation of child-sacrifice (Mic. 6:7). To whom, the Midrash asks, does Micah refer? Only apparently to such as Mesha, the king of Moab, who actually sacrificed his son, and in reality to Isaac, in whose case "the deed was not actually done, yet He accepted it as though it were completed."[47]

This Midrash both astounds and baffles us. It is astoundingly bold to connect what we have viewed as a classical summary of the three-term morality of Judaism with the *Akedah*. It is bolder still to connect both with the explicit condemnation of child-sacrifice. What baffles us is how the intention can be acceptable and even praiseworthy when the deed is abhorrent. We are obliged, however, not to stay baffled but rather to bring our bafflement to the Midrashic author. For it defies all belief that this author, bold enough to make the connections referred to, should himself be unaware of our question—or tell his Midrash without a secret purpose.

On Human Sacrifice, Or the Akedah as Perpetually Reenacted and Superseded Past

We have conceded that a modern Jew, were he addressed as was Abraham, would reject the voice as spurious, i.e., that he would (and should) in this instance side with Kant, for whom this voice is opposed by moral conscience, and not with the Midrash, for which it is opposed by Satan.[48] This concession has perhaps been, if not too quick, at any rate too sweeping. After all, the Torah would bid us act in much the same way as Kant does, for it forbids human sacrifice. Yet unlike Kant the Torah exalts Abraham for what he did (or was prepared to do) at Mount Moriah. Our present question may therefore be formulated as follows: is to reject any possible present *Akedah* necessarily to reject the original *Akedah?*

To begin with it is necessary to identify the ultimate reason why Kant finds himself required to reject the *Akedah* without qualification. His reason is not and cannot be his view that "He who appear[s] to Abraham . . . is God is not certain."[49] The Midrash presumably shares this view, for otherwise it could not let Abraham be effectively tempted by Satan, just as Kant himself lets him be warned by moral conscience. Yet the Midrash sides with Kierkegaard in the view that Abraham can and does have absolute faith, i.e., that he accepts (and that it is possible to accept) with subjective certainty what is objectively not indubitable.[50] Why, then, does Kant side against such a faith and wholly condemn it? The answer is in no doubt: because it is *"absolutely* certain . . . [that a man] may not kill . . . [his] good son."[51]

We must note well the term "absolutely." Moreover, in order not to beg the whole present question from the start, we must rule out every case in which killing is murder. We have noted long ago that the rabbis distinguish between nonmoral laws "to which Satan and the Gentiles object," and moral laws that "had they not been written by God would have had to be written by men,"[52] and that of these latter (which may be said to coincide with the Noaḥidic laws) they would grant, if pressed, that they are rationally discoverable. On the prohibition of murder there is agreement between the ethics of the rabbis and the ethics of the philosophers, and we may note in passing that this connection is so strong in Jewish thinkers such as Maimonides (who derives it from both sources) that he can actually go so far as to use it as his central argument to the effect that the voice demanding Isaac's sacrifice (as well as, incidentally, all prophecy) was, after all, *not* uncertain. It must have been—the Midrash, Kant, and Kierkegaard notwithstanding—objectively certain as well as subjectively accepted. Maimonides writes:

It should not be thought that what . . . [prophets] hear or what appears to them in a parable is not certain . . . just because it comes about in a dream and in a vision. . . . A proof for this is the fact that [Abraham] hastened to slaughter, as he had been commanded, his son, his only son, whom he loved, even though this commandment came to him in a dream or in a vision. For if a dream of prophecy had been obscure for the prophets, or if they had doubts or incertitude concerning what they apprehended in a vision of prophecy, they would not have hastened to do that which is repugnant to nature, and [Abraham's] soul would not have consented to accomplish an act of so great an importance if there had been a doubt about it.[53]

Our present interest in this passage is not epistemological but rather moral and religious. How can there be no doubt whatever about a voice commanding what is "repugnant to nature"? (When we say "no doubt whatever" we include moral and religious doubt, that is, not only doubt as to the authenticity of the voice but also doubt as to its moral and religious acceptability.) Only if the act commanded is not *absolutely* wrong under *all conceivable* circumstances, i.e., if it is not murder but sacrifice, and if it is commanded, not by the false gods who always demand child sacrifice, but rather by the true God who has hitherto not demanded it, and who indeed, according to some rabbinic interpreters, has actually forbidden it since the time of Noah.[54] The rabbis do not criticize but praise Abraham's intention, and this despite the fact that (at least in the Midrashim we have considered) they regard the voice commanding the *Akedah* as objectively uncertain. Being very much of a philosopher and an Aristotelian, Maimonides finds it hard to follow their example, and precisely this fact makes it illuminating why, nevertheless, he does follow it. Abraham

. . . did not hasten to slaughter Isaac because he was afraid that **God** would kill him or make him poor, but solely because of what is incumbent upon the Adamites—namely, to love Him and fear Him, may His name be exalted—and not . . . for any hope of a reward or for fear of punishment.[55]

Maimonides holds that not every killing of a good son comes under the moral category of murder; that at least in principle—though only on the most exacting conditions and, indeed, presumably only in a single case in all of human history—it may come under the religious category of sacrifice.

What, then, makes Kant absolutely certain that the "killing" of a "good" son is wrong under all conceivable circumstances? Not his epistemological disagreement with Maimonides as to the divine voice alone, for this is shared by Kierkegaard and the Midrash. It is, rather an a priori standard of rational morality.

In a general way, this might have been guessed from Kant's previously sketched concept of moral theology.[56] Theological morality accepts laws as moral because they are God-given. Moral theology ascribes them to God because of their intrinsically moral character, which attaches to them quite apart from all God-givenness. This view implies, first, that religious commandments are essentially moral in both content and source;[57] second, that any divine commandment additional to morality, if acceptable at all, must be mediated through morality and certainly cannot be contrary to it; third, that man has, or can have, an a priori conception of God Himself. Kant writes:

Though it does indeed sound dangerous, it is in no way reprehensible to say that every man *creates* God for himself, nay, must make himself such a God according to moral concepts. . . . For . . . even if such a being had appeared to him (if this is possible), he must first of all compare this representation with his ideal in order to judge whether he is entitled to regard it and honor it as a divinity. Hence there can be no religion springing from revelation alone, i.e., without first positing that concept, in its purity, as a touchstone. Without this all reverence for God would be idolatry.[58]

So much for the general grounds of Kant's position toward the *Akedah*. Kant rules out a priori every possible pristine divine commanding Presence of the kind we have found in the three-term morality of Judaism, on behalf and on account of another Presence—pristine, commanding but also universal and therefore in principle incapable of any kind of suspension—the categorical imperative.[59] Whether or not it is tautological to view this Presence as divine as well as moral is immaterial in the present context. Not immaterial is that "empirical" divine voices are acceptable, if at all, only mediately, and that, by virtue of what it said, the voice speaking to Abraham was a priori false. And in obeying that voice Abraham was an "idolater."

However, the general grounds of Kant's moral philosophy no longer suffice for our present purpose. Whatever its merits, our previous exposition of the three-term morality of Judaism has sufficed to cast doubt on the religious adequacy of Kant's two-term morality. This doubt would increase if we had to conclude that, instead of confronting the problem of sacrifice, Kant merely disregards it. We therefore ask whether, in addition to the general resources already cited, Kant's thought has specific resources for dealing with this subject.

We have previously cited one version of the categorical imperative, involving autonomy or self-determination. To advance to our present question we require another, involving the notion of humanity as an end-in-itself.

Suppose there were something whose existence has in itself an absolute value, something which as an end in itself could be a ground of determinate laws, then in it, and in it alone, would there be the ground of a possible categorical imperative.[60]

Kant proceeds beyond mere supposition. Man is in fact an end in himself, if only because he is capable of self-determination and obligated to actualize this capacity. He is a "person" and not a "thing." Hence the imperative:

Act in such a way that you always treat humanity, whether in your own person or in the person of others, never simply as a means, but always at the same time as an end.[61]

So much for the general principle. We now turn to the usually underestimated, but in fact critical, question of specific applications. Significantly Kant's very first example is suicide. A man may risk death under certain circumstances, but under no circumstances may he seek it or bring it about. The suicide is

making use of a person merely as a means to maintain a tolerable state of affairs till the end of his life. But man is not a thing—not something to be used merely as a means: He must always in all his actions be regarded as an end in himself. Hence I cannot dispose of man in my person by maiming, spoiling or killing.[62]

Man cannot deprive himself of his personality so long as one speaks of duties, thus so long as he lives. That man ought to have the authorization to withdraw himself from all obligation, i.e., to be free to act as if no authorization at all were required for this withdrawal, involves a contradiction. To destroy the subject of morality in his own person is tantamount to obliterating from the world, as far as he can, the very existence of morality itself; but morality is, nevertheless, an end in itself. Accordingly, to dispose of oneself as a mere means to some end of one's own liking is to degrade the humanity in one's person (*homo noumenon*), which, after all, was entrusted to man (*homo phaenomenon*) to preserve.[63]

The question of applications is critical because it gives rise to the further question of possible exceptions. Notoriously weak on this latter question, Kant's philosophy has a special and highly significant weakness in the present case—as will be seen, because the problem of sacrifice is involved.

What of Cato who under Caesar "thought that if he could not go on living as Cato he could not go on living at all?"[64] What of Seneca who "anticipated an unjust death sentence" from Nero?[65] What of Curtius who "plunge[d himself] . . . into certain death . . . in order to save [his] country?"[66] What in general of any case of "martyrdom—the deliberate sacrifice of oneself for the good of mankind?"[67] Are all these cases instances of "self-*murder*"[68] when in at least some of them *homo noumenon* is an end in himself even though *homo phaenomenon* has become a means? So profoundly is Kant convinced that the second, as well as the first, is an end in himself that the very most he will do is leave the question open.[69]

Not at all open, however, is the question of religious sacrifice of life. Conceivably in a moral sacrifice *homo noumenon* is the end, and only *homo phaenomenon* a means. In a religious sacrifice-of-life, however, both are means to supposedly higher ends, and Divinity itself rejects any such ends. "A suicide opposes the purpose of his Creator; he arrives in the other world as one who has deserted his post; he must be looked upon as a rebel against God."[70] A man's duty is to preserve his life "until the time comes when God expressly commands us to leave this life."[71] But while such a command may or may not come to us as *moral* sacrifice it a priori cannot ever come to us as *religious* sacrifice.

Suicide is not inadmissible and abominable because God has forbidden it; God has forbidden it because it is abominable in that it degrades man's inner worth below that of the animal creation.[72]

Kant, then, quite unequivocally regards every religious sacrifice of life as a self-murder, for it reduces the human person to a thing. Hence, while at least wondering about such as Cato and

Seneca he simply dismisses Abraham. Indeed, even if per impossibile he granted that Abraham remained a person during the act, his "good son" (a child and no responsible participant) was reduced to a thing from the start.

However, in fastening attention on the *Akedah* (in which, as Kant sees it, Isaac is a thing and Abraham treats him as such) we must under no circumstances overlook the fact that for Kant the hypothetical case of an acceptable yet religious sacrifice never arises. Well aware of the need for moral sacrifice, this latter troubles him only when suicide is involved, for in that case two moral ends are in apparent conflict. Religious sacrifice, in contrast, occasions no trouble even when death or suicide are not involved, for any such sacrifice is in principle to be rejected. Indeed, one may go so far as to say that, so far as Kant is concerned, religious sacrifice is a contradiction in terms. There is sacrifice only when the motive is selfless. Religious sacrifice, however, is either for duty's sake (in which case it is genuine but moral) or for God's sake (in which case it is for extraneous motives and not genuine). The possibility of sacrifice as a direct gift to God motivated by the pure love of God remains totally unexamined. Kant writes:

I take the following proposition to be a principle *requiring no proof.* Whatever, over and above good life-conduct, man fancies he can do to be well-pleasing to God is mere religious illusion and pseudo-service of God.[73]

This conclusion having been reached, the responsible Jewish thinker is required to reinforce his critical attitude toward Kant's entire position, and, much though this may run counter to his own modern proclivities, to hold fast in this attitude to the notion of religious sacrifice. He already rejects Kant's proposition—advanced by him without proof and as requiring no proof—when, though remaining within the sphere of morality, he accepts the three-term morality of Judaism, for he then performs moral commandments for God's sake as well as for their own. He goes further in case he accepts the six hundred and thirteen commandments of traditional Judaism, some of which have no obvious moral content and are thus performable for God's sake alone. He would go further still were he to hold, with Jewish tradition, that while child sacrifice is forbidden and any new *Akedah* is impossible, the original *Akedah* was motivated neither by fear nor by hope but rather by the pure love of God. To be sure, his philosophical responsibility may require him to reject this last-named traditional view. However, it equally prevents him from rejecting it on the grounds of

Kant's philosophy. For, as we have seen, Kant wholly fails to examine the notion of any and all religious sacrifice. His rejection of it, he holds, "requires no proof."

If Kant fails to examine religious sacrifice Kierkegaard is overwhelmed by it. Kierkegaard himself expresses this contrast when he opposes the individual who "determines his relation to the Absolute by his relation to the universal"[74] with the individual who "determines his relation to the universal by his relation to the Absolute."[75] In Kierkegaard's account of this latter relation, however—that of his knight of faith—religious sacrifice threatens morality with destruction.

In posing this threat Kierkegaard and his knight of faith are in marked contrast with virtually the entire Jewish tradition. For Kierkegaard, the ethical is actually suspended in the *Akedah*, and potentially suspended for every knight of faith after Abraham. In Judaism, the Torah ends the possibility of any such suspension, and (as will be seen) the Midrash denies that even in the *Akedah* itself it ever had the form that Kierkegaard ascribes to it. For Kierkegaard, every knight of faith is alone. The Torah relates the members of the covenantal community to each other, and even the Midrashic Abraham is not isolated. In short, whereas Kant bids Jewish thought to reject even the original *Akedah*, Kierkegaard demands of Jewish thought the eternal perpetuation of its possibility. Whereas Kant will not let the Torah rest on Abraham's merit, Kierkegaard would rob us of the Torah, which forbids child sacrifice.

Who is the Kierkegaardian knight of faith? He emerges in contrast with the "moral" or "tragic" hero. Agamemnon is a moral hero when he sacrifices Iphigenia. His sacrifice is for a higher, universal purpose, and he confronts no worse a question than whether the purpose at hand is in fact higher and warrants such a sacrifice. The sacrifice of Isaac at the hands of Abraham, in contrast, suspends the ethical. It is a direct and "absolute duty toward God," and the far worse question is whether there ever can be any such duty and this particular duty. Agamemnon is a tragic as well as moral hero, for he must renounce Iphigenia forever and exists in infinite resignation. Abraham, in contrast, has passed through and beyond this resignation, for since he is a knight of faith, he is paradoxically required both to obey the divine commandment to sacrifice Isaac and to believe the divine promise that Isaac will live.[76] This is why, in case his faith is true, the knight of faith is not at the same time a murderer as well.

The contrast between the two figures would be less sharp, and indeed possibly take a quite different form, were it not for the fact that Agamemnon must and can communicate whereas Abraham is cut off from every human contact. Since his purpose is universal Agamemnon can speak of it to all the assembled Greeks; he "does not enter into any private relationship with the Deity, but for him the ethical is divine."[77] Abraham, in contrast, must remain silent of his purpose even to Sarah, Eliezer, and Isaac himself, for he stands in a relation with the Divine so private that all things universal are suspended.

Why then did Abraham do it? For God's sake and . . . for his own sake. He did it for God's sake because God required this proof of his faith; for his own in order that he might furnish the proof.[78]

Such is the dread of Abraham, the Kierkegaardian knight of faith.

His isolation implies that the dread is not confined to him alone. He does not and cannot suffer it vicariously. Should there ever be another knight of faith, he will be fully as isolated—and his dread will be the same.

In these regions partnership is unthinkable. . . . Even if a man were cowardly and paltry enough to wish to become a knight of faith on the responsibility of an outsider, he will never become one.[79]

The true knight of faith is always absolute isolation.[80]

In the solitude of the universe[he] never hears any human voice but walks alone with his dreadful responsibility.[81]

To sum up, the faith of this figure of the Jewish Bible has no connection with the three-term morality of the Jewish Bible. Quite divorced from passages such as Micah 6:8, this faith is epitomized by a very different passage, taken from the Christian Bible:

If any man cometh to me and hateth not his own father and mother and wife and children and brother and sister, yea, and his own life also, he cannot be my disciple (Luke 14:26).[82]

So much for Kierkegaard's Abraham. What of his Midrashic counterpart? The two share an "absolute relation to the Absolute," i.e., an absolute faith in what objectively is not indubitable. They share, too, the pure love of God. There, however, all resemblance ends, and the Midrashic Abraham escapes the Kierkegaardian categories of "tragic hero" and "knight of faith" alike. Unlike the latter, he has actually renounced Isaac; indeed, even the angels lament that the covenant is broken.[83] Unlike the former, he will not sacrifice Isaac to a higher universal purpose, for he is not told of one and knows of none. Even so, however, he loves God and believes in a purpose. *What purpose?* The Midrashic Abraham does not know what it can be. He knows, however, what it *cannot* be—a private affair between him and God. Could he accept a God who "required this proof of his faith"? Under no circumstances, when he has dared to call Him to account for reasons far less weighty. Could he do it "for his own sake, in order that he might furnish the proof"?[84] Again under no circumstances, for he who was to die contented in the knowledge that Isaac would live could not possibly cherish his own soul above his son's life. Indeed, no Kierkegaardian passage could be more alien to any form of Jewish religiosity than the one just cited, and for any Jewish Abraham to be left without knowledge of a purpose is far better than to be given *this* purpose.

The foregoing characteristics of the Midrashic Abraham all appear in a remarkable dialogue between God and Abraham that takes place after the ordeal is over.

ABRAHAM: One man tempts another, because he knoweth not what is in the heart of his neighbor. But Thou surely didst know that I was ready to sacrifice my son!

GOD: It was manifest to Me, and I foresaw it, that thou wouldst withhold not even thy soul from Me.

ABRAHAM: And why, then, didst Thou afflict me thus?

GOD: It was My wish that the world should become acquainted with thee and should know that it was not without good reason that I have chosen thee from all the nations. Now it has been witnessed unto men that thou fearest God.[85]

The end of the dialogue remains yet to be cited. The part already cited suffices for the distinction between a personal and a private divine-human relationship. Kierkegaard finds it necessary to write an entire chapter entitled, "Was Abraham ethically defensible in keeping silent about his purpose before Sarah, before Eliezer, before Isaac?"[86] The Midrash does not so much as raise this question, for the existence of the silence is denied. Kierkegaard's Abraham cannot communicate, for his relation to God is private. The Midrashic Abraham may and perhaps must communicate; for that his relation to God, while personal, is not private, is evidenced by the purpose of the trial which eventually emerges. Moreover, the Midrashic Abraham in fact communicates, and he does so, above all, to Isaac; and Isaac, accepting and sharing the purpose, responds, "Blessed is the Lord who has this day chosen me to be a burnt-offering before Him."[87] As will be seen, the monumental

[65]

Midrashic response to the *Akedah* is to take it out of the class of child sacrifice altogether and transform it into *Kiddush Hashem*, or martyrdom.[88] But we cannot yet grasp this response, nor is martyrdom as yet our subject.

Our present subject is human community in the presence of God. If this survives even during the *Akedah*, it a fortiori survives for all subsequent members of the covenant begun with Abraham— and, if only they respond to Abraham's own testimony, for the whole human race. Kierkegaard connects the *Akedah* with the Luke passage which (as he interprets it) places every knight of faith into a two-term relation with God in which the ethical is potentially suspended. The Midrash connects the *Akedah* with the Micah passage that places all members of the covenant—and in the end, all men—into a three-term relation in which God, man, and fellowman are all involved.[89]

For Kierkegaard every believer is a potential Abraham. For the Midrash the sons of the covenant are children of Abraham, by whose merit the covenant both was established and survives. We have already noticed that according to a Midrash one of the horns of the ram sacrificed by Abraham was blown by God at Sinai, while the other will be blown to inaugurate the Messianic days.[90] Another Midrash teaches that when the ram's horn is blown in synagogues during the solemn New Year's festival (whose theme is human repentance, divine judgment, and divine-human reconciliation) God, reminded of the *Akedah*, moves from the throne of judgment to the throne of mercy.[91]

What, then, *is* Abraham's "merit"? For Kierkegaard, it is between him and God alone, and consists of his paradoxical faith that he both must sacrifice Isaac and yet will regain him. For the Midrash, it is not between him and God alone, for it lies, while the test lasts, in his self-restraint toward God, and, after it is ended, in his eschatological concern for all the nations and his immediate concern for future Jewish generations. The dialogue already cited goes on as follows:

ABRAHAM: I will not leave this altar until I have said what I have to say.
GOD: Speak whatsoever thou hast to speak.
ABRAHAM: Didst Thou not promise me Thou wouldst let one come forth out of mine own bowels, whose seed should fill the whole earth?
GOD: Yes.
ABRAHAM: Whom didst Thou mean?
GOD: Isaac.

[66]

ABRAHAM: Didst Thou not promise me to make my seed as numerous as the sand of the sea-shore?

GOD: Yes.

ABRAHAM: Through which of my children?

GOD: Through Isaac.

ABRAHAM: I might have reproached Thee, and said, O Lord of the world, yesterday Thou didst tell me, In Isaac shall thy seed be called, and now Thou sayest, Take thy son, thine own son, even Isaac, and offer him for a burnt-offering. But I refrained myself, and I said nothing. Thus mayest Thou, when the children of Israel commit trespasses and because of them fall upon evil times, be mindful of their father Isaac, and forgive their sins and deliver them from suffering.

And so, the dialogue ends, God will sustain the covenant, show mercy in judgment, and bring redemption to all the nations when the final sound of the ram's horn will be heard.[92] Kierkegaard has told us that no knight of faith can rely on an "outsider."[93] The Midrash tells us that Abraham is no outsider. He is the father of every member of the covenant.

Thus, for the present at least, the Kierkegaardian challenge dissolves. This having happened, however, the Kantian challenge re-emerges with new power. If the Torah abhors child sacrifice *now*, how can anyone following the Torah revere Abraham for his willingness to perform it, or call on the God who once commanded it? Kant admittedly fails to examine religious sacrifice. He would have rejected this sacrifice even if he had examined it, and if he had somehow concluded that some kinds of religious sacrifice are possible and necessary. We can suppose a Kant accepting an "absolute relation to the Absolute." What we cannot imagine is a Kant prepared to abandon a second Absolute, i.e., humanity as an end in itself. Nor are we in doubt, in case of clash, as to which Absolute would emerge victorious. The categorical imperative would win for Kant. In his view it should win for us all. In the light of this, it is only a minor matter whether it could have won for Abraham as well. Possibly the ancient patriarch knew and could know only of the first Absolute, in which case one might both absolve him from moral blame and credit him with sincere love of God. The major matter—indeed, in the end the only matter— is that Abraham's love of God, however genuine by his own morally unenlightened standards, would be "idolatrous" by ours. We do not and indeed cannot give Abraham reverence.

For Jewish thought, it would be a sign of apologetically inspired weakness to respond at this late date to Kant's challenge with a wholesale assault on his morality. Such an assault, to be sure, would not lack a degree of plausibility. Kant holds that even "common" —that is, philosophically uninstructed—"reason" knows that man is a person and not a thing. Yet a reason of this sort is not universal even among philosophers, for the Greeks among the ancients had no difficulty with the proposition that some men are slaves,[94] and among the moderns a thinker such as Heidegger puts forward a categorical imperative of sorts yet empties it of its Kantian content.[95] What if, once traced to its roots, the Kantian "person" were in fact the Jewish-Christian image of God, and his "common reason," a secularized faith in that image?

But to advance such criticisms on purely philosophical grounds would be one thing, to use (or abuse) these criticisms for apologetical purposes would be another. Medieval Jewish thinkers rejoiced in the discovery that moral law was rational as well as revealed, and modern Jewish thinkers free of apologetic fears may well wish that philosophers could all be Kantians. (Not accidentally many Jewish treatises, major and minor, have been devoted to the kinship between Judaism and Kantianism.)

Whether or not this wish is realistic, a Jewish reengagement with Kantianism at this point brings to light an insight hitherto concealed, and hence a question hitherto unasked. Jewish and Kantian morality agree that moral law, and hence humanity, has intrinsic value. They disagree in that the one accepts, and the other rejects, pristine moments of divine Presence in which every content and all standards are called into question. Having rejected these latter, Kant can hold fast to the intrinsic value of humanity, for it is ultimate and unchallengeable. But how can Jewish morality hold fast to such value when it accepts pristine moments of divine Presence in which every content and all standards are called into question? Above we found ourselves forced to ask whether, after all, circumstances might not arise in which Jeremiah would call, in the name of his God, for injustice, hatred and murder.

Yet this possibility is an abstract and empty conceit. Jeremiah not only in fact fails to suspend the ethical; it is not concretely conceivable that he should have done so even in the pristine moment when he was first called to his mission. This concrete inconceivability is philosophically intelligible only because this pristine moment occurs in an historical context in which not everything is questionable because something is already revealed; and the morally foremost revelation already given is that man is created in the image of God. The intrinsic value of human personality,

[68]

which is for Kant the possession of common reason, is in Judaism the gift of divine Grace, forever regiven and reappropriated.

This new insight gives rise to a new question in which, once again, the *Akedah* is the touchstone. For Kant's two-term morality, the intrinsic value of moral law and humanity is ultimate. For the three-term morality of Judaism, it is received as divinely given. To be sure, this latter (once the dimension of history is introduced) allows for pristine moments of divine Presence that are pristine only relatively since some value is already given. This possibility, however, cannot extend to all such moments unless radical probing is avoided and, indeed, unless the difference between Jewish and Kantian morality is ultimately to vanish. Thus arises the possibility of the *Akedah*, and along with it the question: must the Jewish thinker either (with Kant) hold fast to the ultimate value of humanity and reject the *Akedah*, or else (with Kierkegaard) hold fast to the *Akedah* and accept the consequence that, radically considered, humanity has intrinsic value only relatively, contingent as it is on an extraneous divine source?

Pre-Kantian Jewish thought did not face this dilemma. The Aristotelian-Maimonidean concept of the "repugnant to nature" falls morally short of the categorical imperative; moreover, the objective certainty attributed by Maimonides to the "empirical" voice speaking to Abraham has vanished under the impact of modern (not exclusively Kantian) criticism.[96] However, once faced with the dilemma by Kant, modern Jewish thought cannot avoid it. Yet we have already warned that it would be rash to assume that one must face it, as it were, nakedly, and that Jewish tradition lacks the spiritual resources that need only be brought to philosophical consciousness in order for the dilemma to be resolved.[97] How can this tradition both abhor child sacrifice and exalt the *Akedah*, never so much as raising the question of whether Abraham was not, after all, a would-be murderer and "idolater"?[98] This question, having forced itself on us again and again, must now at last be answered. What secret purpose may be fathomed in the Midrash in which the *Akedah* is explicitly connected both with the condemnation of child sacrifice and with Micah's classical summary of the three-term morality of Judaism?[99]

Consider a Jew in synagogue on the New Year's festival and hear the Torah portion assigned for that festival—none other than the *Akedah*. Consider his turning, as the festival bids him turn, to the renewal of the Creation, of the creation of man, and of the divine-Jewish covenant. Consider his further recalling, as he listens, the dilemma ascribed by Kierkegaard to a pastor preaching a sermon on this portion of the Torah. If the pastor begins with the *Akedah* he remains with its "dread," unable to pass beyond the beginning. And if, nevertheless, he moves on to the end, he is necessarily glib about the "dread of the beginning."[100] Would the Jewish worshipper recognize this pastor's dilemma as his own? The Kierkegaardian pastor, if a true knight of faith, is an isolated individual; the Jew at prayer is a member of the covenantal community. The first is himself a potential Abraham, and this is why the end of the *Akedah* comes for him after the beginning, as it did for Abraham himself. For the Jew hearing the Torah the beginning comes after the end, for if he now hears the Torah, and possesses the Torah, it is only on account of Abraham's merit. In short, the *Akedah* is present for him as a past, perpetually reenacted and superseded.

Why then, does this Jew, like Kierkegaard, revere Abraham when, like Kant, he considers all present child sacrifice forbidden? *Because of a perpetually reenacted radical surprise.* Kant's "common reason" rules out all surprise when it affirms the intrinsic value of humanity to be simply absolute. To receive the Torah on account of Abraham's merit is, first, to have called all things into question in the sight of Divinity, the intrinsic value of humanity included; second, it is to accept that some things are in question no longer; and third, it is to receive, in surprise as well as gratitude, the value of humanity as a gift that Divinity might have withheld and that is yet given forever.

Kant's common reason and the Torah emerge thus as being in a significant contrast. Immune to surprise from any source, Kant's common reason is *wholly* invulnerable so long as it is not questioned[101] and *indiscriminately* vulnerable once it is questioned.[102] Self-exposed to surprise, the Torah embodies for eternal reenactment the fear and trembling that once gripped Abraham. But precisely this self-exposure makes it *absolutely* immune to *any* child sacrifice, no matter what voice might demand it.

On Kiddush Hashem *or Martyrdom, or the* Akedah *as Present Reality*

In the rabbinic sources we find a legend that seems to explode all mere abstract theorizing—Kant and Kierkegaard, as well as any Jewish notion that the *Akedah* is both safely past and a mere trial. Some sources date the legendary incident during the persecution under Antiochus Epiphanes (167–164 B.C.E.), others, during that under the Roman Emperor Hadrian (135–138 C.E.). The substance of the story is always the same. A mother and her 7 sons are given the choice between idolatry and death; the sons all choose death without hesitation, and each is slaughtered in turn before the mother's eyes.[103] Then, in one version of the tale, the mother

. . . mourning because it had been decreed that [her] . . . sons must be slain, rejoicing . . . because through [her] . . . sons Heaven's glory was sanctified, . . . wept and said to them: "Children, do not be distressed, for to this end you were created—to sanctify in the world the Holy One, blessed be He. Go and tell Father Abraham, 'Let not your head swell with pride. You built one altar, but I built seven altars and on them have offered up my seven sons. What is more: yours was a trial; mine was accomplished fact.' "[104]

What a harrowing legend! But, so we might add quickly, after all a legend only, with doubtful basis in fact. What then shall we make of the following story which we have good reason to take as a factual account?[105] The event occurred in 1096 in the city of Worms, when the crusading mobs fell upon countless Jewish communities, and Jews, having resisted to the end, chose death rather than apostasy, on frequent occasions preferring to kill themselves or each other to being slaughtered. We learn of a certain Rabbi Meshullam Bar Isaac who

in a loud voice . . . called out . . . : "All ye great and small, hearken unto me. Here is my son whom God gave me and to whom my wife Zipporah gave birth in her old age, Isaac is this child's name; and now I shall offer him up as Father Abraham offered up his son Isaac." Whereupon Zipporah besought him: "O my lord, my lord, do not lay thy hand upon the lad whom I raised and brought up after having given birth to him in my old age. Slay me first that I shall not have to behold the death of the child." But he replied, saying: "Not even for a moment shall I delay, for He who gave him to us will take him away to his own portion and lay him to rest in Father Abraham's bosom." And he bound his son Isaac, and picked up the knife to slay his son, and recited the blessing appropriate for slaughter. And the lad replied, "Amen." And the father slew the lad. Then he took his shrieking wife and both of them together left the room; and the vagabonds murdered them. Over such as these, wilt Thou hold Thy peace, O Lord?[106]

Shall we praise Rabbi Meshullam Bar Isaac as a Kierkegaardian knight of faith who "gave the proof God required of him"? Shall we, with Kant, condemn him for "deserting his post" and causing his son to do likewise? Shall we cite against him the Jewish belief that human sacrifice is forbidden—that the *Akedah* is safely past and superseded? We can do none of these things, for in his case— and that of countless others from the time of Antiochus Epiphanes to Nazi Germany—we come upon realities that quite escape the categories hitherto used. The *Akedah* is past? In 1096 it was a ghastly reality. Is the end of the story that God rejects human sacrifice? For the Jews of Mayence and Worms it had a different ending—and it was not a story. How dare we compare or even mention in the same breath a mere legendary sacrifice from the remote past with a present reality? How dare we compare what remained mere intention with one that became literal fact? We must ask how, in the long centuries of Jewish martyrdom, Abraham could have remained a revered example, and are not surprised that the legend arose, directly contrary to Holy Writ, that Abraham actually sacrificed Isaac—that God did not stay Abraham's hand but rather brought a dead Isaac back to life.[107]

What *were* the realities of the Jews of Mayence and Worms? They did not "seek death," knowing full well that the Torah commands the saving of life, one's own included; and, had the possibility existed, they would have done as Maimonides was to recommend a century later—migrate to a land where a Jew can live by the Torah and not die by it.[108] What confronted them, however, was the choice between death and apostasy, and there was grave doubt as to whether the raging mobs would let even would-be apostates live. They chose death, and indeed became "authors" of it; yet, at least in their own understanding, they did not "desert their post" but would have done so had they chosen otherwise. According to Kant (who remains in the realm of abstract universality) a man must preserve his life "until the time comes when God expressly commands us to leave this life."[109] In the concrete situation of the singled out Jews of Mayence and Worms, that time had come when there was no alternative to death but apostasy.

But why suicide? And, to go a vast step further, how could they possibly kill their children? Why not, as Kant bids Cato, stoically await the inevitable? The Jews of Mayence and Worms found it possible to die as well as live in the love of God. Maimonides, who was to ease many troubled consciences by ruling that enforced apostasy is not actual apostasy, nevertheless saw the highest degree of holiness in being found worthy to die for the sanctification of the divine name.[110] Long before him, the mother of the 7 had exclaimed, in a ghastly hyperbole, "To this end you were created."[111] In a previously cited Midrash the ram's horn reminds God of the *Akedah*, causing Him to judge Israel in mercy because of Abraham's merit.[112] From Gaon Saadiah (862–942) we learn that this same horn also reminds Israel to be "ready at all times [like Isaac] to offer . . . [their lives] for the sanctification of

His name."[113] They must be ready in case events occur that prove that Abraham's testimony to the nations had not been enough.

But *was* Isaac ready? And was his namesake ready, the son of Rabbi Meshullam Bar Isaac? The Midrashic Isaac, unlike both the Kantian and the Kierkegaardian, is no helpless, immature, and unsuspecting victim but rather a knowing, willing, adult participant. He is a grown man, 37 years of age, and (as the Midrash goes out of its way to stress) no aged father could have bound such a man without his consent.[114] The Midrashic Isaac joins his father in praising God, and responds "Amen" to the latter's blessing; and what is done by him in mere legend is done by his namesake, the son of Rabbi Meshullam, in literal fact. The Midrash takes the monumental step of transmuting the *Akedah* from child sacrifice into *Kiddush Hashem*, or martyrdom;[115] as for countless Jewish men, women and children from Antiochus Epiphanes to Hitler, they took the altogether staggering leap from intention to execution.

How shall the modern, philosophically instructed Jew so much as begin to come to grips with Jewish martyrdom? That he will look in vain to Kant is already evident from the use of Kantian terms in the preceding several paragraphs—terms too abstractly universalistic to come anywhere near doing justice to the singled out Jewish condition. Kant does leave room for *moral* "martyrdom —the deliberate sacrifice of oneself for the good of mankind."[116] That he can make nothing of *religious* martyrdom might be guessed from our previous account of religious sacrifice, and is confirmed by the fact that the Kantian Jesus is a moral hero who may risk death but in no sense seek it or be author of it; the Jesus who wills his Father's will when the hour of martyrdom has come escapes the Kantian scope.[117] Moreover, his martyrs are all presumably heroic soldiers, leaders, prophets, philosophers, adult fighters for truth and goodness. To think of a singled out community composed of men, women, and children, we may be sure, never enters his mind. In short, *Jewish* martyrdom for the sanctification of the divine name, though having a long history in Kant's Europe, is, so far as Kant is concerned, as though it had never been.

Far more surprisingly, the same is true of Kierkegaard as well. Unlike Kant, Kierkegaard not only considers religious martyrdom, he agonizes over it. He writes an essay entitled "Does a Man have the right to let himself be killed for the Truth?"[118] Yet despite its universal title the essay speaks of none but Christian martyrs and, indeed, does not hesitate to assert that "Christianity invented the possibility of martyrdom."[119] (The Abraham praised so eloquently

[73]

elsewhere, it is clear, is a proto-Christian and nothing else.) Jews do appear in the essay, not, however, as martyrs, but as Christ-killers.[120]

But, for all this, are his reflections on Christian martyrdom relevant to Jewish martyrdom? They are not. They may or may not be valid for the Christian would-be martyr to his truth. For the Jewish situation they are without substance and relevance.

Consider Kierkegaard's argument. That Christ could sacrifice his life out of love one can understand; but how could his love allow him to let others become guilty of his murder? Did not love require of him to be "more yielding?"[121] But Christ was the Truth as well as Love. Hence

... he wills his death. Yet in this ... he did not, like a man, tempt God. His free decision to die is in eternal harmony with the will of the Father. When a man wills his death he tempts God; for no man may presume to such harmony with God.[122]

Does a mere man, then, have the right to let himself be killed for the Truth even when he is, as Christian, in possession of the Truth—if this makes others guilty of murder?

Does my duty toward the Truth give me *this* right? Or does my duty toward my fellowmen require that I compromise the Truth some-what?[123]

The question arises because the would-be martyr would not be killed if he *did* compromise somewhat, a fact that makes others quite rightly say that the martyr's death is his own fault. "And yet, if he gave his life for the Truth he was, in the noblest sense, innocent."[124]

The conclusion emerging from these tortuous reflections is that the contemporary Christian, at any rate, has no right to expose himself to martyrdom. Possibly his ancestors had this right, for they witnessed to the Christian Truth against pagan falsehood. Vis-à-vis other Christians, however, no Christian "may pretend to be in possession of the absolute Truth."[125] To be more yielding is not only his human right but also his Christian duty.

Did the Jews of Mayence and Worms have the choice of not singling themselves out by "compromising the Truth somewhat"? They *were being* singled out, and had the choice only between faithfulness unto death and total apostasy. In choosing death, did they witness to "absolute Truth" against total falsehood? Al-though given every reason to consider Christianity false, they made no necessary judgment about the Christianity of Christians but only about their own Judaism: they must remain faithful to the divine-Jewish covenant. Could each person choose as an individual? They were singled out as a community, with fathers facing a necessity never dreamt of by Kierkegaard—that of choosing with and in behalf of their children. In making their choice, did the Jews of Mayence and Worms let the crusading mobs become guilty of murder? These mobs were already bent on murder, not because of anything Jews had done or would do, but simply because they existed. Moreover, one might add that Rabbi Meshullam Bar Isaac relieved their gentle consciences of at least one murder—that of Isaac, the namesake of the ancient patriarch.

Thus only one of Kierkegaard's questions remains, and even this must be restated in order to be applicable. Kierkegaard writes: "When a man wills his death, he tempts God, for no man may presume to such harmony with God."[126] Did Rabbi Meshullam Bar Isaac have the duty to choose apostasy above truth, in the hope that lives might thus have been saved?

For a believing Jew, this is the ultimate question. Survival—including one's own—ranks high among his God-given duties. (Indeed—though Jews prior to the Nazi holocaust could not know of this—a time would come when it would rank highest, after Jews had been confronted not with death as one of two choices but with total extermination.) Maimonides still ranks survival high even when the price is enforced apostasy, for he rules that such an apostate is guiltless and remains a member of the covenantal community. Yet in his view this guiltless apostate has broken at least one commandment, the sanctification of the divine name; and he who observes that commandment "has been found worthy by God of reaching the highest stage."[127] Can a Jew accept a God who ranks this stage highest? Can he ever accept himself or his children as singled out for that stage, so long as survival still remains a possible alternative?

The Midrashic Abraham could accept the *Akedah* only on condition that it had a purpose, and on the further condition that this purpose was not between God and himself alone. Generations to come were to see that Abraham's merit no longer seemed operative; confronted with the *Akedah* as a *present* demand, they were forced to ask what was its present purpose. Abraham had witnessed to the nations, yet, to judge by Antiochus Epiphanes, Hadrian, the crusading mobs, and countless others, his testimony had been in vain.[128] Was any justifiable purpose served by any new *Akedah*, and if so what was that purpose?

To these tormenting questions, Jewish martyrs and those remembering their martyrdom were able to give only fragmentary

[75]

and even conflicting answers. Possibly the purpose of Jewish martyrdom lies in the hereafter.[129] Possibly Jewish martyrs atone for the world's sins as well as for their own.[130] Perhaps, most extreme of all, there are times when God says, as He did to the prophet Ezechiel, "As I live . . . , I will not be inquired of by you." (Ez. 20:3)[131] Only one thing remained constant in all these conflicting and fragmentary answers: that, for the sake of both God and the world, a Jew must not leave his covenantal post. With this one absolute commitment made, it is impossible to rule out extreme situations in which the divine name can no longer be sanctified in the world through life, but only through death.

The Midrash tells how once Nebuchadnezzar erected an idol and assembled three men from every nation to bow down to it. Hananiah, Mishael, and Azariah, the three Jews selected, consulted the prophet Ezechiel as to their duty, and the prophet, citing Isaiah, advised them to flee and hide. But who, the three asked, would then testify against the idols? Whereupon Ezechiel, consulting with God, said: "Sovereign of the universe, Hananiah, Mishael and Azariah seek to give their lives for the sanctification of Thy name. Will Thou stand by them or no?" God replied, "I will not stand by them, as it is written . . . 'As I live . . . , I will not be inquired of by you.'" (Ez. 20:3) Ezechiel broke into tears, for did not Scripture say that these three alone were left in Judah, and would not this small remnant now perish? Yet Hananiah, Mishael, and Azariah, informed of the divine reply, said: "Whether He stands by us or does not stand by us, we will sacrifice our lives for the sanctification of God's name."

Who are the three pillars on which God has established the world? The Midrash ends with this question and replies that some say it is Abraham, Isaac, and Jacob; others, Hananiah, Mishael, and Azariah.[132]

The Impossible Question

The following is part of an eye-witness account of what occurred on October 5, 1942 in Dubno in the Ukraine, when thousands of Jewish men, women, and children were rounded up, told to undress, were shot, and, alive or dead, thrown into ditches. The witness writes:

Without weeping or lamenting, these people undressed, stood together in family groups, kissed and said farewell . . . During the fifteen minutes or so while I watched I heard no laments or appeals to be spared. I noticed a family of about eight, a man and a woman of about

[76]

fifty, with their children, approximately one, eight and ten years old, as well as two adult daughters between twenty and twenty-four. A white-haired old woman held the baby, sang to him, and tickled him, and the baby shrieked with pleasure—all this while the parents looked on with tears in their eyes. The father held the boy of about ten by his hand and spoke softly to him, while the boy struggled to hold back his tears. The father pointed to the sky, stroked the boy's head, and seemed to explain something to him. . . .

The witness ends: "The above is the pure truth, so help me God."[133]

What did the father explain to the son? We shall never know. What was there to explain? That, given a choice between apostasy and death, a Jew must choose death? Jews in Nazi Europe were not given this choice. That a Jew could still choose *how* if not *whether* to die, and that the manner of his death would be a testimony to the nations? But diabolic cunning would be used to blot out all signs that they had ever lived, and the world was showing even then that it cared little whether they lived or died, and less how they died. That God does not break His covenant with Israel? This was the lament of the angels when Abraham raised his knife, but God stayed Abraham's hand and stilled their lament. What did the angels do when they saw Auschwitz, Bergen-Belsen, Maidenek, Buchenwald? And where was God?

A Jew after Auschwitz cannot and dare not give answers. He may and must give a response. The core of every possible response is that just as Abraham, the mother of the 7, Rabbi Meshullam Bar Isaac, and countless and nameless others refused to abandon their Jewish post, so must he—but that after the martyrdom of Auschwitz, forever unfathomable and without equal anywhere, Jewish life is more sacred than Jewish death, even if it is for the sanctification of the divine name.

Chapter 3

MOSES AND THE HEGELIANS

JEWISH EXISTENCE IN THE MODERN WORLD

INTRODUCTION

Concerning Moses, the greatest Jewish prophet, Moses Maimonides, the greatest Jewish philosopher, asserted that he defies all comparisons.[1] In his *Guide for the Perplexed* he did not shrink from a philosophical investigation of prophecy, or from the attempt, bold for any medieval thinker, of mediating the sharp dualism between the "natural" endowments of reason and the "supernatural" gift of revelation. Nevertheless—and in view of his philosophical mediating activities this fact stands out clearly and firmly—he considered Moses to be unique in all of history. There never had been nor would ever be a prophet like Moses; and as incomparable as Moses himself was and always would be was the Torah, which was given to him at Sinai. Such was the verdict of one whose learning, wisdom and fidelity gave rise to the saying: "From Moses to Moses there was none like Moses."[2]

This verdict of the greatest medieval Jewish philosopher is both shared and dialectically transformed by the greatest modern Christian philosopher. In his *Lectures On The Philosophy of Religion* G. F. W. Hegel writes as follows:

Moses is called the law-giver of the Jews. But he was not for the Jews what Lykurgos and Solon were to the Greeks. The latter two gave as men their own laws. Moses only made the laws of Jehovah known: it was Jehovah Himself who, according to the story, engraved them on stone. Attached to the most trifling regulations, the arrangements of the tabernacle, the usages in connection with sacrifices, and everything relating to all other kinds of ceremonial, one finds in the Bible the formula "Jehovah saith." All law is given by the Lord and is thus entirely positive commandment. There is in it a formal, absolute authority. The particular elements in the political system are not, generally speaking, developed out of a universal purpose and are, further, not left for man to determine in detail, for the [divine] Unity does not permit human caprice, human reason, to exist alongside it, and political change is in every instance called a falling away from God. Rather is the particular something determined by God, and hence regarded as eternally established. Here the eternal laws of what is right, of moral-

[81]

ity, are placed in the same rank and stated in equally positive form as the most trifling regulations. *This constitutes a strong contrast to the conception which we have of God. . . .*[3]

The medieval Jewish philosopher upholds a Mosaic law unchangeable until the Messianic days. His modern Christian (or post-Christian) critic considers this the authentic Jewish view—and declares that "we" have surpassed it.

Hegel's criticism differs in kind from those dealt with earlier in this book. Empiricists and Kantians disregard history. For Hegel it is central. The God of Elijah and that of Abraham are assailed by their modern philosophical critics by timeless standards as timeless falsehoods. In criticizing the God of Moses, Hegel refers to the "strong contrast" with the conception that "we"—the modern secular-Protestant world—have of God; and his comparison between the laws of Moses and those of Lykurgos and Solon is not between simple falsehood and simple truth but rather between two partial truths—now both superseded. The empiricists' Elijah and the Kantian Abraham are straight obscurantists, by the standards, respectively, of scientific and moral enlightenment. The Hegelian Moses is no simple obscurantist, and indeed his people are praised for the "marvellous steadfastness" with which they adhere to His laws. If nevertheless the God of Moses is subject to criticism (and Jewish steadfastness is at the same time "fanatical stubbornness"), it is because even in ancient times Judaism was only a partial truth. And if "we" can recognize this partial truth as partial, it is because we possess a universal, comprehensive Truth in which all partial truths, the Jewish included, are both preserved and superseded. The God of Moses is not a simple, unhistorical falsehood; He is an anachronism.

To put it mildly, this charge is not original with Hegel. In Christian theology it begins with Paul. In modern philosophy and philosophically minded history it is found wherever religious history is understood as a liberalistic evolutionary process from particularistic to universalistic "God-ideas," for in such schemes Judaism appears with depressing regularity as somehow beneath the standards of "modern universalism." Yet among modern philosophers—the argument with Christian theology is outside our present inquiry—Hegel alone (Hegelians only excepted) deserves to be taken seriously by modern Jewish thinkers. For all its supposedly deep immersion in historical realities, a work such as A. J. Toynbee's *A Study of History* criticizes Jewish "parochialism" in the light of empty, unhistorical, syncretistic abstractions, and his criticism amounts to little more than the liberalistic platitude that men should rise from the stepping stones of their particularistic selves to higher, more universal things. No religious Jew, however extreme in his parochialism, would recognize his religion in Toynbee's caricatures. (Nor would *any* religious man exchange his concrete religious reality for Toynbee's lifeless abstractions.)

Like the liberals, Hegel affirms a religious evolution from particularism to universalism. However, under no circumstances may his doctrine be confused with an "evolution of God-ideas" that judges all living religions by subjectivist, abstract, humanly invented standards—and inevitably destroys them without discrimination. Hegel differs in at least three crucial particulars. First, he begins by taking all serious forms of religious life as they take themselves, that is, not as the human self's solitary disport with its own ideas or emotions, but rather as actual, lived relations between the human and the Divine. Second, he does not judge forms of religious life in the light of subjectivist conceptions externally and arbitrarily brought to them, but rather tries to bring to consciousness an inner logic already within them. And if, third, he nevertheless rises above such a phenomenological understanding to philosophical judgment and criticism, it is because judgment and criticism somehow forced upon thought by religious life itself, (although, to be sure, not by religious life alone). Religions oppose each other with absolute and hence irreconcilable claims. Hegel accepts these claims but rejects their absoluteness. The core of his philosophy of religion—perhaps of his philosophy as a whole—is a mediating thought-activity that transforms all absolute into relative religious conflicts, thus aiming at an absolute, all-comprehensive Truth in which all partial truths are both preserved and superseded.

This is, of course, a monumental undertaking, and the central question is whether, and if so on what conditions, it is possible. There is at least one condition about which Hegel himself is in no doubt: the goal yet to be made actual by his all-mediating thought is attainable only if it is somehow already actual in historical life. Thus Hegel, like the liberals, claims for the modern world—not merely for his own philosophical thought—a vast religious superiority over the whole of man's religious past.

The liberals merely claim this superiority by presupposed and hence arbitrary standards. Hegel seeks to demonstrate it. And since "demonstration" means "all-mediating comprehensiveness," Hegel finds himself required to do a "justice" to the superseded past that liberal evolutionism would find neither possible nor necessary. Past religious truth must be preserved as well as super-seded by the higher modern religious Truth, and shown to be so by Hegel's philosophy. Hence it must be said that Hegel alone (Hegelians only excepted) has a genuinely philosophical concept of religious-truth-become-anachronistic.

To do justice to the actual world is thus an intrinsic part of Hegel's philosophical program. We on our part, however, would fail to do justice to Hegel were we to concentrate on his program alone. The heart and soul of this thought lies in the labor of execution. For Hegel, mediation is the law of all things, divine as well as human. Yet all depends on the recognition that he does not, by an arbitrary, external, a priori fiat, merely assert a "law of universal mediation," thus presupposing justice to the phe-nomena—and ipso facto failing to do it. His thought is self-im-mersed in and self-exposed to the phenomena, risking at every step of its labor the chance that the mediation sought remains either fragmented or proves wholly impossible. In view of the vast variety and complexity of the facts of religious life (as well as of the enormity of his philosophical aim), one may safely anticipate that Hegel's thought does less than complete justice to the phe-nomena. The astounding fact is how much justice it does.

In no case is such justice more astounding than in that of Judaism. Jewish scholars have not failed to note in Hegel's account of the Jewish religion what do indeed seem to be serious if not scandalous omissions and distortions.[4] Yet any Jewish thinker must, before all else, be greatly surprised by the fact that, in the case of Judaism, Hegel's philosophy metes out any kind of justice at all.

Four considerations may be adduced in ascending order of im-portance. First, the hoary legend of Jewish "barren legalism" was still uncritically accepted in Hegel's time, and Hegel (who in-herited it from Kant) had himself perpetuated it in his so-called *Early Theological Writings*. Second, Hegel's time, if any in all of history, seemed to confirm this legend, for German culture was at its peak, Jewish religious life (in Germany at least) at its nadir, and "cultured" German Jews rushed in droves to the baptismal font, considering it, as the most famous of them put it, as their "entrance ticket" to Europe.[5] Third—here we turn from non-philosophical to philosophical considerations—Hegel's mature philosophy by no means *compelled* him to revise his early estimate of Judaism, for it recognized in history contingent fact wholly devoid of spiritual truth.[6] Finally—here we come to the crux—a conscious self-exposure on Hegel's part, not to a mere image of Judaism of his own making, but to actual Jewish religious realities, called into question, not some minor aspects of his thought, but nothing less than his system as a whole.

This may seem a grandiose if not wholly irresponsible assertion, and, indeed, all that follows will be required to explicate and defend it. For the present, prima facie plausibility alone is required, and this may be furnished by a sketch of significant contrasts.

Self-exposed to the "actual world," Hegel's all-mediating thought is, by its own admission and insistence, vulnerable to charges of "injustice" done to the world. Such charges were to come after Hegel's death, at one extreme, from Karl Marx on behalf of the alienated proletariat and, at the other, from Søren Kierkegaard on behalf of the "existing" Christian individual. To this day both charges are widely considered too profound to be disregarded by the Hegelian system, and too radical to be assimilated. Yet the facts pointed to by neither thinker can match the threat to Hegel's system represented by Jewish history—a fact confronted by Hegel himself.

Had Hegel been alive he might have relativized the Marxist protest (made on behalf of man alone), on the one hand, by extending his own thought beyond its bourgeois limits and, on the other, by giving that protest a posthumanist, religious direction. To Kierkegaard's protest (unlike that of Marx, made on behalf of both God and man) he might have replied that his "existing individual," like Hegel's own, was a Christian, and that since the Christian God had rendered the divine-human incommensurability commensurate, Kierkegaard's isolation from man or God was less significant than he imagined.

Neither of these possible Hegelian responses were adequate to the challenge of Jewish history. That trimillennial fact, confronted as such by Hegel himself, bears witness (unlike the merely modern proletariat and its spokesman Marx) to both God and man in *all* history. Unlike Kierkegaard and indeed any Christian, it bears witness to their ultimate incommensurability. Jewish religious existence bears witness through the ages to the absoluteness of at least two distinctions—between God and man, and between the one true God and all the false. On its part, Hegel's philosophy seeks to mediate all absolute distinctions, not excluding those between God and man and true and false gods. No more radical contrast is possible, and had Hegel simply dismissed the fact of Jewish history—as a fossil, a curiosity, a mere fact without spiritual truth—one would not be surprised.

It therefore testifies to an altogether exceptional philosophical integrity that Hegel spurned this easy course, and occupied himself with Jewish history throughout his life, increasingly attempting to do it justice. His biographer Karl Rosenkranz writes:

Hegel's view of Jewish history varied greatly at different times. The phenomenon both repelled and fascinated him, and vexed him as a dark riddle throughout his life. At times, as in the *Phenomenology*, he ignored it. At other times, as in the *Philosophy of Right*, he placed it in close proximity to the Germanic Spirit. At other times again, such as in the *Philosophy of Religion*, he placed it on a par with Greek and Roman history, as together constituting the immediate forms of spiritual individuality. Finally—in the *Philosophy of History*—he made Jewish history part of the Persian Empire. All these are . . . justified aspects . . . but only the whole can satisfy.[7]

Less pious Hegelians than Rosenkranz may not share his last-named opinion; indeed, Hegel himself may have had his doubts.

Hegel is the only non-Jewish modern philosopher of first rank to take Judaism in its own right seriously. Even so, however, it may seem wayward for a contemporary Jewish thinker to take *him* seriously. The contemporary historian will object that his image of Judaism is dated if only because postbiblical, rabbinic sources are ignored. His philosophical colleague will object that while Hegelian fragments remain alive, his system does not. Both may unite to assert that the charge of anachronism directed against Judaism, at least in its Hegelian form, is itself anachronistic.

Yet Hegel's philosophical history is not ordinary history; its power to challenge Jewish religious existence does not depend on the achievement of its maximal goals; and despite its failure to reach these goals it remains the deepest modern philosophical challenge to Jewish religious existence to this day. We shall dwell briefly on these three points—on the third only cursorily since perforce the whole remainder of this chapter is required for its full explication.

First, to cite, say, rabbinic sources against Hegel would be easy but, by itself, off the mark. On the one hand, Hegel's use of biblical sources seems as arbitrary as his failure to use rabbinic ones. On the other hand, while ignoring postbiblical Jewish religion, he by no means ignores postbiblical Jewish history. Related to the modern "Germanic" world, this history is in some sense dialectically superior to the entire Christian Middle Ages. Transformed in Spinozism into the form of thought, it is the indispensable beginning of all modern philosophy. These two examples suffice to show that Hegel's failure vis-à-vis Judaism (if such it is) is not a historian's failure, such as prejudice, unfamiliarity with sources, and the like. It is a philosopher's failure. Hegel is a philosophical historian; and his goal in this capacity is to comprehend Jewish history within the context of "world history."

This overall Hegelian goal (to turn from the first quarter of objectors to the second) is not invalidated by Hegel's failure, readily admitted by the present writer, to attain his maximal aims. Marxism and existentialism might be called as witnesses to its lasting significance. More pertinent is the fact that, unless deliberately self-ghettoized, the Jewish religious thinker must sooner or later himself attempt to do from one extreme what is done most radically by Hegel's thought from the other. Hegel permits each historical self-understanding, the Jewish included, its own scope, and then mediates and resolves the conflicts between them. The Jewish religious self-understanding is world-historical from a Jewish point of view; the Hegelian philosophical comprehension is world-historical from a "world-historical" point of view; and it is its claim to do justice to all points of view which makes its own point of view "world-historical."[8] But can a Jewish religious thinker—or, at any rate, one who is modern—fail to ask how his own point of view stands related to others?

To perceive the full power of this question three points must be made about the Jewish religious self-understanding. First— like Hegel's philosophical comprehension and unlike much religious self-understanding—the Jewish religious self-understanding is itself historical: Jewish religious existence is *between* Creation (or Fall or Exodus) and the Messianic future. Second—again like Hegel's philosophical comprehension—this religious self-understanding is *world*-historical: the beginning and end of history are universal, and Jewish existence between these extremes is that of a *witness* in which the abstractions "particular" and "universal" are concretely intertwined. Third—and this is decisive—unless Jewish religious existence is to be not only *in* history but also somehow *of* it, it must sooner or later, and certainly in the modern world, relate itself not only to non-Jewish world history but also to non-Jewish ways of understanding it. But once it makes this attempt from its *own* point of view it comes face to face with the Hegelian mediation of *all* points of view from a world-historical point of view.

Hegel's comprehension of world history therefore confronts the Jewish religious self-understanding with a radical challenge, and this does not vanish if Hegel's own point of view should prove to be less world-historical than he imagines. This challenge may be expressed in the form of a dilemma. Either the Jew keeps himself immune to all changes of a merely "worldly" history; assuming that nothing decisive can happen to his religious self-understanding between Sinai and the Messianic days, he remains indiscriminately indifferent to the Greek-Roman world (which considers him an exclusivist "enemy of mankind"), the medieval Catholic world (which makes him a religious anachronism shut away in ghettoes), and the modern secular-Protestant world (which invites him, qua man, back into history on condition that, qua Jew, he stays out of it): but then he cuts off his own history from world history, reduces himself to a worldless monk, and confines the present effectiveness of the God of all history to Jewish history, all of which is contrary to central Jewish religious commitments. Or else he insists on being of history as well as in it, open to epoch-making changes in world history that might affect his religious self-understanding; but then this self-understanding is rendered questionable by all epoch-making changes; indeed, the possibility arises that Jewish religious existence is wholly superseded. Put in its most radical (i.e., Hegelian) form, this dilemma raises the spectre of "anachronism" in either case—in the first case, through a Jewish opting out of world history; in the second, through voluntary self-dissolution into it. So radical is the challenge of Hegelianism to the Jewish self-understanding.

But might not Judaism challenge Hegelianism as radically as Hegelianism challenges Judaism? Hegel's philosophy mediates from an external and superior point of view between Jewish history and, respectively, the ancient Greek-Roman, medieval Catholic, and modern secular-Protestant worlds. What if, in point of historical fact, Hegel's external mediations of Jewish history with the periods of world history were matched by *internal* Jewish *self*-mediations *in response* to the epoch-making changes which are cited by Hegel against it?

This question has never been asked. It does not occur in Hegel's thought. It has not occurred to Jewish Hegelians or anti-Hegelians. Yet once it is asked, Hegel's understanding of Jewish history, his understanding of world history, and indeed his world-historical standpoint are all called into question. What if *some* distinctions— between God and man, and between the one true God and all the false—were in fact as absolute as they are held to be by the Jewish religious self-understanding? Or, to put it more cautiously, what if the Jewish religious self-understanding has been able to hold fast to these distinctions in response to three thousand years of world-historical change rather than at the price of withdrawal from it? Only an actual encounter between Judaism and Hegelianism can give an answer to this question. One outcome, however, is clear from the start. Should the question we have asked have an affirmative answer, Jewish history will become a far darker "riddle" to any form of Hegelianism than even the master dreamt of.

HEGEL'S ACCOUNT OF JUDAISM

Previously in this book we initiated encounters between Judaism and modern philosophy. Our present encounter will be in the nature of a response, for Hegel already has an encounter with Judaism in his own right.

On first sight this distinction between, say, Kant and Hegel is hardly justified, for Hegel's account of Judaism seems to differ from Kant's only in being more detailed and to be no less a caricature. In both philosophies Judaism figures as the chief villain, illustrating the vices, respectively, of "theological morality" and of religious "positivity"; and there may seem little to choose between Kant's recommendation of "euthanasia" for Judaism and Hegel's demonstration that it is anachronistic. What can one say on behalf of either thinker, then, except that they took their cue on "Jewish legalism" from Spinoza and Moses Mendelssohn, and thus cannot be overly blamed if they relied on Jewish authorities?

But on closer inspection Kant never tries to understand Judaism whereas Hegel makes a serious, even desperate, attempt to do it justice. Kant takes no serious look at either Judaism or his own standards before concluding that its euthanasia will benefit one and all, not least the Jewish people itself.[9] When judging Judaism to be anachronistic Hegel not only examines the phenomenon seriously (if, to be sure, inadequately), he also examines the standards by which he does the judging. And both examinations are sufficiently deep that Jewish religious existence, supposedly over and done with in the Christian world if indeed not already in the Greek-Roman period preceding it, keeps reappearing in contexts that, it is true, dialectically transform it but that do not, at any rate, simply dispose of it. To expand somewhat on this fact already briefly referred to, the God of Israel alone survives the death of all ancient gods in the Roman pantheon; the "people of Israel" is "held ready" for some true (if negative) purpose by "Spirit and its world" beyond the Christian Middle Ages;[10] and there is room for both the Jewish God and the Jewish people even in the modern world. Of the God this is clear, for the God of Israel assumes in Spinozism the form of Thought. Of the people it is not so clear.

Yet it will be seen that a brief and cryptic note in Hegel's *Philosophy of Right*[11] can mean nothing else than that there is a future for the Jewish people in the modern world, the dialectical dissipation of its religious past notwithstanding—a view lending poetic if no other truth to the fact that the first modern Zionist philosophy (that of Moses Hess) is recognizably Hegelian.[12] These are the results of Hegel's effort to do Jewish history justice.

Such results would never have come to pass had Hegel's mature thought not turned sharply from the standpoint of his so-called *Early Theological Writings*. These early fragments, never intended for publication, remain with a dualism wholly alien to his mature philosophy. A religion of true inwardness is contrasted with one of mere "positivity" or external observance, and of this latter Judaism serves as the prime example. To be sure, Hegel surpasses Kant even then in historical sensitivity, and his brief recourse to an unhistorical, mystic-romantic divine-human "union" is accompanied by a tragic awareness of divine-human "nonunion" in actual history. Even so, however, there remains a dualism between sheer virtue or spirit and sheer vice or letter and, as has happened with such melancholy monotony in the history of Christendom, Judaism is the chief villain. No matter how the realm of religious truth is circumscribed—and on this subject Hegel's views shift quickly in this early period—Judaism falls outside it.

In Hegel's mature thought Judaism is drawn into the sphere of religious truth.[13] This monumental change is part and parcel of a no less monumental change in Hegel's philosophy of religion as a whole. First, every trace of subjectivism (Kantian or romantic), if ever genuinely present at all, has disappeared: the religious fact for philosophical thought is not subjective or human, but rather (as all serious religious self-understanding takes it to be) subjective-objective, or a human-divine relationship. Second, this latter relationship is characterized by divine-human nonunion *as well as* divine-human union: the tragic realism that in the *Early Theological Writings* falls outside the realm of religious truth now lies within it. Of these two doctrines the first is already present in Hegel's transitional romantic phase. But not until the second is fully developed has his religious thought reached maturity.

Hegel's mature doctrine is as follows. Without divine-human union there is no genuine religion but only mutual divine-human indifference and irrelevance. (Deism, ancient and modern, is no genuine religion but only a disguise for lack of religion.) Without divine-human nonunion religion is idolatrous or frivolous: the first if the divine Infinity is reduced to sheer finitude; the second if the human self has fled from its real finitude into the shapeless "fog" of an infinite but unreal pious emotion. Hegel holds that no genuine religion is simply idolatrous, for the divine Infinity is at work in every such religion even if it does not, or only inadequately does, become conscious *for* it. He also contrasts romantic frivolousness with Christian seriousness. The one flees from the actual divine-human discord into the sheer union of mere feeling. The other finds its climax in the Easter—a "union of union and nonunion"[14] that both preserves and conquers the Good Friday, i.e., the whole pain of absolute discord.

Within this overall conception, Judaism appears as the stern, stubborn, incorruptible witness to divine-human nonunion. The Jewish God is one, infinite, universal, wholly incommensurate with multiplicity, finitude, particularity. On his part, His human worshipper exists in stark human finitude and particularity, a "family" even when "expanded into a nation."[15] Hegel sees a "strange, infinitely harsh, the harshest contrast"[16] in this divine-human relationship, and everything will in the end depend on why he sees a harsh contrast here and how he copes with it. For the present, however, all attention must be focused on his view that the Jewish divine-human relationship is a dimension of religious truth despite, indeed because of, this contrast. *In spite* of it: Judaism is by no means (like Deism) a mutual divine-human indifference or irrelevance; within the divine-Jewish nonunion there lives a real union when man recognizes God as Lord and himself as servant, and when God assumes lordship over him. *Because* of the contrast: the Jewish testimony to the divine-human nonunion has an absolute right over all efforts to deny or dissipate either the finitude of the human or the infinity of the Divine. Moreover, it has a role within the total realm of religious truth that is unique and indispensable. The Jewish fear of the Lord is not one wisdom beside others. It is the beginning of all religious wisdom.

The philosopher can elicit from Judaism (as from every genuine religion) a "metaphysical notion." The Divine is "infinite Power." A Power is infinite only if it is not beside or indifferent to the finite but rather Power *over* it. It is divine only if it is not sheer Power (no object of possible worship) but rather "Power of *Wisdom*." The world of finitude is "absolutely posited" by this Power, the "purpose" being divine lordship over the "world." Such, in utmost brevity, is the metaphysical notion of Judaism.[17]

It would be a mere philosopher's abstraction except for its "realization." This occurs in and for the religious consciousness— in Judaism, in a human acceptance of both world and human self as products of a divine *creatio ex nihilo*. In this acceptance, divine Power reveals itself as Goodness and Justice. Divine goodness is absolute, manifesting itself not in *what* finite things are but rather in *that* they are at all: granted independent existence, despite their finitude, side by side with the divine Infinity. (For idolatrous or atheistic consciousness the existence of the world is an unquestioned fact. For Jewish consciousness it is *the* primordial miracle, for the world is finite and God is infinite.) No less absolute is divine Justice, its primordial manifestation being the revelation that over against the divine Infinity the finite owns no claims. By virtue of divine Goodness the world is forever already created and forever being maintained. By virtue of divine Justice it is forever destined to perish. He who in the beginning alone was will alone be in the end.[18]

This realization of the metaphysical notion of Judaism brings about the "demythologization" (*Entgöttlichung*) of the world. In nature religions the natural is itself divine, and even for Greek religion (no nature religion) the world is "full of gods" (Thales). Because in Judaism nature is posited by the Divine it is itself undivine, and this is true as well of man or "finite spirit": all finite things are divinely posited. Only on this "prosaic" presupposition can there be miracles. When, as in Indian religion, the Divine and the human freely intermingle, "everything is intrinsically topsy-turvey."[19] Only when the world is in principle distinct from the Divine can it have a finite order of its own, and only then can there be "sporadic manifestations of God in something particular."[20] Such manifestations must here be possible and indeed necessary, for the distinction between God and a divinely posited world takes place in a religious consciousness *existing in the world*. To the "prose"—in contemporary language, secularity—of the world corresponds "holiness" in Divinity, and the religious consciousness is the place in which this "prose" and this "holiness" are united even as they are held apart. But how could this be unless the Divine broke into man's wordly consciousness?

This "place," however, would be subjective only (i.e., divorced both from an objective God and the "actual world") were it mere consciousness. There must be, and is, an acting out in which the objective God, the actual world, and existing man in his psychosomatic totality are all involved. This occurs when men "walk before God" so as to give Him "honor" in the "world."[21]

This honor is given in an affirmation of the divine Infinity by the finite self, which is at the same time that self's self-negation. No less essential than this, however, is the finite self's self-affirmation.

[92]

Greeks submit to a blind divine Fate; Jews have trust in a divine Wisdom that will confirm the worshipping self not in spite of but precisely because of and *in* his human finitude. According to Hegel, there is fragmentation in this togetherness of finite self-negation and self-affirmation; even so there is truth in it. The Jewish "confidence" that "he who does right will fare well . . . is [not only] a basic trait of the Jewish people [but also] . . . one which is admirable."²²

No less admirable (and ultimately for the same reason) is Jewish "steadfastness," a "fanaticism of stubbornness."²³ On the one hand, Jews worship the one, infinite, universal God, rejecting all finite, particularistic deities. On the other hand, they remain one particular "family" even when "expanded into a nation," refusing to "absorb alien forms of religious worship." We have already seen that Hegel finds a "strange, infinitely harsh, the harshest contrast" in this relation. We now see him specify this contrast as between "the universal God . . . of heaven and earth . . . [and] . . . His limited . . . purpose in but one family . . . in the historical world," that is, between "the demand that all nations give praise to His name [and His] real work [which consists] only . . . in the external, internal, political, ethical existence" of this one people.²⁴

Hegel might have trivialized this contrast in the fashion of subsequent evolutionary liberalism, either by reducing the God of Israel to a mere tribal deity, or by dissipating the actual Jewish "family" into an abstract sect of "monotheists," or by contriving an "evolutionary process" from the one to the other in which the *terminus a quo* never meets the *terminus ad quem*. He resists that (crypto- or pseudo-Protestant) temptation. It is precisely *in* his finite, human, Jewish particularity that the Jew worships a God who *is* God for him only because He transcends all finitude and particularity. Furthermore, the Jew not only *does* hold fast to this contrast, he *must* hold fast to it and endure it. In Hegel's view this contrast could be overcome (rather than merely evaded) only by means of a divine-human mediation in which at once the Divine concretized its own Infinity in finite human particularity while, as part of the same mediation, the particularity and finitude of the human were somehow raised and transfigured. Lacking a mediation of this sort, the Jew must hold fast to the contrast: to let go of it would be to lapse either into frivolousness (a flight from his actual Jewish particularity into some such abstraction as humanity-in-general) or idolatry (the reduction of the Lord of Creation to a tribal deity). In spurning both, the Jew is the uncorrupted witness to the incommensurability of the Divine in its universality and the human in its particularity; and precisely this fidelity is "admirable." Hence the authentic core of Jewish religious existence is a "renunciation of renunciation."[25] The worship of the infinite divine Power can be nothing less than the total self-renunciation of human finitude. This, however, would be a sheer self-dissipation were there not also a "renunciation of renunciation"—a "confidence" in a divine Wisdom that will confirm man precisely in his human finitude. Thus, "submission, renunciation, the recognition of the . . . purposive divine Power restores Job's former good fortune. Pure confidence, the intuition of the . . . purposive divine Power comes first; but it carries in train temporal good fortune."[26]

Thus, in brief, the Jew gives honor to God in the world. Yet this "realization" of the "metaphysical notion" of Judaism would remain unreal in an unreal world if it remained in heart and thought alone. It assumes actuality in the actual world only as it permeates and transforms the whole length and breadth of real life—in the "labor" of *cult*.[27] Jewish cult is obedience to a God-given law in the fear of the Lord.

Fear remains animal so long as it is dispersed into many fears geared to finite objects. Fear of the Lord, being one infinite fear, far from itself animal, on the contrary drives out all the many fears. And while the animal affirms its animality as it is gripped by fear, the Jewish fear of the Lord dissipates human selfhood into nothingness. Yet, in the concrete labor of cultic life, as in the abstract consciousness of heart and thought, the Jew renounces renunciation. He finds himself confirmed in his human, particular, finitude in the very act of surrendering both. In recognizing God as Lord, the Jew finds himself recognized as servant, both by the Lord and by himself. "The fear in which the servant regards himself as servant restores his being to him."[28]

This restoration manifests itself in obedience to a God-given law. We have already seen Hegel contrast the man-made laws of Lykurgos and Solon with the God-given law of Moses. It has now come to light that Jewish "positivity" is by no means a contingent and unspiritual trait to be done away with in the religious life, and to be ignored by philosophic thought. Since God and man are incommensurable in Judaism, the God-given law must be, for Hegel, "positive" in both content and origin. "The most trifling ordinances" not only must coexist with "the eternal laws of right and morality," resting as they do on a divine authority incommensurable with all things human, they must also be "of the same rank." Nor can they be alterable by human action, and human freedom must be confined to accepting obedience. Hence "the details of the political constitution" must all be determined—divinely, indiscriminately, and once and for all; they are neither left for the human will or reason to determine, nor in themselves determined with reference to a universal purpose. As for every kind of "political change," it is apostasy.

This acceptance [of the service of the Lord] is once and for all. *It takes the place of reconciliation and redemption.* In themselves reconciliation and redemption have already taken place, reflecting a choice by divine Grace apart from all [human] freedom.[29]

So much, for the present, in exposition of Hegel's account of Judaism. To this account he adds the observation that the God of Moses is in "strong contrast" to the conception that "we" have of God.[30] It is not yet clear who this "we" is and how "our" conception of God is arrived at. One thing, however, already is clear: "our" conception of God is superior to that ascribed to Judaism; indeed, without this assumption the account itself (though as yet shorn almost wholly of all criticism) would be impossible. For reasons that have yet to emerge, Jewish religious existence, though an indispensable aspect of the total religious Truth, is now as such an anachronism.

A PRELIMINARY CONFRONTATION

We may pause for a preliminary confrontation between the Hegelian philosophical comprehension of Judaism and the Jewish religious self-understanding—preliminary because the grounds of the first have not yet emerged and thus the comprehension itself is left incomplete. To say first things first, Hegel's search for the inner logic of the Jewish divine-human relationship shows a sure grasp of its core. Undeceived by all liberalistic tribal deities, universal God-ideas and evolutionary processes inserted between them, it takes a firm hold of the fact central to the Jewish religious self-understanding: the living relation between a God who is Lord of Creation and one singular human family. We shall see Hegel do Judaism less than justice. That he metes out some justice is clear from the start.

Indeed, much in the above account passes the scrutiny of the most normative and exacting (i.e., rabbinic) Jewish standards, and this despite the fact that Hegel nowhere shows signs of acquaintance with Talmudic or Midrashic sources. Thus, to give some examples, the rabbis may affirm an "oral Torah" that interprets and develops the "written" one, yet insist that the first is *in* the second, not a "free" human alteration of it; or they may search for "reasons behind the commandments" (*ta'ame mitzvot*), yet stress the validity of the commandments whether or not reasons are found. Even modern nonorthodox Judaism pays at least liturgical (if no other) homage to the "positivity" of the Torah in retaining its reading in the weekly Sabbath service. One must add at once, to be sure, that the positivity of the law of Moses does not render the rabbis incapable of union with its divine Giver: His law can be, and ought to be, observed for its own (and His) sake rather than merely for extraneous motives. But Hegel himself (unlike Kant and similar critics of "Jewish legalism") understands the law of Moses, its positivity notwithstanding, not as a bar between divine Giver and human recipient, but rather as a bridge.[31] (Indeed, this is his decisive superiority over Kant in his comprehension of Judaism.) And that a bridge not wholly unlike that seen by Hegel may remain even if the law itself is abandoned is illustrated when as antinomian a Jewish thinker as Martin Buber affirms an immediate (albeit, to be sure, not "harsh") relation between a divine "Thou" who is "eternal," and a human "I" who remains particular, finite and human. Still more illustrative is that thinker's detection of an immediate divine kingship over an assembly of tribes in the pristine biblical sources.[32] Clearly, the "contrast" between the one Infinite, universal Divinity and one particular family is as central to any genuine Jewish religious self-understanding as it is to Hegel's philosophical comprehension. Indeed, one may say that on no other grounds could the Jewish people have survived through the ages. (Thus either of the extremes imagined by liberalistic ideology—a clinging to a merely "tribal" deity and an abstract "monotheism"—would have foredoomed this people to extinction.) Much has happened in more than three thousand years to shake the Jewish "confidence" that Hegel considers admirable. Yet this confidence—and the Jewish people—survives to this day.

Prima facie at least, Hegel's philosophical comprehension of the central Jewish religious fact is as sound as his hold of the fact itself. How could a divine "Thou"—or King—possess infinity unless the finite "I"—or family or nation—renounced themselves radically in His presence? And how could, nevertheless, an immediate relation exist between these two incommensurables unless there were also, and at the same time, "renunciation of renunciation"?

Yet Hegel's core philosophical concept is prima facie as unsound as it is sound. (We say "prima facie" in both cases since the Hegelian grounds of this concept have yet to emerge.) To begin with a by no means random example—for to Hegel Job is the pious Jew par excellence—the Hegelian Job can receive the gift of an all-restoring divine Goodness only after a total surrender to the divine Power. In contrast, the biblical Job (and any Jewish, as distinct from Christian, understanding of him) lodges a radical protest that remains incommensurable with the divine Presence even when this latter manifests itself as absolute Power.[33]

This example once cited, others more central to our purpose become inescapable. Hegel both praises the "firm" Jewish refusal to "assimilate alien forms of worship" and criticizes this Jewish lack of universalism. The Maccabees were able to reject Hellenistic gods while yet absorbing secular Hellenistic culture.[34] Rabbinic loyalty to the Sinaitic covenant went together with their belief in a Noaḥidic covenant and with the conviction that "righteous Gentiles" are equal to the high priest in the sight of God. The Hegelian Jewish "particularism"—"God is God of His people only and not of all men"[35]—reaches prima facie absurdity with his statement that the Jewish doctrine of creation had effective reality not in Judaism but only in Christianity.[36] One Talmudic rabbi sums up the whole Torah with the verse, "This is the Book of the generations of man" (Gen. 5:1);[37] and orthodox Jews still thank God daily for renewing the creation.

No less prima facie absurd than Hegel's "Jewish particularism," is his (as will be seen, related) "Jewish unfreedom." Hegel's Jewish God is Lord only, worshipped in nothing but fear. The rabbinic God is Father as well as King, worshipped in love as well as fear.[38] The Hegelian Mosaic law is purely positive, and Moses himself a sheer instrument. The rabbinic Moses is no sheer instrument, and the rabbis themselves are so "free" in their interpretation of his law that Moses himself, listening in heaven, cannot understand it.[39] To come to the climactic point, Hegel's Sinaitic legislation "takes the place of reconciliation and redemption . . . and reflects a divine Grace apart from all [human] freedom." In the rabbinic self-understanding, human freedom as well as divine Grace is involved in the Sinaitic event;[40] and, far from taking the place of redemption, it points to a Messianic future that is the joint achievement of human freedom and divine Grace. Something, it seems, is seriously wrong.

What is wrong, however, is not Hegel's mere ignorance of the rabbinic sources; and the wrong cannot be detected, let alone rectified, by our mere citations of these. For as we now turn from rabbinic to biblical sources, the Jewish religious self-understanding still remains radically at odds with Hegel's philosophical comprehension of it. Presumably any philosophical account of the "inner logic" or "essence" of a form of religious life is problematic in being perforce selective in its use of the sources. Hegel's selectivity vis-à-vis biblical Judaism, however, is either scandalously arbitrary —or else has a philosophical justification that has yet to emerge.

Consider the concepts of universalism and freedom that will turn out to be crucial (as well as related). Hegel writes:

The Jewish God is the God of Abraham, Isaac and Jacob, the God who has led Israel out of Egypt; and there is not the slightest reflection that God has acted affirmatively among other nations as well.[41]

To cite no earlier sources, what of prophetic universalism? What of Amos' explicit connection of Israel's exodus from Egypt with that of Philistines from Caphtor and Aram from Kir? (Amos 9:7) Hegel disposes of prophetic universalism as follows:

The honor of God is to become manifest among all nations; especially among the later prophets this universality appears as the higher demand. Isaiah makes God say, "I will make priests and levites of those Gentiles who become worshipers of Jehovah." (Isa. 66:21) All this, however, is later; according to the dominant ground-idea (*Grundidee*) the Jews are the chosen people, and universality is thus reduced to particularity.[42]

But what if (as modern, sometimes Hegelian Jewish thinkers were to argue) prophetic "universalism" is implicit in an original "particularism"? Or, far more importantly, what if according to the biblical self-understanding itself God chooses Israel for purposes transcending Israel from the start? What *Grundidee* (or characteristics of the *Grundidee* Hegel adduces) deprives such universalism of truth or authenticity—when in contrast Hegel permits New Testament Christianity to explicate its universalistic implications through nothing less than world history, not despite but because of *its* scandal of particularity? According to Hegel, it is the "lack of freedom" in biblical Judaism. The biblical Jew can self-actively transform the world, and he can be "reconciled" with God: a union of the two relations is impossible. Any Jewish "freedom" over against God is perforce a "falling away" from His law and an act of rebellion. In short, biblical Judaism implies, for man, a stance of frozen and passive obedience; for God, a stance of frozen and commanding otherness; and for the law which alone can span the gulf between these two incommensurables an unalterable, uninterpretable, indiscriminately valid "positivity."

[98]

With this conclusion, Hegel's ignorance of rabbinic Judaism becomes a merely derivative issue, for had he been acquainted with it, he would have been forced to deal with it as he in fact dealt with prophetic universalism.

Yet Hegel's Jewish unfreedom is as much at odds with the biblical sources as is his Jewish particularism, which is derived from it. The biblical Jew accepts the divine law as freely as does his rabbinic descendant who is its interpreter; and acceptance is in either case in both love and fear. To go further, such is and remains his freedom over against God that, having accepted God's law, he does nothing less than hold God responsible for its terms. There is, in short, a divine-Jewish covenant, and such is the extent of its mutuality that God may respond to an antidivine human act by *Himself* accepting its consequences. Thus "political change"—such as the demand for a human king, the kingship of God notwithstanding—is, to be sure, in the first instance a "falling away from God"; yet in the end it is divinely accepted. Such is the significance of this particular acceptance that the descendant of David, the human king, is the Messiah himself. But in Hegel's account of Judaism there are two features that startle above all others. One is that he mentions the concept of covenant but can make nothing of it. The other is that, incredible though it may seem, the Messianic belief is wholly omitted—a fact the more startling because in his *Early Theological Writings* Hegel himself had seen the essence of Judaism in Messianism.[43]

Two explanations are possible for this extraordinary state of affairs. Of these, one—that Hegel claims to find his *Grundidee* of Judaism in the biblical sources—would be convenient for the modern Jewish thinker who can then dispose of his account of Judaism by means of mere citations; it would, however, imply an arbitrariness on Hegel's part that, in his case, defies all belief. We must therefore resort to the other explanation: Hegel (at least in part) brings his *Grundidee* to the biblical sources, with a philosophical justification that has yet to emerge; and until it has emerged, the question of Hegel's philosophical comprehension of Judaism and the Jewish religious testimony against that comprehension remains wholly open. In short, the encounter between Judaism and Hegelianism that we aim at has yet to come.

In seeking the philosophical grounds for Hegel's *Grundidee* of Judaism the temptation to take a giant leap straightway into the complete and self-completing Hegelian system must be resisted. This latter, to be sure, being an infinite, self-explicating Thought-activity that mediates all things, divine as well as human, may well produce in this process a *Grundidee* that both does its own kind of justice to Judaism and yet proves it superseded. However, we have noted from the start a radical conflict between Hegel's philosophical commitment to universal mediation and the Jewish religious commitment to at least two absolute distinctions—between the divine and the human, and between the one true God and all the false. A straight leap into Hegel's system would merely concretize this abstract conflict into one between Hegel's *Grundidee* of Judaism and Jewish protests against the injustice of this "justice"—and remain as barren as before.

As well as rule out from the start possibilities of significant confrontation, such a leap would also disregard the historicity of both Judaism and Hegelianism that, as will be seen, creates these possibilities. Of the historicity of Judaism we have yet to speak. To the historicity of Hegel's thought we have already referred, with the assertion that it does far greater justice to historical life (and hence to Jewish historical life) than is held by his panlogistic interpreters. Rather than impose *ab extra* a "law" of universal mediation upon historical life, it somehow (it is not immediately clear how and by what right) observes mediation as already present in historical life—a presence on which his philosophy itself depends. And whereas the ultimate mediation occurs nowhere except in Hegel's modern philosophical thought, this latter, by Hegel's own admission and insistence, is possible only because of a mediation already present in modern historical life. In short, the Hegelian "we" we are in search of—the "we" whose concept of God renders the God of Moses anachronistic and enables philosophical thought to prove Him so—consists, at least in the first instance, not of philosophical minds inhabiting the Hegelian system. It consists of authentic inhabitants of the modern secular-Protestant world.

But a straight recourse to Hegel's "modern world" would be a leap hardly less radical than one into the Hegelian system—and would produce results still more barren. Who or what will identify the authentic inhabitant of the modern world? Or judge in an abstract conflict between him and the Jewish believer? If, as Hegel holds, mediation is already present in historical life, Hegel's modern world must itself be shown by philosophical observation to be the product of historical mediation. And if the Jewish religious self-understanding is to be, not merely in history but of it as well, it must display its powers for self-mediation in response to all epoch-making events that call it into question. Moreover, this being an encounter between Judaism and Hegelianism, the confrontation between Hegel's mediating in "world history" and Jewish self-mediating responses to it must begin where Hegel sees it begin—in the "meeting" between Jewish "East" and Greek-Roman "West."

ATHENS AND JERUSALEM

The theme "Athens and Jerusalem" is well-nigh inexhaustible. Not so when our task is confined to the clash between Hegel's philosophical observation of Athens and Jerusalem and the response in history by Jerusalem to Athens and her works. Hegel observes a conflict between Jewish "East" and Greek—or Greek-Roman—"West,"[44] and he seeks to mediate that conflict from a standpoint external and superior to it.[45] On its part, Jewish religious existence is historically involved in that conflict and, as will be seen, is able at its own standpoint to meet the challenge of Greece with a self-exposing, self-transforming, self-mediating response. To be sure (as is already obvious and will emerge more fully in due course), Hegel's *Grundidee* of Judaism rules out all genuine responses to history in Judaism, and while this Hegelian claim is as yet far from justified or even fully developed, it clearly cannot be met with random illustrations of the banal truth that in empirical history all things are possible.[46] Yet since by its own admission and insistence Hegel's philosophy remains self-exposed to all genuine protests against its comprehensiveness, an epoch-making response on the part of the Jewish "East" to the Greek "West" might conceivably call into question, not only the *Grundidee* ascribed by Hegel to Judaism, but nothing less than the world-historical standpoint that Hegel's philosophy must claim when it generates the *Idee*—in short, nothing less than Hegel's system as a whole. The religious believer will in any case resist the claims of a philosophical standpoint purportedly more ultimate than his own—the Jewish believer more so than most when he stands in his stark human finitude before an uncompromisingly infinite Divinity. His resistance will acquire a new quality if in point of historical fact his faith has exposed itself to conflicting realities—religious, secular, philosophical—and emerged unvanquished. Hegel himself sees Jewish existence persist through his "ancient," "medieval," and "modern" worlds and remains, for all his mediating efforts, with a "riddle." What if every Hegelian mediation of Jewish history with an epoch in world history were matched, unrecognized by Hegel, by a Jewish self-mediation? This question, already generally raised, now finds its first, and in some respects crucial, test.

Jewish history repels Hegel even as it fascinates him. With Greece he has a lifelong affinity. Neither view is, in Hegel's case, reducible to mere personal or historical prejudice, and, unlike virtually all his contemporaries, the mature Hegel both does Jerusalem increasing justice and becomes increasingly sober about Athens. "We" cannot return or wish to return to ancient Greece, for its spirit is irretrievably past; and what makes it past is its lack of precisely what Judea possesses.[47]

Then why are "we" nevertheless "at home" with the Greeks? Because they, like ourselves, are at home in the world. The animal is by nature at home in nature. Man (no mere animal) is at home in the "world" (not mere nature) only by virtue of his "free" self-activity. Being the author of such activity, "Greece is the mother of the wisdom of the world, i.e., of the consciousness . . . that the world too has validity."[48]

This "wisdom" and "freedom" would be trite (and Hegel's assertions about Greek uniqueness, manifestly false), if both were merely finite. Men everywhere clear forests, plow fields, form societies, and build cities. Greek "wisdom" and "freedom" deserve this Hegelian title only by virtue of a religious (or quasireligious) dimension of infinity. The laws that govern the Greek city states are "divine" even though their authors, Lykurgos and Solon, are human. Divinity attaches as well to the "beauty" of Greek worship, despite its bondage to man-made statues. Most eminently is this true of Greek philosophy, for this, like all philosophy worthy of the name, is a rise to Divinity in the realm of thought.[49] Greek man, then, is at home in the world because Divinity is immanent both in this world and in his own relation to it. Thus he is free, and thus his wisdom is not of this or that but of the world.

Such, at any rate, is Greek historical experience, and this, not some random philosophical view, is what presently matters. Athens herself is permitted to speak by Hegel's philosophy—and as she speaks she supplies standards for judging Jerusalem. As for Hegel's philosophy, it merely brings Athens and Jerusalem together in thought, and then, as it were, simply looks on.

This looking on, however, has a feature that brings to light at least one Hegelian philosophical commitment. His philosophy will not suspend all judgment and merely look on. Still less will it simply side either with Athens or with Jerusalem.[50] It rather

perceives truth in both, in spite and indeed because of their contrast. In spite of it: there *is* truth in both for a philosophy that has
rid itself of all arbitrary prejudices. Because of it: the truth in each
reveals a falsehood in the other. This view on Hegel's part, to be
sure, represents a philosophical commitment that may be questioned. It is, however, not unsupported. As will be seen, the truth
and falsehood, far from an assertion unique to Hegel's philosophy,
has revealed itself, so Hegel holds, in world history long before
Hegel's philosophy has come upon the scene.

As Hegel's philosophy observes the Greek-Jewish contrast it
finds its first support (though incomplete) for what hitherto in
this discourse has seemed a wholly arbitrary judgment. It is the
fact of Greece, not some arbitrarily imported philosophical category, that—at least in the first instance—both reveals and serves
to criticize "Jewish unfreedom." Jewish fidelity to a God-given
law is unfree when contrasted, and thought together, with Greek
homage to a law man-made and yet divine. Divine transcendence
in Judaism becomes sheer lordship when made to meet the
"beauty" of Greek divine immanence. And as at length Greek
philosophical thought achieves a pure divine-human union it reveals and criticizes what would remain otherwise revealed less
starkly if not wholly concealed—the absoluteness of divine-human
nonunion in Judaism. According to an old Jewish legend Plato
studied under Moses. In Hegel's view Plato, had he ever met
Moses, would not have recognized his God as divine. To be sure,
the God of the philosophers is ultimately also the God of Abraham,
Isaac, and Jacob. This fact, however, is wholly unknown in both
Athens and Jerusalem, and is disclosed in its final significance only
by Hegel's thought.

This last view implies that for Hegel's observing thought Jerusalem is a critique of Athens even as Athens is a critique of
Jerusalem. To the Greek exposure of Jewish unfreedom (or
divine-human nonunion) corresponds a Jewish exposure of the
limitations of Greek freedom (or divine-human union). As the
Jew bears witness to a "holy" Infinity, the beautiful Greek
statues are revealed, to be sure, as true insofar as they are beautiful
but as false insofar as they are gods. And as the Jew testifies that
all are slaves of the transcendent Lord, the fact is disclosed that in
Greece only some are free—and the others are slaves of mere men.
Only in one sphere—that of philosophy of which, incidentally,
Jerusalem is incapable[51]—does Athens achieve a pure finite-infinite,
divine-human union; but this is at the price of a self-confinement
to thought ultimately tantamount to a flight from the world. The

Jew, in contrast, perseveres in his service *in* the world of a God who is Lord *of* it. As for us moderns, we may be at home with the poetry that is Greece; yet we can worship a Greek god no more than an Indian cow,[52] thus finding ourselves, at least with regard to religious worship, far closer to the Jewish prose that, overwhelmed by the divine "holiness," has demythologized (*entgöttlicht*) the world from the start.

Then—to repeat—why "our" closer affinity with Athens? Because of one crucial advantage of Athens over Jerusalem. Serving his transcendent Lord, the Jew must remain unmoved in His service; or, if and when he moves, his movement is a "falling away from God." Because His Divinity is immanent, the Greek can self-actively transform his condition and at least partly transcend its limitations. Initially no less particularistic than the Jewish, his existence has a nisus toward universality. And thus it can come to pass that the gods of the Greek West are demythologized, not only in the external encounter with the Jewish East, but also by the West itself—by Greek philosophy in the realm of thought and by the Roman Empire in the realm of life. The Greek advantage, then, is that it is historical, or capable of dialectical self-development. "Unfree" Judaism, in contrast, lacks this capacity—and the fact that it has nevertheless persisted will turn out to be the core of Hegel's puzzlement.

It would be untrue to Hegel's thought to view this freedom and this unfreedom as simple strength and simple weakness. On the one hand, the Greek-Roman West cannot transcend absolutely the limitations of its origin. On the other, the Jewish East resists rightly absorption by the West as this latter expands and universalizes its scope.

Neither Greek philosophical thought nor Roman political life transcend absolutely their common mythological origin. The Platonic *Republic* can destroy the city state but not restore Greek political life; and indeed ancient philosophy as a whole, confined to thought from the start, seeks in its Neoplatonic end refuge in a wholly worldless God. On its part, the Roman Empire is a godless world: in the pantheon the gods are not only all assembled but also made subservient to a merely human-political use and thus destroyed. Moreover, as human emperors move into the vacated sphere they become emperor-gods, and the ancient West, self-liberated from the gods, becomes self-enslaved to men. Thus the Greek-Roman world not only fails to transcend the limitations of its "freedom;" it comes to *recognize* this inability when, taken as a whole, it turns into an "unhappy" conflict between a "free" philosophical flight to a worldless God and a self-enslaved life in a godless world.

This "unhappiness" reveals the Western "untruth" to the West from within. It is also revealed by the Jewish East from without. Lacking Western "freedom," this latter also lacks its limitations. Alone of all the ancient gods, the God of Israel is neither assembled in nor destroyed by the Roman pantheon. And the Jew, however unfree in His service, participates neither in the philosophical flight from the world nor in the political self-enslavement in the world in which the Greek-Roman West ends. He continues, unmoved and unmoving, in his service *in* the world of a God who is Lord *of* it. And this unmoved and unmoving testimony reveals the untruth in the West.

It is important to stress that the Jewish testimony must be simply unmoved and unmoving. This becomes manifest as Hegel's *Grundidee* of Judaism, hitherto seemingly an abstract and arbitrary philosopher's construction, now assumes a more concrete shape and significance. Hegel's thought has observed Athens and Jerusalem lay claim to a divine-human reality. Recognizing both claims and, as it were, placing them into the same space, it has seen them jostle each other. They cannot destroy each other. Neither can they unite in a weak compromise: only by destroying his "beautiful" freedom could the Greek submit to the Jewish transcendent Other; and only by blaspheming against his "Holy" One could the Jew arrogate unto himself any Greek-Roman freedom. Doubtless compromises abound; however, these belong to merely empirical history and are without world-historical significance. The *Grundidee* Hegel seeks in both Athens and Jerusalem is their unsullied essence, and only insofar as historical "existence" is bound up with that essence do both have "actuality."[53]

Has Hegel's philosophy, as thus far developed, managed to demonstrate that the response of a Jerusalem true to her essence to the challenge of Athens *must be* unmoved and unmoving? By no means, for on Hegel's own showing, his own philosophical *Grundidee* of Judaism could not have emerged within the limits of the ancient world. Not in the Greek-Roman West: this, its philosophy included, understands the Jew at best as a fanatical obscurantist, and at worst as an "enemy of mankind." Not in the Jewish East if only because to its self-understanding the concepts of covenant and Messiah, absent in Hegel's *Idee*, are altogether central. Hegel's philosophical observation of the Greek-Jewish contrast has therefore given flesh and bones to his *Grundidee* of

Judaism (and to the unfreedom and immobility implied in it); it has done so, however, only on the basis of as yet unexpressed and certainly unjustified philosophical assumptions that leave that *Grundidee* itself still unjustified and, indeed, far even from fully expressed.

For this reason, it is, at least at this juncture in our developing confrontation, a matter of momentous import that in point of historical fact Jerusalem, confronted by Athens, was not confined to the Hegelian alternatives of surrender and an historically sterile fidelity. We have seen Hegel mediate between Athens and Jerusalem, from a standpoint, external and superior to both, whose justification has yet to show itself. We shall now see Maccabean Judaism exposed (and self-exposed) to the challenge of Hellenism —and give a self-mediating response to the challenge whose consequences, for Jewish if indeed not for world history, reverberate to this day.

Of the period preceding and including the Maccabean revolt (167–162 B.C.E.) the historian Elias Bickerman writes boldly but correctly that "never before and never thereafter was the spiritual existence of Israel so imperiled."[54] No peril would have existed at all had Greek culture been or remained particularistic; and had this culture not been of universal attractiveness the peril would not have been spiritual. In fact, however, Greek culture, "from its beginnings . . . supranational, because the Greeks never constituted a unified state,"[55] posed the peril referred to once it had so developed its initial trait that "a man became a 'Hellene' without at the same time forsaking his gods and his people, but merely by adopting Hellenic culture." Hellenic culture tolerated rather than repressed religious difference. And if precisely this tolerant universalism posed a mortal threat, it was because it forced faithful Jews—not merely the compromisers and the indifferent—to ask whether the time had not come to match tolerance with tolerance, to merge with the Hellenic world and to

. . . remove everything which smacked of separation, of the "ghetto": Sabbath observance, beards, circumcision, and that namelessness of God which was otherwise to be met with only among the most primitive peoples.

For

. . . to a man of the Hellenistic age this "separation from the nations" could be regarded as nothing else than the expression of a Jewish "hatred of mankind." Favorably disposed critics have endeavored to explain the withdrawal of the Jews from history as a consequence of the "bad experience of their expulsion from Egypt," and to exculpate it on such grounds; but no one outside Jewry itself has ever recognized positive merit in the separation.

The unprecedented challenge of the Hellenistic age, then, was that it forced Jews themselves—including and perhaps above all the most deeply committed—to ask whether there was merit in further separation, or whether the time had not come "to accept Western culture fully."

What, unless the challenge was simply rejected, were the basic alternatives? One—"to renounce the ancestral religion, to which any participation in the cult of the gods was an abomination"— was obvious and total surrender. Less obvious, and hence far more perilous, was surrender in what for a time must have seemed the sole other alternative: a "modernization" of the ancient law that, matching tolerance with tolerance, "preserve[d] those character- istics of the Jewish religion which suited the Greek taste [such as] the imageless God . . . [but] remove[d] everything which smacked of separation," with the overall goal of giving "the 'God of the Jews' [a place in] the general pantheon." Tolerance may indeed have been the original motive among Jews supporting this latter alternative. Yet never in Jewish history has tolerance so radically turned into self-destructive tyranny.

In 167 B.C.E. King Antiochus IV Epiphanes passed a decree rescinding the law of Moses, making capital offenses of sanctifica- tion of Sabbath and New Moon, and instituting pagan services in the Jerusalem Temple. Tradition has it that this decree (which sparked the Maccabean revolt) was the work of a power-drunk king (nicknamed Epimanes—"the mad one"). In reality it owed its inspiration to Hellenizing Jewish leaders who, long bent on "accommodating traditional Judaism to the times," at length en- listed non-Jewish government force. In their own eyes, these leaders were not traitors or apostates. They were a "reform party," concerned not to destroy Judaism but rather to preserve it. Yet had their efforts succeeded, they would have destroyed Judaism from within far more thoroughly than any external enemy.

In their revolt the Maccabean leaders might have simply dis- regarded the challenge of Hellenism and invoked the ancient covenant. Had they done no more, their war, even if militarily successful, would have been without epoch-making results; their cause would have died, if not sooner, after 70 C.E.; and, on our part, we would have at this stage no grounds for calling Hegel's *Grundidee* of Judaism into question. What, then, was the actual Maccabean response to the Hellenistic challenge?

Mattathias does not dispute the right of the ruler to alter the laws of peoples subject to him; he does oppose an order of the king which is at variance with the revealed commandment of God. The struggle is . . . between earthly power and the law of the state of God.

The speech in which Mattathias says these things, while doubtless apocryphal, contains an indisputably historical distinction. The distinction, moreover, is in germ epoch-making. Without discriminations between the "state of God" and "earthly power" Jewish religious existence could not have survived in and beyond the Hellenistic age. There could have been no peace: not that of 163 B.C.E. in which "the government . . . consented to *tolerate* the Jewish religion," nor that of 162 B.C.E. in which "the *dominion* of the Torah was fully restored." In any total, unmediated, life-and-death struggle between the Eastern Jewish "state of God" and the Western Greek-Roman "earthly power" there is no doubt as to which would have been destroyed. Mattathias' distinction is unprecedented, profound and of epoch-making consequences for all of subsequent Jewish religious existence.

Like all distinctions of this kind, however, it did not and could not stand in abstract isolation. The state of God was distinguished from earthly power: the war between them related the two as well. In the early days of the revolt the Maccabees, aim as they did to preserve the state of God, refused to fight on the Sabbath, only to be slaughtered wholesale by the forces of the earthly power. Faced with the prospect of a state of God that was pure but dead, they were forced into the decision to fight on the Sabbath, for defense if not for attack. Thus the fateful question arose: could one violate the Sabbath in order to preserve it?

No less fateful was the Maccabean answer: yes, if the "violation" was no violation at all, but rather a justified interpretation. Prior to this answer, there seemed only two alternatives. The earthly power could force violations of the law of God upon the defenders of the state of God, thus making them accomplices in its desecration. Or these defenders could remove the state of God from the reach of the earthly power, by making it a state of the spirit only, unfit for flesh-and-blood inhabitants. In giving a third alternative the Maccabees recognized the crucial question of the hour: could a "state of God" exist in history so long as there was history, that is, an "earthly power" in potential or actual conflict with it? Their epoch-making response was, in effect, that the Sabbath was made for man, not man for the Sabbath.

It is not clear, nor does it matter, whether the Maccabees gave their answer in full awareness of its implications. What matters is that, when these implications became manifest to the Maccabees, they did not retreat. The "privilege of interpreting the Torah," such as it was, had hitherto been "vested with the high priest and his council." These latter, however, were the leaders of the "reform party." Wittingly or unwittingly, Mattathias (an unknown priest at the time) made himself into a rival government of the state of God when he appropriated that privilege. To go further, he also raised a question far transcending the immediate conflict, and this almost certainly unwittingly: what was the relation between the interpretation of the *Torah* (changing with historical circumstances and presumably human) and the *Torah* itself (unchangeable and divine?) This question, once raised within Jewish religious existence, was never again to vanish. Thus Mattathias' "resolve [concerning the Sabbath] constituted a turning point in Jewish history."

That the Maccabees *recognized* their resolve for what it was is sufficiently proved by a single dramatic example. Never before in Jewish history "had a festival been instituted by human hands." When Judah Maccabee, victorious, *himself* instituted the Hanukah festival, his act was, first, in Judaism an "innovation without precedent"; it was, second, "in complete accord with the usage of the Greeks"; third—and this is crucial—it was a use of Greek custom for the glory and in the service of the God of Israel.

. . . Judah imitated the practice of his enemies but at the same time incorporated it into Judaism. This was the first step along the path which was to constitute the historic mission of Hasmoneanism—the introduction of Hellenic usages into Judaism without a sacrifice of Judaism. No one any longer celebrates the Greek festivals that served as Judah's example. But the eight-branched candelabrum, a symbol, again, that imitates a pagan usage, is lighted on Kislev 25 the world over, in countries Judah never knew about, in Sydney as in New York, in Berlin as in Capetown.

The reform party wished to assimilate the Torah to Hellenism; the Maccabees wished to incorporate Hellenic culture in the Torah.

Here is the core of the self-exposed, self-mediating response of Jerusalem to the challenge of Athens and all her works.

We need not and cannot pursue the consequences of this response—which include Pharisaic and rabbinic Judaism and by some stretch of the philosophic imagination Alexandrian and medieval Jewish philosophy as well—in order to ask: how does this self-mediating response of Jerusalem to Athens stand related to Hegel's philosophical mediation between Jerusalem and Athens, perceived from a standpoint external and superior to both?

Prima facie, Hegel's philosophy is refuted by history. The Hegelian Jewish "holiness" is incompatible with "free" Greek self-activity; yet the Pharisees (following the Maccabean lead) adopted "a Hellenic, one might say a Platonic notion that education could . . . transform the individual and the whole people"— and made "the ideal to fashion a Greek . . ; gentleman" subserve the biblical precept, "Ye shall be unto Me a holy people and a holy nation." Hegel's (man-made) Greek and (God-given) Jewish laws are in absolute conflict; the Pharisees (unlike the Sadducees and like the Greeks) acknowledge "an 'unwritten law' (*agraphos nomos*) which is preserved not on stone or paper but lives and moves in the actions of the people"—and make this Greek law Jewish by letting it not "negate the written law" but rather serve as a "fence for the Torah." Hegel's *Grundidee* of Judaism, insofar as it emerges from a sheer observation of Athens and Jerusalem, lies in shambles.

If nevertheless this conclusion is prima facie only, it is because Hegel's observation is not sheer but rather rests on philosophical grounds that have yet to emerge. Even so, however, the facts of ancient Jewish history have served clearly to lay the onus of proof on Hegel. Were he to be incapable of proof, Jewish history would have to exact his concession that Jerusalem's self-mediating response to the challenge of Athens is a world-historical accomplishment; that, accepting Greek-Roman "culture" while yet rejecting its "religion," Jerusalem achieves vis-à-vis Athens an epoch-making reaffirmation of her two absolute distinctions—between God and man, and between the one true God and all the false.

It would, however, be premature to exact the Hegelian proof at the present stage of the developing encounter. For in Hegel's view his proof cannot emerge in philosophy prior to the emergence in history of a Truth higher than that found in either Athens and Jerusalem; of a Truth nonexistent in the entire ancient world.

"OLD" AND "NEW" JERUSALEM

According to Hegel this higher Truth has come into the world with the advent of Christianity—a "jolt" so momentous as to transform all world-history, philosophy itself included. With this altogether central assertion his philosophy at once declares itself to be either in some sense Christian or in some sense post-Christian, and thus under no circumstances a neutral observer of any Jewish-Christian confrontation. Hence whereas hitherto Athens and Jerusalem were both permitted to speak by Hegel's philosophy, and observed as each other's judges, the great difference now emerges that the "old" Jerusalem is no longer permitted to speak with her own voice against the claims of the "new." Yet we on our part would do no justice to Hegel's philosophy were we to ignore his justice (such as it is) to Judaism. For Hegel's philosophy cannot simply assert its own Christian or post-Christian status; in order to be or remain philosophy, it must demonstrate that status, and (since "demonstration" means "all-comprehensiveness") this involves a justice to all religions (and hence to the Jewish religion) such as no religion, the Christian included, is able to mete out. In Hegel's view any simple endorsement of Christian against Jewish claims would ipso facto be guilty of one-sidedness. And the result of the Hegelian "justice" is that, despite the uneven contest, Jewish religious existence survives throughout the entire Christian Middle Ages—as a true (albeit negative) witness against the untruth that remains in that period.

These preliminary reflections serve now, as before, to limit our theme. The many-sided theme "Athens and Jerusalem" has found much genuine debate; the still more many-sided theme " 'old' and 'new' Jerusalem," virtually none. In nearly two millennia of Jewish-Christian coexistence the Christian majority has been as unwilling or unable to listen as the Jewish minority has been unfree (outwardly, and hence often also inwardly) to speak; and even now any mutuality in Christian-Jewish dialogue has little substance. The obvious must therefore, nevertheless, be said—that the present encounter is not between Judaism and Christianity, but merely between Hegel's philosophical comprehension of the medieval-Christian world and normative Jewish responses to the Middle Ages.

In Hegel's view the Christian "jolt" is prepared albeit not necessitated by a commingling of Jewish East with the Greek-Roman West.[56] On the Jewish side, the falsehood in its divine-human nonunion comes at length into Jewish consciousness as its service of the transcendent Lord, compelled to seek but unable to find the Divine through the law, turns from confidence into painful longing. On the Greek-Roman side, the falsehood in its divine-human union comes to consciousness in that unhappy tension between a free philosophical flight to a worldless God and political self-enslavement in a godless world with which the whole pagan world comes to its end. The commingling of Jewish pain and Greek-Roman unhappiness makes the time ripe for an unheard-of composition—a God who in the extreme of His Jewish transcendence Himself enters into an immanence so extreme as to reveal that the Greek-Roman gods, far from too anthropomorphic, were not anthropomorphic enough. The good news of this absolute reconciliation of the Divine and the human removes the falsehood from both Athens and Jerusalem, while preserving their truth. In the terms of Athens, it renders free, not merely *some* men by virtue only of what they *do*—aesthetic, political, philosophical self-activity—but rather *all* men by virtue of what they *are:* recognized in and indeed because of their human finitude by the divine Infinity, and hence raised *as men* above slavery. In Jerusalem's terms the Christian good news is put differently: it replaces the law—which "takes the place of reconciliation and redemption" —with *actual* reconciliation and redemption: Divinity, on the one hand, lowers itself and assumes human flesh and death, and, on the other, raises men above mere finitude by its death of death, i.e., the Holy Spirit. Thus, in brief outline, history itself reveals what we have thus far come upon only as an (incompletely developed) commitment in Hegel's philosophy—the higher Truth that Jewish East and Greek-Roman West each contains both truth and falsehood. It will emerge that Hegel's thought will require this historical revelation for its own justification, and that so long as its implications are not fully explicit his *Grundidee* of Judaism will remain partly obscure.

We have heard Athens and Jerusalem themselves speak. The same is now true of the new Jerusalem if no longer of the old. It is clearly New Testament, Pauline, Trinitarian Christianity, however, with two radical qualifications. The first is radical enough: by itself, New Testament Christianity is only faith in the absolute divine-human reconciliation; its realization occurs only as in the Christian Middle Ages a "sacred" world takes shape, on the one hand, in the life-aspect of Christian cult, and, on the other, in the thought-aspect of Christian theological thought. Still more radical is the second qualification: the process of realization remains in principle arrested during the entire Christian Middle Ages, and does not become fully actual in the "actual world" until the rise of the modern "free" secular-Protestant world—and Hegel's own philosophy comprehends that world and, in so doing, completes the realization itself.[57]

How, within its medieval limits as perceived by Hegel, does the new Jerusalem testify against the old? We have seen how

Hegel's *Grundidee* of Judaism takes shape in the encounter between Athens and Jerusalem, and also how Jerusalem's response to Athens breaks the limitations that might be put on her, either by Athens herself or by Hegel on Athens' behalf. The challenge of Athens and the response of Jerusalem are both transcended as the Hegelian *Idee* now takes profounder shape in the testimony of the new Jerusalem. That the Jew must "renounce" his finitude before the divine Infinity; that he must "renounce renunciation" if he is, nevertheless, to persist as finite before that Infinity; and that there is both truth and falsehood in the resulting "admirable confidence" that constitutes his religious existence: all this could not have been disclosed, either by Athens, or by her philosophy, or by a strictly neutral observation of the clash between Athens and Jerusalem. It *is* disclosed (in life if not yet in philosophical thought) by the death and resurrection of the Christ. Vis-à-vis Athens and all her works the Maccabees could affirm a freedom, genuine yet human, in the service of a God who is transcendent and yet accessible. Both sides of this affirmation are now superseded. For the crucified and resurrected Christ reveals, negatively, that, radically considered, any merely human freedom remains ultimately unfree, and that any Divinity that remains confined to Divinity, remains ultimately inaccessible. The positive counterpart of this negative revelation is that, in its Jewish no less than its Greek form, the divine-human, infinite-finite, transcendent-immanent dichotomy must be, and in fact is, mediated.

Hegel requires this Christian testimony against Judaism. He cannot, however, simply endorse it. He could not do so even in the modern world (where it becomes fully explicit), much less in the medieval world where, so he holds, the Christian "inversion" of the world remains in principle arrested. It follows that Hegel's *Grundidee* of Judaism could have emerged in the medieval no more than in the ancient world. The God of Moses, in Himself an anachronism since the advent of the Christ, does not become an anachronism in and for medieval Christian life, nor prove Himself so for medieval philosophy. As will be seen, Jewish religious existence remains an authentic witness until the rise of the modern world.

Hegel's view of the limitations of the Christian Middle Ages is briefly as follows.[58] The New Testament reveals the incursion of God into flesh. The "freedom" thus initiated remains incomplete until it has revolutionized the world. Throughout the entire Middle Ages, however, this process remains arrested. There appeared and was bound to appear a profound split between a "sacred" heaven and an "unsanctified" earth. The God descended to earth remained, after all, confined to heaven, leaving earth itself in its Roman condition. The Holy Roman Empire was both holy and Roman; it could be both only by virtue of a dichotomy between a holy power that was mere church and a secular power that, if anything, became less "free" than it had been in the ancient world. Even Christians, become "free" in the sight of God, remained "unfree" in the sight of feudal princes. As for Jews, they lost even such freedom in the new Roman Empire as had been theirs in the old. The old, though considering them enemies of mankind, made them Roman citizens even when they retained their faith. The new considered them enemies of God Himself, and reduced them to "chamber serfs." This last observation is not Hegel's own, for he pays little heed to the medieval Jewish fate. Yet it wholly accords with his views as to the "untruth" persisting throughout the medieval Christian world.

If in Hegel's view this fateful sacred-profane split was inevitable, so was its nemesis. The earth, left "unsanctified," entered into the medieval heaven and at length destroyed it. For the crusaders themselves, their arrival at Jerusalem was a climactic experience. For Hegel's philosophical observation, the event is revelatory of the untruth of the whole Middle Ages, and the beginning of their decline.

In the medieval Christian world Truth remains a heavenly truth only, a Beyond. Actuality, the earthly element, is consequently God-forsaken and hence arbitrary; a few individuals are holy, not the others. In these others we see the holiness of the moment in the quarter of an hour of worship, and then for weeks a life of rudest selfishness and violence and of the most ruthless passion. Individuals fall from one extreme into the other, from the extreme of rude excess, lawlessness, barbarism and self-will, into the renunciation of all things without exception, the conquest of all desires.

The great army of the Crusaders give us the best example of this. They march forth on a holy errand, but on the way they give vent to all the passions, and in this the leaders show the example; the individuals allow themselves to fall into violence and heinous sin. Their march accomplished, though with an utter lack of judgment and foresight, and with a loss of thousands on the way, Jerusalem is reached: it is beautiful, when Jerusalem comes in view, to see them all do penance in contrition of heart, falling on their faces and reverently adoring. But this is only a moment which follows upon months of frenzy, foolishness and grossness, which displayed itself everywhere on their march. Animated by the loftiest bravery, they go on to storm and conquer the sacred citadel, and then bathe themselves in blood, revel in endless cruelties, and rage with a brutal ferocity. . . .[59]

The medieval Jewish fate, had Hegel paid attention to it, might have illustrated his point most poignantly. The crusading mobs showed all their "brutal ferocity" (and no "lofty bravery") when they slaughtered wholesale Jewish men, women, and children in the cities on the Rhine. On their part, the local bishops tried to save Jews "as men"—but were hampered by the doctrine that, since these men were Jews, they were enemies of God and beyond the pale of humanity. For the end as well as for the crisis of the medieval-Christian world Jewish fate might have served as Hegel's most poignant example. The Spanish Inquisition divorced heaven and earth when it burned Jewish bodies to save Jewish souls. "Unsanctified earth" destroyed "sacred heaven" when even properly and safely converted Jews were hounded to the fourth and fifth generation—a medieval anticipation of Hitler.

Hegel, though failing to give these examples, might well have given them, for his philosophical observation of the Christian Middle Ages does not exclude the appearance of the Jewish people as *objects*. If Jews *as subjects* cannot appear, it is because of Hegel's view that the right of Jerusalem to be heard has vanished once the new Jerusalem has come on the scene.[60] Hence as we now turn from Hegel's mediation of Jewish history with world history in the medieval period to the Jewish self-mediating response *to* that period, we must take great care to listen to the actual Jewish response, not to a response that others (Hegel included) might ascribe to it. As for Hegel's own "justice" to Jewish religious existence, this must be watched with special care in this particular period. Had Hegel considered the Maccabean response to the challenge of Hellenism, he might have done it a measure of justice, for (as we have seen) he permitted Jerusalem to speak against Athens with her own voice. Granting her no such permission vis-à-vis the "new" Jerusalem, it is a priori certain that he can do no justice to Jewish responses to medieval challenges. Yet the crucial Jewish response—rabbinic Judaism—far exceeds Maccabean Judaism in depth and world-historical significance. Perhaps it is no mere accident (such as unfamiliarity with the sources) that Talmud and Midrash do not appear in Hegel's philosophy.

The Maccabees had won a victory. Ever since 70 C.E., the rabbis lived with an unprecedented defeat. Yet such was their unprecedented response as to make the "riddle" of Jewish history nowhere deeper for Hegel's philosophy than in the long medieval night. However, precisely because a priori Hegel can do no justice to medieval Jewish history we must watch closely every trace of such justice as he metes out.

Under no circumstances may rabbinic Judaism be mistaken for a response by an "old" Jerusalem to the challenge of a "new." To view it as such—not to speak of mistaking all the staged medieval Christian-Jewish debates for dialogues essential to the medieval Jewish self-understanding—would be not only to lapse into a time-honored Christian prejudice but also to fail to challenge Hegelianism at a pivotal point in its self-understanding. For Hegel's world-historical comprehension from his world-historical point of view (which has yet to prove itself so), the jolt ending one world and beginning another is Christianity. For the Jewish religious self-understanding (which, if world-historical, is so from a Jewish point of view), the jolt is the destruction of the Temple and of the state of God in 70 C.E. It was, to be sure, the old, "profane" Roman Empire that produced that catastrophe. However, when the new "holy" Roman Empire replaced it, it did not heal the hurt of the Jewish people; indeed, the catastrophe deepened. Many responses appeared. Sadduceean-style (and, subsequently, Karaite) Judaism remained in frozen immobility. Essene, apocalyptic (and, subsequently, Kabbalistic) Judaism resorted to flight from history. Only one response was to become normative. Rabbinic Judaism alone held fast to the God of Creation, to the Jewish "family expanded into a nation"—and confronted the catastrophe head-on.

By the standards of Hegel's (as yet insufficiently explicated and philosophically altogether unjustified) *Grundidee* of Judaism, the catastrophe of 70 C.E. should have left Jewish religious existence with nothing but "pain." With the Temple and the state of God destroyed, any *simply* positive law of Moses had been rendered inapplicable: Jewish self-renunciation through obedience was impossible. Rendered doubly impossible was any Jewish "renunciation of renunciation," for along with the possibility of "doing right" all grounds had vanished for the belief that those doing right would "fare well." This latter belief, to be sure, could never have been crude. (One wonders why Hegel makes nothing of the fact that the Book of Job is not history, but a tale.) The fact of exile, however, now destroyed that belief for the entire people. In short, the Sinaitic law, had it ever "taken the place of reconciliation and redemption," could now be taken as such no longer. There might have been simple despair—one kind of end to the

[116]

Jewish people. There might have been recourse to a new religion
—another kind of end. (According to Hegel himself there was
the puzzling fact of continued existence in sheer pain, endured
willingly for no purpose and hence intelligible not as the acting
of subjects, but only as the suffering of objects used by the World
Spirit.) A response to the catastrophe, through the Torah, for the
sake of its Giver should have been impossible.

To be sure, there had been a previous exile. But the Babylonian
exile both inspired and fulfilled the hope for an early restoration;
moreover, it produced the response that if Israel did not now fare
well, it was only because she had not done right. But while Jeremiah could view Nebuchadnezzar as God's own instrument, no
rabbi could view Titus in the same light; and any surviving belief
that God's ways are evident in catastrophe was suspended when
in 135 c.e. Hadrian transformed Jerusalem into a pagan city.[61]
Moreover, hopes for any early restoration were known to be un-
realistic by the rabbis themselves—and have remained unfulfilled
to this day.[62] To sum up, while the first exile, though epoch-
making for the Jewish religious self-understanding, might conceivably fit into Hegel's *Grundidee* of Judaism, the second leaves
us with but two possibilities: either Judaism became a fossil in,
70 c.e., or Hegel's *Grundidee* of Judaism is radically false.

For the sake of a genuine encounter between Judaism and Hegelianism this either/or must not be set up either too sharply or
prematurely. Not too sharply: we must describe, as far as possible, the un-Hegelian rabbinic response to exile in Hegelian (or
quasi-Hegelian) terms. Not prematurely: we must not forget
that while (as has been shown) the onus of proof rests upon
Hegel, that proof cannot show itself until his philosophy has
wholly emerged.

The Maccabees interpreted the "law of God" in order to save
the "state of God." The rabbis were faced with the fact of that
state destroyed. The Maccabees and their Pharisaic successors
may or may not have confronted the question of how any justified
interpretation of a God-given law could itself be human. The
rabbis, faced with drastic catastrophe, could not avoid that question. Either mere man arrogates unto himself the right of radical
interpretation; but then the law of God becomes a mere pious
fiction if indeed not a swindle; or else that law is and remains genuinely divine: but then the interpretation is not merely human but
rather itself divinely inspired. The rabbis embarked firmly on the
second course: an oral Torah, additional to the written, had been
given at Sinai itself. And the whole, vast, unique world of the

Talmud is in the end nothing but the creative tension between the two Torahs.

Hegel's written law of Moses must be "positive" if the divine-human gulf is to be bridged. Merely by virtue of being oral, the oral Torah cannot be so, but is rather impossible without human self-activity. The rabbinic Halachah is produced by the self-activity of study, interpretation, and debate. The rabbinic Haggadah reflects awareness of this fact, for example when it pictures Moses, listening in heaven to rabbinic interpretations of his own Torah, as unable to understand it.[63] By the standards of Hegel's *Grundidee* of Judaism, the rabbis should have produced a new religion. The fact that they did not is a testimony against that *Idee*—the first truly radical testimony we have come upon in this discourse.

We have noted, though hitherto as a mere datum in the biblical sources, that Hegel can make nothing of the fact that "political change," though initially a "falling away from God," is in the end accepted by God Himself. This fact now reveals itself as all along part and parcel of the inner logic of the Jewish religious self-understanding, disclosing a vast discrepancy between this inner logic and what Hegel considers to be the inner logic of Judaism. The core concept of the Jewish religious self-understanding is not a "positive" law of Moses but rather a divine-Jewish covenant. Like the first, the second establishes a relation between the one and infinite God and one particular human "family"; but wholly unlike the first, the second does not produce a harsh contrast, but rather an intimate mutuality, the incommensurability of divine Infinity and human finitude notwithstanding. We have seen that Hegel surpasses Kant in his recognition that the law of Moses is a bridge between the Divine and the human, rather than a bar. It now emerges that he fails to pass beyond Kant when he, too, fails to recognize the Grace that is in that "law."[64]

Had Hegel permitted rabbinic Judaism to speak with its own voice he could not have dismissed its concept of covenant (as he did in the case of the Bible) as a mere fact without spiritual truth. With the state of God destroyed, how would the law of God remain a present reality instead of a mere dead memory or an ineffectual hope? Only by virtue of "free" human self-activity. And how, with the house of God destroyed, could the interpretation and observance of the law of God remain a bridge between Him and its human recipients? Only if this God Himself remained accessible in both the interpretation and the observance. Rabbinic Judaism responded to the fact of exile by carrying the Torah into exile—and the Midrash considers God Himself, the Lord of Creation, self-exiled on account of His love for Israel and the world.[65] So sharply is Hegel's harsh contrast contradicted by the covenantal intimacy of the Jewish religious self-understanding.

Covenantal intimacy, however, is only one aspect of the rabbinic testimony against Hegel's *Grundidee* of Judaism. The other is the Messianic expectation. So closely are these two aspects connected that Hegel, had he done justice to the one, would of necessity have faced the task of doing justice to the other as well. The exile of a God who is and remains Lord can only be self-exile; and the Love that produces this result would destroy divine Power unless this self-exile pointed to redemption; indeed, to a redemption ultimately universal in scope.[66] Covenant and Messiah, though present in biblical Judaism, could seem to Hegel to be marginal to the inner logic of Judaism. In the case of rabbinic Judaism this is impossible. Had Hegel's thought permitted rabbinic Judaism to speak with its own voice these two doctrines would necessarily have moved from the margin to the center. And the Jewish people would have become *subjects* witnessing *against* the medieval "untruth" focused upon them, and *to* a future light.

For it is against Hegel's own medieval untruth that rabbinic Judaism testifies, and, moreover, supremely so in what Hegel himself considers its supreme medieval disclosure. The Jews in the cities on the Rhine, given the choice between death and apostasy by the crusaders, chose death without hesitation. Their martyrdom bore witness against the unredeemedness *of earth*, and to an *earthly* redemption yet to come.

This testimony, to be sure, is in behalf of the two absolute distinctions of Judaism—between man and God, and between the one true God and all the false; and it is not prejudice or carelessness on Hegel's part but rather the belief that the Christian jolt has superseded these two distinctions that makes him disregard the medieval Jewish testimony. In view of this, however, it is remarkable that Hegel does not do total injustice to medieval Jewish history; that, unable to disregard it, he does it a peculiar justice of his own. To be sure, the Jewish religious self-understanding is no longer a subject in the Christian Middle Ages. Neither, however, is it a mere object, i.e., a fossil, anachronism, or the object of the wrath of a true God it has rejected.

It was hitherto stressed that the "true" Christian "content" supersedes the truths of Athens and Jerusalem. It must now be added that this content has an "untrue form"—the split between sacred heaven and profane earth—which has no precedent in either

Athens or Jerusalem, and which therefore leaves aspects in both unvanquished. On one side, Greek philosophy, become subservient to medieval ecclesiastic authority, longs, as it were, for the recovery of its former freedom. On the other side (and this is our present concern), Jewish religious existence, however deaf to the good news of the transcendent-Lord-become-immanent, is a true witness against the medieval Christian falsehood when it longs, however painfully and vainly, for a salvation that is not in heaven but rather on earth. Hegel makes this point—briefly, cryptically, but in a passage placed so strategically as to be unmistakable in its importance—when he states that the Jewish people was "held in readiness" by nothing less than "Spirit and its world" and represented the "infinite pain" of the entire Middle Ages—the witness par excellence to the "untruth" of that world-historical epoch.[67]

The same passage proceeds to assert, however, that in the modern world the medieval untruth vanishes and the Jewish testimony is superseded. The modern world is the "absolute turning point" that transfigures "absolute negativity" into "infinite positivity." "The principle of the unity of the divine nature and the human," in itself actual ever since the jolt of Christianity, is at length "grasped by" spiritual *self*-activity. Only then a "we" can appear in the realm of life whose "concept of God" renders the God of Moses wholly anachronistic. And only then can a philosophy appear in the realm of thought—Hegel's own—that will produce a *Grundidee* that *demonstrates* that the religious truth of Judaism is both absorbed and, as such, superseded.

JEWISH EXISTENCE IN THE BOURGEOIS-PROTESTANT WORLD[68]

Hegel's "absolute turning point" is produced by three distinct but interrelated modern revolutions: the Protestant Reformation (in which the Christian God descends from a medieval heaven into a modern "heart" on earth); an infinitely "free" self-activity reflected in diverse secular forms such as modern science, morality and, above all, the modern state (in which man storms all the heavens); and a philosophical rebellion against its medieval servitude, which recovers its ancient Greek freedom in the modern form of subjectivity and culminates in an absolutely self-active thought inclusive of all reality—the Hegelian system.

The three revolutions are certainly distinct. Thus a veritable gulf may seem to yawn between a Protestant piety that, however emancipated in its "free" inwardness from all ecclesiastical authorities, remains receptive of divine Grace and thus "pious," and the wholly impious French revolution, which makes human autonomy its supreme principle in its conquest of the external world. Less obvious, but no less serious, is the contrast between these two revolutions taken together (which occur in historical life), and the third (which occurs in philosophical thought). Freedom or self-activity in the first two is limited by the fact that it exists in and for men of flesh and blood. In the third it is unlimited—but confined to thought. A significant and influential distinction between a "standpoint of life" and a "standpoint of thought" has come to consciousness in German philosophy ever since Kant. In Hegel's thought it has become wholly self-conscious and all-pervasive.[69]

But if Hegel's three modern revolutions were distinct only, there would be no absolute turning point in modern world history, no concept of God that would make the God of Moses anachronistic, and no philosophy productive of a *Grundidee* that would prove Him anachronistic. Hegel himself criticizes Protestant inwardness when it is and remains inward only, that is, indifferent or hostile to the external world, and, had he considered the matter, might well have found truth vis-à-vis such indifference or hostility in a Jewish stubbornness that, however unfree in the service of its transcendent Lord, at any rate serves Him in the actual, psychosomatic world.[70] Likewise, he sees the nemesis of French revolutionary "freedom" (which absolutizes a merely human freedom and thus turns it into an idol) in French revolutionary "terror," and—once again if he had considered the matter—he might have seen truth in the Jewish Lord insofar as He testifies against that idolatry. The law of Moses, to be sure, makes impossible revolutionary freedom—but also revolutionary terror.

Would the third revolution—modern philosophy self-completed in the Hegelian system—by itself render Jewish religious existence anachronistic? Taking a firm stand against Hegel's panlogistic interpreters, we have already answered this question negatively *in abstracto*. Our answer is no different as Hegel's system now appears in its concrete historical setting. In Hegel's view modern philosophy begins with "war" upon religion but ends with the Hegelian "peace."[71] Most certainly both Judaism and Christianity would be forced to offer resistance in the war; possibly Christianity might join Judaism in offering resistance to the philosophical peace offer as well. But—and this is the crux—on Hegel's own admission and insistence, in any such war between life and thought life would emerge victorious.

The last point is important and controversial enough to need spelling out in some detail. According to Hegel, modern philosophic freedom takes the form of an infinitely self-productive subjectivity or autonomy. For this reason its Cartesian and Spinozistic origins show an absolute hostility to any and all religion because of its "form" of receptivity: modern philosophy is like "a young eagle, a bird of prey which strikes religion down." That this attack provokes religious protests is evident. Not evident (but affirmed by Hegel) is that, since the attack is in thought only while the protests take place in the religious life, the contest reveals one-sidedness in both contestants and that this one-sidedness may count against religion but counts decisively against philosophy. In any case, Hegel's own philosophy can become "science" only if it can overcome this one-sidedness, that is, if it can make a "peace" with religion in which all truth, the religious included, is preserved and united, and all things, divine as well as human, are mediated.[72]

But what if this peace itself were the product of thought alone? Here it is at least doubtful whether the Christian religion can or must accept a peace if the philosophy offering it not only differs from the Christian religious self-understanding (as it does and must), but also is a thought-activity only, over against and in contrast with the Christian religious life. Not doubtful at all is the case of Judaism. The Jewish religious self-understanding would not only protest against the Hegelian mediation of all things, but also would do so successfully. The continued testimony of the Jewish religious life to its two absolute distinctions—between the Divine and the human, and between the one true God and all the false— would by itself suffice to refute Hegel's all-comprehensive Truth, were this latter confined to thought alone. Indeed, vis-à-vis such a testimony in the religious life this philosophy would show itself to be, like its Neoplatonic ancestor, in flight from the world. The claim on which it stakes everything, however, is that, unlike that ancestor in the ancient world, it can stay with the modern world.

The three revolutions that produce and constitute the modern world are interrelated as well as distinct. Only thus can there be an "absolute turning point" in the modern world; only thus can there be a modern "we" whose God-concept renders that of Moses wholly anachronistic; and only thus can there be a philosophy —Hegel's own—productive of a *Grundidee* of Judaism that both does total justice to the truth of Judaism and yet wholly absorbs it. Here at last comes to light the world-historical standpoint ascribed by Hegel both to the modern world and to his own philosophical system. To light as well comes the reason for the inconclusiveness of our previous encounters between the Jewish religious self-understanding and Hegel's philosophical comprehension of it.

That encounter reveals itself as being, and implicitly having been all along, a version of the theme "Jewish existence in the modern world." It is, to be sure, one version only; its treatment, like that of the previous themes "Athens and Jerusalem" and " 'old' and 'new' Jerusalem," will have to be limited. But what it lacks in breadth it more than makes up for in depth: no modern philosopher (his heirs not excepted) combines as radical a claim for modernity with as profound a regard for religious tradition; as for justice to Judaism in the context of this dual commitment, Hegel has no peer.

In Hegel's view the modern Protestant "heart" contains the "true content" of the Christian divine-human unity; it can hope to overcome its "untrue form" (receptive inwardness) only as this latter seeks, rather than shuts itself off from, self-active secular expression in the external world. On its part, modern secular self-activity possesses the "true form" (infinite or autonomous freedom); the "true content" eludes it as a mere Kantian ideal or a Fichtean fragmented reality until it passes beyond sheer—scientific, moral, political—acting to see and accept a religious source in all its acting. Only in this secular-religious union—"implicitly" actual in the modern world and destined to remain creative diversity in all its future explications—does the "principle of the unity of the divine nature and the human" come to life in modern spiritual self-activity, and is "grasped" as such by it. This grasp, first, constitutes the turn from "absolute negativity" to "infinite positivity": the self-differentiating whole of modern secular-Protestant "freedom" unites a divine-human "union" in which all divine-human "nonunion" is forever already overcome in the Easter of the Protestant "heart," with a self-active secular "self-confidence" that forever faces a "nonunion" *yet to be* overcome. It brings to life, second, a "we" that wholly internalizes the God of Moses and raises his Jewish servant above his servitude. This grasp, finally, renders possible the rise of an infinitely self-active, all-mediating, divine-human Thought productive of a *Grundidee* that both preserves the truth of Jewish religious existence and supersedes it. We have stressed that on Hegel's own admission this feat remains impossible so long as it is one of thought only. It becomes possible and actual —so Hegel teaches—for a philosophical thought that merely completes and brings to absolute self-consciousness a divine-human mediation that, except for that completion and mediation, is already complete in historical life. Only thus does Hegel's thought mediate the ultimate dichotomy—i.e., between itself and life—and "over-reaches" life.[73]

For our purposes it must be noted with special care—with a view to subsequent left-wing Hegelianism, on the one hand, and any Jewish response to the challenge of Hegelianism, on the other —that neither Hegel's "modern world" nor his philosophical thought dissipates either the Divine into the human, or the human into the Divine, or the distinction between the two; and indeed, if any of these dissipations occurred, the supposedly world-historical standpoint of both Hegel's modern world and his own philosophical system would at once show themselves to be mere expressions of one particular historical period inflated by delusions of grandeur. In Hegel's modern world the otherness of the Divine is grasped as a divine self-othering in the human, making the self-activity that does the grasping *itself* more-than-human; and what is true of Hegel's modern world in life is true of his own philosophy in thought. Only because divine otherness is thus preserved does Hegel's "identity of the divine nature and the human" not become either an immediate absurdity or an immediate triviality.[74] Here we have the ultimate reason why the Jewish witness to the otherness of God, unshaken in this testimony by three millennia, is genuinely challenged; or in other words, why Hegel's *Grundidee* of Judaism has real power—when hitherto in this discourse, to put it bluntly, it seemed unworthy of a great philosopher.

What, then, *is* the power of that *Idee?* First, the Christian "un-heard of" composition of the Divine and the human becomes trivial or absurd unless it is recognized as indeed unheard of, and philosophical thought can accomplish and hold fast to this recognition only if it can point to a human testimony to the otherness of the Divine prior to the Truth of the divine self-othering in the human. (Thus one might say that, had Hegel not found this testimony in Judaism, he would have been forced to invent it.) Second, the divine-human composition must remain unheard of, the Truth of the divine self-othering in the human notwithstanding. (Thus if divine otherness simply vanished, either in modern religious representational life, or in modern secular self-activity, or in modern philosophical thought, what to begin with was neither absurd nor trivial would in due course assume one of these two qualities, and no witness would show this as clearly as the faithful Jew.) Third, if Hegel's "identity of the divine nature and the human" is and remains unheard of in the modern world and nevertheless actual (and is so comprehended by Hegel's philosophy), then Hegel's *Grundidee* of Judaism is indeed nothing less than what it claims to be, i.e., the true philosophical grasp of both the truth and the falsehood of Judaism.

For at long last we have discovered the ultimate reason why the concept of covenant does not appear in Hegel's account of Judaism, and why Jewish Messianism is not even mentioned: by the standards of a divine-human freedom, which is a divine self-othering in the human, any freedom remains "unfree" which remains human in its relation to the Divine; and any God is Lord only who remains other-than-human in His relation to the human. It is by this standard that Hegel sees the truth of Judaism in its relation between the universal Divinity and one particular family. It is by this standard, too, that he sees a harsh contrast in that relation, and yet a greatness precisely in that harshness, which would be destroyed by petty or unauthentic compromises. However, it is by this standard, too, that the truth of Judaism is both preserved and superseded. Such is Hegel's "world-historical" comprehension of Judaism.

More precisely, such is its negative aspect. A positive counterpart has yet to show itself. Hegel's philosophical comprehension can demonstrate its own comprehensiveness (and hence its world-historical status) only if no truth, however partial, disappears within the whole without a trace.[75] Much to his credit, Hegel makes Judaism no exception to this dialectical requirement. Thus the "Lord" of Judaism does not disappear as He loses His otherness within the context of the modern "infinite positivity"; He is transfigured into the Spinozistic "Substance." And this latter is as world-historical as was its ancient counterpart. Once the Jewish "fear of the Lord" was the beginning of all religious wisdom. Now the beginning of all modern philosophical wisdom is the Spinozistic God.

This transfiguration of the Jewish God, however, remains doubly one-sided. The Jewish God is liberated in Spinozism from His premodern otherness; yet this occurs at the double price of an abstractly universal indifference to all particularity, and of a flight from life into mere thought. Once the particular Jewish family served its transcendent Lord in the world; this unfree relationship possesses both truth and falsehood compared to Spinozistic "acosmism."

Hegel's philosophical mediation of Jewish religious existence would therefore remain fragmentary unless both its terms were preserved, that is, the Jewish family as well as its Lord. That family has preserved itself in Hegel's thought until the modern "absolute turning point" from "absolute negativity" to "infinite positivity." We ask: what happens thereafter to the flesh-and-blood people, when it evidently cannot, and is not meant to, dissipate itself into bloodless Spinozistic thought?

On this altogether crucial question there would appear to be in all of Hegel's writings only a single and, moreover, cryptic footnote. Hegel here calls for the emancipation of the Jewish people in the modern state, in itself no mean commitment in the Germany of his time. More significant still is his reason: the Jews are, "above all, men." But what is "humanity?" Not, Hegel tells us, a "flat, abstract quality."[76] Such a quality is affirmed by Enlightenment emancipators when they propose to give to Jews "as men" everything, and to Jews "as Jews," nothing. Since Hegel rejects such abstract dichotomies he seems to say nothing less than that the modern state is not wholly free until it makes Jews *as Jews* wholly free, and that, on their part, Jews can make modern freedom their own and yet remain Jews. But what will be the Jewish people once it has superseded its "unfree" religious past? We search Hegel's writings in vain for an answer. His philosophical comprehension of Jewish history has been permeated throughout by a sense of riddle. On a note of riddle it ends.

That Hegel's philosophy has no pat solutions to the problem "Jewish existence in the modern world" is to its credit. For as we now turn from Hegel's mediation of Jewish existence with the "modern world" to Jewish responses to that world we shall be faced with many riddles ourselves. And while we can find all sorts of responses, ranging from unbending attempts to ignore the modern world to ill-disguised surrenders to it, we cannot find self-exposed, self-mediating, yet normatively Jewish responses of the kind discovered earlier in this discourse—not among Jews in Hegel's own time, nor, for that matter, among their descendants throughout the nineteenth century. Not until the twentieth century did responses of this sort come upon the historical scene, and by then it was clear to all except sundry retarded theologians and way-out secularist ideologues that Hegel's "modern world" lay in ruins.[77]

We may begin with a group of Jewish intellectuals immediately under Hegel's own influence. In 1819 7 young men foregathered in Berlin to form an association subsequently named *Verein für die Kultur und Wissenschaft der Juden*, whose express purpose was to bring about a Jewish renewal in the light of the requirements of modernity. The 7 were by no means all equally acquainted with or influenced by Hegel's thought. Yet their common convictions were recognizably Hegelian. No salvation lay in the stance of the previous generation—a merely negative *Aufklärung* that one-sidedly rejected Jewish tradition, dissolved Jews into men-in-general, and thus was left with an "empty abstraction."[78] No better was romantic particularism, a vain and reactionary hankering after a lost past. The requirement was a new synthesis that would transfigure the Jewish past in the light of modernity, and replace the "empty abstraction" with "another content."[79] As for the nature of this content—with or without Hegel—one thing was agreed on by all the seven. Negatively, the "first dogma"[80] of the members of the *Verein* was that conversion to Christianity was inadmissible. Positively, it was the conviction—vague, but seemingly firm—that "if we feel the inner necessity of our continued existence [as Jews], then its inner possibility is undeniable."[81]

The *Verein* lasted for only 5 years. Eduard Gans, its leading spirit, embraced Christianity one year after its dissolution and became a Berlin professor. Heinrich Heine, its greatest genius, accused Gans of opportunism,[82] but soon himself accepted baptism as the "entrance ticket" to European culture. (Even so, torn between Judaism and Europe to the end of his life, he remains the greatest, if tragic, Jewish witness of his generation.) Only in one of the original members, Leopold Zunz, did the original Jewish impulse of the *Verein* bear a modern Jewish fruit: Zunz became the founder of modern Jewish scholarship. Yet neither in Zunz's own case nor in that of likeminded devotees of the nineteenth century so-called *Wissenschaft des Judentums* was it ever wholly clear whether the new discipline was to be an enterprise wholly neutral to Jewish life, an instrument for its renewal, or, as one of them put it, a "decent burial" of more than three thousand years of Jewish existence.[83]

Doubtless many features were responsible for the failure of the *Verein*. We have already stressed that the zenith of German culture coincided with the nadir in German-Jewish religious life—a fact that made Heine later judge that the members of the *Verein*, while "gifted men of profound heart," had merely tried to "save a long lost cause."[84] Yet Heinrich Graetz was astute when he blamed the failure on Hegelian ideas. In one of his three remarkable addresses Gans—not only the leading spirit of the *Verein* but also the most thorough Hegelian—said the following:

Only a jarring independence which is reflected only on itself is to be done away with [in Jewish existence], not an independence subordinate to the whole ... which is not required to lose its own substance. That wherein it merges (*aufgeht*) is to be enriched by what has become part of it; it is not merely to become poorer by having lost an opposition. ... The specific character [of present day Europe is] ... the fulness and richness of its particularities ... The comforting lesson of history, properly understood, is that everything passes away (*vorübergeht*) without vanishing (*vergehen*), and that everything persists which is long considered past. Hence neither can the Jews perish nor Judaism dissolve; but in the great movement of the whole it shall seem to have perished and yet live on as the current lives on in the ocean.[85]

Rarely if ever has any Jewish Hegelian placed so complete and indeed childlike a confidence in Hegel's modern Europe—and in its capacity to do Jewish history "justice."

Yet rarely, too, has Hegel's own conception appeared in a more dubious light than in this connection. When, in Hegel's own time or before or after, has Christian or post-Christian Europe ever fully recognized Jews *as Jews?* As for any European willingness (or capacity) to incorporate in its own substance the "fulness and richness" of the Jewish "particularity," this was always fictitious. (To this day some Germans and German Jews speak of a once-existing "German Jewish symbiosis." In fact, there was much Jewish giving to German culture, often to the point of total self-sacrifice; there never was any German reciprocating.)[86] The unphilosophically minded, but level-headed and stoutly Jewish Heinrich Graetz has therefore right on his side when he considers the utterances of Gans as mere "muddiness," "eccentricity," and "Hegelian gibberish."[87]

Gans writes under the direct influence of Hegel's thought. That the challenge of Hegel does not vanish with the advent of a more sober detachment is illustrated by two later nineteenth century Jewish thinkers. Samuel Hirsch (1815–1889) and Moses Hess (1812–1875) wrote their relevant works after the heyday of Hegel's philosophy had passed.[88] Their thought is critical of Hegel and in some respects even anti-Hegelian. It remains Hegelian in judging divine-human otherness to be anachronistic, and in seeking to reform or revolutionize Jewish existence lest it, too, become anachronistic. Both men find many treasures on the way. Their goal, however, is abortive. At one extreme, Hirsch internalizes the Lord of the divine-Jewish covenant so as to transfigure Him into the divine principle immanent in Jewish "freedom"; but in this process the flesh-and-blood Jewish people is dissolved into abstract missionaries of an Idea.

At the other extreme, Hess preserves the people and indeed is the first Zionist thinker; but he can save the universal Jewish God from reduction to a tribal product of a "free" Jewish "genius" only at the price of an eschatological optimism much less realistic than Hegel's own. To be sure, for Hegel himself the "Sabbath of history" has already arrived, whereas for his left-wing follower we are only "on the eve" of it.[89] Yet the master's own Sabbath requires a persisting "workaday week" if it is to be and remain historical. The disciple, in contrast, expects and demands a Sabbath that will wholly transfigure the week—and is left with the choice either of imposing on "Jewish genius" a universal burden such as no flesh-and-blood people can bear, or of reducing that genius, its God included, to but one instrument in the orchestra of nations. Once the universal Lord of all Creation was able to single out the particular Jewish family. This possibility has now vanished at both extremes. And the cause is that on the crucial point—Hegel's modern "grasp" of "the identity of the divine nature and the human"—both thinkers uncritically surrender.

The responses thus far considered are way-out extremes wholly unrepresentative of the Jewish people in nineteenth-century Western Europe. They increase in representativeness as we move from the extremes closer to the middle. This fact may be viewed in two ways. One is that nineteenth-century Jews moved half-heartedly, compromisingly, and apologetically in their response to the challenge of modernity, and faced up only indirectly (if at all) to its maximal (i.e., Hegelian) form. The other is that, in this particular case, there was steadfastness and good sense in this very lack of radicalism, that is, a distrust in the maximal (i.e., Hegelian) self-appraisal of the modern world. Viewed in this light, this response, however unimpressive by the Hegelian (or quasi-Hegelian) standards of religious profundity and radical readiness for win-all-or-lose-all historical self-exposure, must be viewed positively—as it were, as a holding operation. To accept this latter evaluation is not to deny validity in the former—the view that these holding operations do not constitute, but merely postpone, a radical Jewish self-exposure and response to the modern world in its maximal, Hegelian claims.

The liberal Abraham Geiger (1810–1874) and the neo-orthodox Samson Raphael Hirsch (1808–1888) may serve as examples of nineteenth-century Jewish holding operations. Both thinkers are self-exposed to the modern world. Neither is radically self-exposed in a win-all-or-lose-all posture. Both risk or sacrifice part of the Jewish religious past, though the one does so joyously, consciously, and without misgivings, while the other, if without misgivings, does his sacrificing only because the fact remains largely unconscious. Because of their lack of radicalism, the basic categories of neither thinker bear much profound or critical inspection. Yet this weakness cannot hide a strength—a firm rootedness in the Jewish substance, which, incidentally, in a twentieth-century perspective shows far more unity among them than was perceived by the two men themselves; their nineteenth century quarrels set them apart.

Such Geigerian categories as "religious creativity," "historical development," and "universalistic significance" remain superficial so long as the basic issue—the destiny of the divine-Jewish covenant in the modern world—does not come under explicit scrutiny. Nor are they deepened by the manner in which Geiger himself bolsters them—his scholarly demonstrations that Judaism never lacked the above-mentioned qualities he ascribes to it. Geiger's achievement lies in the quality of his Jewish scholarship, not in the ideological use he makes of it; and if this is a religious as well as a scholarly achievement, it is because there are elements in the Jewish substance that remain not negotiable.[90]

These are the strengths and weaknesses of the liberal Geiger. Those of the neo-orthodox Hirsch are oppositely distributed.[91] Unlike Geiger, Hirsch firmly holds fast to the ancient divine-Jewish covenant, and indeed, his orthodoxy is founded upon it. Yet he finds it necessary to reinforce this commitment by external standards derived from the modern world. Thus it is not clear whether his ideal of a "Yisroel-Man" is found in the Torah or (at least in large measure) read into it with the help of idealistic philosophy; and the consequence of this ambiguity is that, despite Hirsch's insistence on the Messianic significance of the flesh-and-blood Jewish people, he comes close to replacing it with a spiritualized, quasi-Protestant abstraction. Indeed, as the most astute student of this period in the history of Judaism has observed, Hirsch goes so far as to project this spiritualized conception into ancient Judaism itself with his view that the Jewish state always was but a means to the "spiritual mission of Israel."[92] In Geiger's case, the Jewish substance survives, at least in part, despite ill-fitting and inadequate modern categories. In the case of Hirsch, the categories, traditional, fitting, and profound albeit radically questionable in the modern world, do not succeed in leaving the Jewish substance wholly intact. Both men conduct holding operations and nothing more.

Yet by any fair and realistic standard the positive aspect in the work of these two thinkers (and others who might have been cited) has the edge over the negative. In Hegel's vision modern

European freedom is at least "implicitly" actual for all men and groups of men. Marx's "proletariat" only excepted, no group of nineteenth-century Europeans has had as much cause to doubt that vision as the Jews of Europe. Hedged between Christian reactionaries on the right (who would deny, obstruct, or delay their emancipation) and Enlightenment liberals on the left (who would grant it only on condition that they weaken if not surrender their Jewishness), only deluded, servile, or self-hating Jews could see any truth in the Hegelian vision. Realistic, steadfast, or self-respecting Jews were bound to question if not altogether reject it, and to defend their Jewish substance by whatever means they could. If their responses to modernity were less self-exposed than self-protective, and shot through with conscious and unconscious apologetics, this fact reflects less on nineteenth-century Judaism than on nineteenth-century Europe. The left demanded that, alone of all men, the Jews become men-in-general; the right, that they be more German than the Germans and more French than the French. Vis-à-vis Jews if nowhere else, the abstractions "mankind" and "nation" became absolute principles. As for the universal mediation supposedly manifest in Hegel's modern Europe, Jews, at any rate, experienced no trace of it.

Hegel's Europe was destroyed by the first World War—an event that he had held could not happen. Remarkably (however belatedly and fragmentarily), two Jewish thinkers gave a radical Jewish response to Hegel's Europe and its maximal (i.e., Hegelian) self-interpretation—one in the trenches, the other even before the catastrophe had occurred. Hermann Cohen and Franz Rosenzweig, taken together, may be viewed as such a response. Also—though this is a subject transcending our present scope—their work, together with that of Martin Buber, marks the beginnings of a liberated modern Jewish philosophy.[93]

Jewish thinkers prior to Cohen were apt to project into the future what to Hegel himself was already implicitly present. This turn of thought, hitherto peripheral, moves for Cohen into the centre. Moreover, the future becomes radical. No mere reformed version of the present, it is Messianic. Indeed, Cohen's entire thought is Messianism, and he finds its ultimate ground, not in aspects of the modern world—secular morality, the Protestant spirit, or, for that matter, philosophical reason itself—but rather in an explicitly Jewish article of faith. He writes:

Prophetic Messianism . . . is the most tremendous idea which [rational or philosophic] ethics must borrow and absorb from a reality alien to philosophical methodology.[94]

No modern Jewish philosopher prior to Cohen had the philosophical courage to make such an affirmation; none had the philosophical ability to make it stick. To the basic dilemma of modern Jewish thought of ignoring, or submitting to, modern thought and its standards, Cohen responds with a third alternative: in its pivotal point modern philosophy (and hence the modern world) stands itself in need of foundations originally, if no longer exclusively, Jewish in character.[95] Thus Cohen first takes a step without which a truly free Jewish response to all modern philosophy—Kantian, Marxist, or existentialist no less than Hegelian—is in principle impossible.

Cohen assails Hegel's maximal self-understanding of the modern world in behalf of the Jewish Messianism Hegel ignores. His disciple Franz Rosenzweig levels his attack in behalf of the God of Sinai, whom Hegel himself considers central to Judaism, but anachronistic for "us." In his own way each thinker aims at the core of Hegel's modern world—the "identity of the divine nature and the human." Yet with respect to radicalism the teacher must yield to the disciple. Cohen's "God-Idea" merely projects Hegel's own divine-human identity into the absolute, i.e., Messianic future. Rosenzweig's "new thinking" has passed through that identity, exposed it as a false abstraction of mere thought, and only after having done so reaffirms the present otherness of the God of Sinai. Hence the much misunderstood, seemingly arbitrary, yet in fact unerringly precise departure of *The Star of Redemption* with God, World and Man as "empirically" ultimate "data." Hence too the startling boldness of a purely philosophical, hence "universal," "system" in which, nevertheless, the divine-Jewish covenant is central in all its stark particularity. An astute critic observes that

... whereas the classic work of what is called Jewish medieval philosophy, the [Maimonidean] *Guide for the Perplexed*, is primarily not a philosophical book but a Jewish book, Franz Rosenzweig's *Star of Redemption* is primarily not a Jewish book but a "system of philosophy."[96]

The medieval Jewish thinker must confront Greek (i.e., pagan) philosophy only insofar as it conflicts with his Judaism. His modern counterpart must be more radical. Modern philosophy is not obviously pagan and indeed claims absolute universality; and in its profoundest (i.e., Hegelian) form this claim becomes one of comprehensiveness. The Jewish thinker can confront this challenge only by exposing his own Judaism to it wholly and without remainder; and he can achieve its uncompromising recovery only after so total a self-exposure. It is significant that Franz Rosen-zweig began his career with a great work on Hegel,[97] subsequently wrote the "system of philosophy" that recovered his Judaism for him—and finally declared that he no longer needed that system.

But if Cohen and Rosenzweig may thus be viewed as long-delayed radical Jewish responses to the maximal (i.e., Hegelian) self-understanding of the modern world, these responses would nevertheless appear to be fragmentary, or, more precisely, one-sided. For all its Jewishness Cohen's neo-Kantianism is Hegelian enough to internalize both the God of Moses and the prophetic Messiah,[98] and the result is that the flesh-and-blood people of the covenant remain as abstract missionaries of the Idea as they had been for Samuel Hirsch. And Rosenzweig's anti-Hegelian "system" remains Hegelian enough to be able to restore the divine-Jewish covenant only at the price of leaving it as unhistorical as it had been for Hegel himself. So far does Cohen go in his idealistic, quasi-Protestant dissipation of the flesh-and-blood people as in all seriousness to assert that, of all peoples, this people alone may not have a state of its own if it is to remain true to its Messianic mission.[99] And so strong is the Hegelian element that persists in Rosenzweig's *Star* as to make possible the affirmation that Chris-tianity alone is *of* history while Judaism is merely *in* it, unmoved between Sinai and the Messianic days.[100] Neither thinker could have foreseen two events that, soon after their deaths, were to re-turn this people into history, and indeed place it into what Hegel might have considered its center. Yet the fact remains that Jewish death at Auschwitz and rebirth at Jerusalem have made both thinkers more dated in certain respects than premodern, rabbinic Judaism.

Their datedness lies in a one-sided, crypto-Protestant fideism[101] alien to Jewish existence, always rightly opposed by an equally onesided "national" or "Zionist" secularism, and now wholly anach-ronistic. The Nazi holocaust was a crime at once religious and secular, aimed at both the death of the Jewish faith and the death of Jews regardless of faith or lack of faith. The Zion that has arisen from the ashes is both "secular" and "religious" and a witness against that dichotomy. Hegel's premodern Jerusalem antedates the split between religiosity and secularity introduced by Chris-tianity. The reborn Jewish Jerusalem of our own time has begun to supersede that split.

Hegel's philosophy does not allow either for the particular facts of the idolatry of Auschwitz or a Jewish Jerusalem reborn, and how it might respond to these facts will be a speculative question.[102] Not speculative is his response to the general fact of modern spiritual decay. While Hegel never despaired of the modern bourgeois-Protestant world his *Philosophy of Religion* ends, nevertheless, with sad reflections upon contemporary spiritual decay. Protestant faith may affirm that "the very gates of hell cannot prevail against the Kingdom of God." What if faith is itself in a state of decay? What if, correspondingly, political life is "inactive and without confidence," so much so that no philosophical efforts can revive it? Philosophic thought—so Hegel ends—has in that case no choice but to flee into a "separate sanctuary" and to "leave to the world the task of settling how it might find its way out of its present state of disruption."[103]

Hegel never connects such reflections (in any case marginal in his thought) with the question of Jewish destiny in the modern world. Had he done so, what might have been his answer? Neo-platonic thought once found divine-human union at the price of flight from the ancient world, and the Jewish role then had been to persist in serving *in* the world a God who was Lord *of* it. This role is over and done with in case Hegel's own thought, unlike its ancient predecessor, can *stay with* the world. But what if, against its central intention, it too is forced into flight? Hegel never raises this question. We shall have to raise it in his behalf.

LEFT-WING HEGELIANISM AND "THE JEWISH PROBLEM"

How Hegel might have responded to the questions just asked will be risky speculation. The response of his left-wing followers is a matter of historical record. We have thus far taken the Hegelian system as it takes itself. It was to be proved dramatically, however, that his system lends itself to an internal "transformation" that (1) holds fast to Hegel's own maximal claims in behalf of the modern world, (2) moves into the center the recognition of contemporary "disruption," which for Hegel himself remains marginal, and (3) yet wholly unlike Hegel stays with this disrupted modern world instead of resorting to flight from it. To consider the relation between this transformation and a correspondingly transformed image of Judaism will be a task whose importance one cannot exaggerate.

The left-wing Hegelian feat is in essence astonishingly simple. Hegel's philosophy has rightly mediated the divine-human difference and opposition in thought. It has rightly insisted that this mediation would be quite chimerical unless it were already somehow actual in historical life. Finally, it is right in maintaining that its own world—the bourgeois-Protestant world[104]—is the conclusive divine-human mediation and thus of world-historical significance. Only in one fundamental point is Hegel's philosophy radically mistaken; the correction of this one error, however, "transforms" everything. Hegel's "ultimate" world is in truth the penultimate world, and his philosophy, the penultimate philosophy. In its secular aspect, that world is free in idea only, not yet in concrete reality. In its religious aspect it is true and ultimate insofar as it is Protestant, but remains false and penultimate insofar as it remains religious. Taken as a whole, it calls for one final revolution, whose negative aspect is to destroy the Christian-Protestant God (and *ipso facto* all possible gods), while its positive aspect is, for the first time in all of history, to produce an "existence" that, both *absolutely* free and *concretely* human, has been all along the unrecognized and unrealized "human essence."[105] In this revolution what in Hegel's world is the "identity of the divine nature and the human" becomes the appropriation of the divine nature *by* the human.

So much for the transformation of Hegel's modern world. His philosophical comprehension of that world undergoes a corresponding transformation. Mistaking its own world for ultimate, Hegel's thought, on the one hand, understands itself as divine-human, and, on the other hand, culminates in "interpreting" the world. To correct this error is to make philosophical thought human, and, at the same time, to make it pass beyond merely "interpreting" to "changing" the world.[106] Thus Hegel's "owl of Minerva" (which rises to flight only with the coming of dusk) becomes the "cock" that announces and indeed *helps produce* a new day. More precisely, it will be *the* day.

The left-wing Hegelians were involved in internecine quarrels, some petty, others momentous. Yet the views just outlined were shared, among others, by Arnold Ruge (1803–1880), Ludwig Feuerbach (1804–1872), Bruno Bauer (1809–1882) and Karl Marx (1818–1883);[107] and the example of Ernst Bloch (1885–   ) suffices to show that they have not vanished from the contemporary scene. These views were summed up perfectly by none other than Marx himself, in a passage that deserves to be quoted:

For Germany, the criticism of religion has been largely completed; and the criticism of religion is the premise of all criticism. . . . Man, who looked for a superman in the fantastic reality of heaven and found nothing there but the reflection of himself, will no longer be disposed to find but a semblance of himself, the non-human (*Unmensch*) where he seeks and must seek true reality.

The basis of religious criticism is: Man makes religion, religion does not make man . . . Religion is the self-consciousness and self-feeling of man, who either has not yet found himself or has already lost himself again. But man is no abstract being, squatting outside the world. Man is the world of man, the state, society. This state, this society produce religion, an inverted world-consciousness, because they are an inverted world. Religion . . . is the fantastic realization of the human essence because the human essence has no reality. The struggle against religion is therefore indirectly the struggle against that world whose spiritual aroma is religion.

Religious suffering is the expression of real suffering and at the same time the protest against real suffering. Religion is the sigh of the oppressed creature, the heart of a heartless world. . . . It is the opium of the people.

The abolition of religion as the illusory happiness of the people is required for their real happiness. The demand to give up the illusions is a call to give up a condition which needs illusions. . . .

The criticism of religion disillusions man to make him think and act to shape his reality like a man who has been disillusioned and . . . will revolve around himself and therefore around his true sun. Religion is only the illusory sun which revolves around man as long as he does not revolve around himself. . . .

The criticism of heaven turns into the criticism of the earth, the criticism of religion into the criticism of right, and the criticism of theology into the criticism of politics. . . .

Luther, to be sure, overcame bondage based on devotion by replacing it with bondage based on conviction. He shattered faith in authority by restoring the authority of faith. He turned priests into laymen by turning laymen into priests. He freed man from outward religiosity by making religiosity the inwardness of man. He emancipated the body from its chains by putting chains on the heart.

But if Protestantism was not the true solution, it was the true formulation of the problem. The question was no longer the struggle of the layman against the priest external to him but the struggle against his own inner priest, his priestly nature. And if the Protestant transformation of German laymen into priests emancipated the lay popes—the princes with their clerical set, the privileged, and the Philistine—the philosophical transformation of priestly Germans into men will emancipate the people. . . .[108]

Virtually any left-wing Hegelian might have written this passage, though none as brilliantly. A few representative examples will suffice. Ruge rhetorically asks, "Is the highest (i.e., free) being man himself, or something alien to man not of this world?"[109]

He answers with a "negating and postulating activism" that will produce a "humanized world of liberated men."[110] Bauer (in whose view Christianity has destroyed the freedom of classical antiquity) wants to negate this negation by reviving a pre-Christian Germanic supposed free "right of conquest."[111] Feuerbach (who "transforms" all divine into human attributes) wants to make this transformation actual in life by making religion into politics:

The true state is unlimited, infinite, true, complete, divine Man. Only the state is Man. The state is self-determined, self-related, absolute Man.[112]

These and other passages disclose for us the first element of common doctrine among all the left-wing Hegelians—an inseparable connection between the negation of all past and possible gods, and an affirmation of a future Man whose unprecedented "freedom" will be the positive counterpart of his self-produced godlessness.

Is Marx an exception to this generalization? He differs from his fellow left-wing Hegelians only in degree and not in principle. For while the early Marx already distinguishes between a religious criticism already done and a social criticism yet to be done, he cannot divorce the two entirely. And while the late, so-called scientific, Marx may have become indifferent to religion, only a persistent dialectical negation of religion can account for expectations which are nothing short of Messianic.

So much, then, for the first common element in left-wing Hegelianism. It is by no means the only one. The left-wing Hegelians are not postreligious atheists; they are post-Christian, or, more precisely, post-Protestant atheists. Hegel's "identity of the divine nature and the human" becomes actual not in a generally religious but rather in a specifically Christian-Protestant world. As the left-wing Hegelians "transform" Hegel's identity into an appropriation of the divine nature by the human, it must under no circumstances be overlooked that they affirm and produce, not a generally postreligious, but rather a specifically post-Christian-Protestant world. Hegel's all-comprehensive philosophy requires, not "religion" but Protestant Christianity. His left-wing disciples require, directly Hegel's "modern world," and indirectly, the Christianity that is part of it. In short, Hegel preserves Christianity, his left-wing followers destroy it, but both require it. (That this is in each case Hegel's Christian self-understanding, not necessarily every Christian self-understanding, need hardly be added.)

The assertion just made is doubtless debatable. Also, if true, it will be crucial for any encounter between Judaism and left-wing

Hegelianism. It is therefore necessary to pause briefly for some expansion and corroboration. Unlike Enlightenment deists, Hegel knows no such thing as religious-truth-in-general but only degrees of such truth. Unlike Enlightenment atheists, the left-wing Hegelians affirm degrees of religious falsehood. In Hegel's view Protestant Christianity is the absolutely true content, untrue only in form. In the view of the left-wing-Hegelians this religion, to be sure, is false in content as well as form. It is, however, the least false religion in both respects. Hence, negatively, its death is ipso facto the death of all possible religions, while, positively, its life and death is the dialectical presupposition of the final truth that (to cite Feuerbach's version) will

... reduce theology to anthropology ... [and] exalt anthropology to theology, very much as Christianity while lowering God into man, made man into God.[113]

The Protestant-Christian presuppositions of left-wing Hegelianism are not equally obvious or prominent in every case. In no case, however, are they wholly absent, and this despite the fact that the respective evaluations of Christianity differ radically. Thus at one extreme Feuerbach (who, despite his atheism, has a deep regard for the Christian religion) sees the humanization of God and the deification of man already in Protestantism, so that all that remains is the "transformation" of religious falsehood into humanistic truth. At the other extreme Bauer "no longer seeks to humanize the 'essence' of Christianity but to demonstrate its 'inhumanity' "; indeed, viewing Christianity as *the* misfortune of the world," he wants nothing less than a "total de-Christianization."[114] Even so it does not occur to him to want to restore the "free" ancient world. The Christian subversion of the ancient world was a dialectical necessity, and the "free" atheism that will arise from the negation of this negation will not only be anti-Christian but post-Christian as well.

Once again, as before, Marx may seem to be the great exception. (Certainly the "scientific materialism" of Marxist orthodoxy would look quite odd unless it rejected all religion simply as religion and without discrimination.) Yet once again, as before, Marx differs from his colleagues only in degrees. The previously cited passage is enough to show that Marx's negation of religion is not indiscriminate; and in a recent work Marx is called "the last of the Lutherans."[115]

Under these circumstances, we are in pursuit of no mere piecemeal or parochial objective when we now turn to the image of

Judaism in left-wing Hegelianism. His dialectical requirements compel Hegel to try to do Judaism justice in the process of proving it anachronistic. His left-wing followers face the same requirement under transformed conditions. Hence nothing is more wayward (and, possibly, escapist as well) than the view that the left-wing Hegelian image of Judaism is a mere detail without universal significance. Indeed, we shall be forced to conclude that any version of left-wing Hegelianism that does Judaism no kind of justice stands for that reason alone, and by its own dialectical standards, in need of total reexamination.

Feuerbach gives the first left-wing Hegelian image of Judaism. And, brief though his account is, it remains normative for the whole nineteenth century. Only the twentieth-century thinker Bloch tells a new tale.

The "principle" of Judaism, Feuerbach declares, is "egoism." The Greek beholds, admires, worships nature. Believing it to have been created for his benefit, the Jew "makes nature the abject vassal for his selfish interest, of his practical egoism." Hence

... eating is the most solemn act, the initiation of the Jewish religion. In eating the Israelite celebrates and renews the act of creation; in eating man declares nature to be an insignificant object.

Judaism thus begins with egoism. It also remains confined to it.

The Greeks looked abroad into the wide world that they might extend their sphere of vision; the Jews to this day pray with their faces to Jerusalem.

Judaism thus contrasts unfavorably with Greek (and indeed all) polytheism by virtue of its "egoism." It contrasts unfavorably with Christianity by virtue of its "unfreedom."

The Christian religion distinguishes inward moral purity from external physical purity; the Israelites identified the two. In relation to the Israelitish religion, the Christian religion is one of criticism and freedom. The Israelite trusted himself to do nothing except what was commanded by God; he was without will even in external things; the authority of religion extended itself even to his food. The Christian religion, on the other hand, in all these things made man dependent on himself, i.e., it placed in man what the Israelite placed outside himself in God. In relation to the Israelite, the Christian is a ... free thinker.

Are there, then, two vices in Judaism, egoism, and unfreedom or positivity? In Feuerbach's view, Jewish positivity ultimately *is* egoism.

The supranaturalistic egoism of the Jews did not proceed from the Creator, but conversely, the latter from the former. In the creation the Israelite justified his egoism at the bar of his reason.

Jehovah is the ego of Israel, which regards itself as the end and aim, the Lord of nature. . . . If, in the course of time, the idea of Jehovah expanded itself in individual minds, and his love was extended, as by the writer of the book of Jonah, to man in general, this does not belong to the essential character of the Israelitish religion.[116]

In short, Judaism *is* egoism, and, what is more, an egoism that is beyond redemption. Feuerbach stresses this last point when, unlike Hegel himself, he takes note of the Talmud—only to assert that Talmudic Judaism too is egoistic.

Can Feuerbach's Judaism, like Hegel's, be considered a serious philosophical conception? Not for an instant. In the picture he draws Jewish "initiation" is eating (a use of nature), not circumcision (which symbolizes that such use has sharp limits). His contrast between Judaism and Christianity disregards that in Judaism human righteousness is worthy in the sight of God, while in Pauline-Augustinian-Lutheran Christianity man is worthless until redeemed by a Grace entirely arbitrary. But why go on? There is no point. Indeed, one is tempted to dismiss this caricature of Judaism as the work of an ex-Christian thinker who has rejected Christianity but not Christian antisemitism.

Yet the question of how a serious thinker could produce such a caricature cannot be avoided. Several explanations are possible. The most fruitful understands Feuerbach's image of Judaism as part of his "transformation" of Hegelianism.[117]

Like Hegel, Feuerbach detects a contrast between the one infinite God of Judaism and the particular Jewish family. Like Hegel, too, he finds this contrast harsh and hence rules out—in his case, however, without a moment's thought—the covenantal and Messianic beliefs. But wholly unlike Hegel he makes no attempt to wrestle with, let alone appreciate and understand in its own terms, the otherness of the God of Judaism for the simple reason that, in his view, there is not and never was such an otherness, and, indeed, no God. Hence Hegel's profound if ultimately inadequate concept of a Jewish "renunciation of renunciation" (which, let it be stressed, includes an anything-but-egoistical "renunciation"[118] as an indispensable element) shrivels for Feuerbach into a crude, one-dimensional egoism projected on a nonexistent Deity. Similarly, while in Hegel's view the "firm" Jewish refusal to "assimilate alien forms of worship" is "admirable," in Feuerbach's eyes it is merely "immovable."[119] As for citations from the

Talmud, Hegel's ignorance is to be preferred to Feuerbach's "knowledge," for his authority is Eisenmenger's *Entdecktes Judentum*[120]—one of the worst antisemitic concoctions of all time. No one seems to have emphasized or even noticed this last fact— a minor scandal in philosophical scholarship.

The failure to expose Feuerbach's caricature of Judaism is a major scandal, and in theology and philosophy as well as merely in scholarship. For since in every dialectical philosophy one gross lapse reverberates throughout the whole, to overlook, or make nothing of, Feuerbach's radical injustice to Judaism is necessarily to blind oneself to the repercussions of this injustice in Feuerbach's entire thought.

This is illustrated by a justly famous essay of Karl Barth's.[121] This essay makes two fundamental assertions: that the atheist Feuerbach remains "more theological than . . . many [Christian] theologians, . . . in closest loyalty to traditional material," challenging Christian faith more radically than Kant and Hegel; and that, despite these merits, Feuerbach's conclusion is in Christian eyes "quite extraordinarily, almost nauseatingly trivial."[122] It is Barth's great merit to have seen this strange state of affairs. He is unable, however, to explain it.

He would have succeeded had he exposed and criticized Feuerbach's caricature of Judaism. (Instead—a depressingly familiar phenomenon—he simply ignores it.) Why is Feuerbach trivial in Christian eyes when Hegel is not? Had Barth not ignored the image of Judaism in both thinkers he would have found his answer. Hegel's divine-human composition not only *is* but *remains* unheard of, and the good news of the Easter remains not only ever-good but also ever-new; and to hold fast to this union of union and nonunion Hegel requires the faithful Jewish testimony to divine-human nonunion. Feuerbach, in contrast, transforms all divine into *simply*, that is, one-dimensionally human, attributes, a reduction that is impossible without a corresponding reduction of Hegel's Jewish renunciation of renunciation to a one-dimensional Jewish egoism. It matters little whether in Feuerbach's thought an original undialectical anti-Judaism has in train a trivialization of Christianity, or whether an original reductionist humanism necessitates a caricature of Judaism; for the results are the same. Feuerbach's "elevation of anthropology to theology" remains an empty proclamation that elevates nothing. And historic justice is done to his thought when it is attacked, not only (as we have seen) for triviality from the neo-orthodox Christian right, but also (as remains to be seen) for abstractness from the atheistic left. Unfortunately, in these attacks, so far as Judaism is concerned, the left did even worse than the right. Barth merely ignores Feuerbach's Jewish egoism. The left-wing Hegelians accept that caricature and transform it in the light of their own dialectical requirements.

Feuerbach devotes only a brief chapter in his best-known work to Judaism. Bruno Bauer is the author of a large and influential tract solely devoted to "the Jewish problem."[123] Bauer's left-wing Hegelianism, such as it is, advances beyond Feuerbach in "concreteness," for whereas the latter thinker merely exalts a "future politics," the former is engaged in actual, historically oriented, political thinking. However, advance is in this case a doubtful virtue. In advancing beyond Feuerbach, Bauer not only augments his defects but also produces doctrines for whose absurdities he can claim sole, if dubious, credit. Bauer writes:

A truth is true only once—at the moment of time when it is conceived in human consciousness, and only as long as it fights side by side with the spirit of history, until it is assimilated completely by the latter, that is, subjected to criticism, and its dissolution becomes the fertile soil for the growing of a new form of truth. The fire worship of the Parsees, too, was true once. So was the law of Jehovah.[124]

This single passage (except for Bauer's view that his own "criticism" has finally disposed of the Jewish-Christian and thus all religious conflict)[125] suffices completely to sum up Bauer's left-wing Hegelianism insofar as it concerns our present purpose. The first fact to note is therefore that if Bauer surpasses Feuerbach in historical concreteness (being in this respect closer to Hegel himself), it is only by virtue of a simplicistic vulgarization of Hegel that is almost beyond belief.[126] Hegel makes God act in history. For Bauer "the spirit of history" is itself divine. Hegel distinguishes between historical sequence and dialectical advance. For Bauer this difference disappears. Hegel's "actuality of the rational"—to be sure, a controversial dictum but in Hegel's thought subtle and carefully weighed[127]—degenerates in Bauer into an ideological weapon enabling its wielder according to whim to use "facts" to strike at theories, and "theories" to strike at facts.

Bauer's image of Judaism, far from the result of an independent study of the sources, is simply that of Feuerbach, and all that is new is that he develops that image in the light of his own ideological requirements. Indeed, one could virtually deduce the one from the other were it not for the complicating factor, already mentioned, that for Bauer Christianity is "the misfortune of the world." Feuerbach blames Judaism for falling short of Christianity. Others, such as Nietzsche, were to blame it for having produced Christianity. Bauer manages to combine both criticisms—a feat accomplished not without a certain perverse brilliance.

How does Judaism fall short of Christianity? As in Feuerbach, by virtue of its "egoism." Judaism only "satisfies man preoccupied with . . . nature . . . , who wants to see himself merely independent of nature." In contrast, "Christianity says: man is everything, is God, is all-comprehensive and all-powerful, and merely expresses this truth in a still religious manner when it says: only one, i.e., Christ, is the man who is everything."[128] "Unfree" Jewish service, then, is overcome in Christian "freedom."[129]

Then how, falling short of Christianity, is Judaism at the same time responsible for Christianity? Because Christianity is "Judaism become complete." "Christianity originated when in a weak hour the masculine spirit of Greek philosophy and classical culture became intermingled with a Judaism which happened to be in a state of lust." (Bauer does not explain the Greek weakness, to say nothing of the Jewish lust.) The result of this disastrous alliance was a Christianity

pushing inhumanity to a point more extreme than any other religion, indeed, to its absolute peak. Having grasped the most unlimited concept of mankind, it perverted and distorted it in a religious form which was bound to make the human essence itself inhuman. Jewish inhumanity is not pushed that far.

How, then, can Judaism be both responsible for and inferior to Christianity? Because the Christian universalization of Jewish "egoism" is the dialectically necessary condition for human self-liberation. Indeed, the struggle for human self-liberation is implicit in Christianity; in Judaism it is not.

Jewish Jesuitism is that cleverness with which sensuous need satisfies itself . . . Christian Jesuitism, in contrast, is the hellish theoretical labor of spirit struggling for its freedom.[130]

Hence in any conflict between these two "egoistic" Jesuitisms, it is the relatively harmless Jewish one, not the disastrous Christian one, which is without historic rights.

Not the daughter is ungrateful toward the mother, but the mother does not want to acknowledge the daughter. The daughter has the higher right. . . . If one wants to call both sides egoistical, then the daughter is selfish for wanting her own way and progress, and the mother because she wants her own way and no progress. . . . The Christian religion is the abolition of Judaism, therefore it also abolishes Jewish exclusiveness. This is true, however, insofar as it is really the perfection of Jewish exclusiveness.[131]

This, it may be thought, is bad enough. But worse is yet to come as the hitherto "abstract" terms turn into "concrete," i.e., political ones. Jewish emancipation in nineteenth-century Germany is the sorry tale of a weak minority having to fight for elementary rights that in more advanced Western states were taken for granted. Hegel, as we have seen, supports Jewish emancipation. Bauer, though far to his left and writing many years later, devotes a whole treatise to opposing it. No wonder German Jews, turned rightward in their uneven battles, felt stabbed in the back.[132]

Bauer asserts: neither Jew nor Christian is emancipated in the present Christian state, and Jews, rather than fight for rights within the present state, ought to fight for the freedom of all in the future secular state. This kind of argument, morally dubious enough in its abstract liberal form, becomes altogether ominous in Bauer's concrete left-wing Hegelian form. In the liberal version Jews must fight for the freedom of all to have the right to fight for their own freedom, regardless of any special disabilities they may suffer. In Bauer's version the Jew must cease to be a Jew if he is to have the right to any kind of freedom at all. Indeed, even if he makes no demands for emancipation, a Jew arrogates to himself a "privilege" merely by remaining a Jew: "the idea of privilege is intertwined with . . . [the Jew's] nature." As for his both remaining a Jew and yet demanding emancipation, this is morally self-contradictory. It is not altogether far-fetched to see loom behind Bauer's nineteenth-century "moral" demand for the Jew's voluntary self-dissolution the twentieth-century "moral" right to exterminate him.

What is the source of Bauer's Jewish "idea of privilege"? Nothing but Feuerbach's "Jewish egoism," and, far from concerned to test this against historical fact, Bauer merely tests and transforms this conception in the light of his own ideological requirements. (If "ideology" is a scheme concerned only with its own coherence and quite indifferent to historical fact, then Bauer is the nineteenth-century left-wing ideologue par excellence, though he has found successors exceeding him on both right and left in the twentieth century.)

Disregarding historical fact, does Bauer's ideology allow at least such elementary moral distinctions as between the "privilege" of the Christian state to oppress its Jewish minority and the "privilege" of that minority of merely existing? By no means. Christian intolerance is nothing but universalized Jewish "egoism," a fact that deprives Jews of every right of complaint. To go further, Jewish "fanaticism," being particularist in its egoism, is merely petty, while Christian fanaticism, having become universalized, has had "blessed periods to give them a special splendor." Thus "the fire of Christian love" shone when St. Augustine commanded the persecution of the heretics, when the crusaders were on their way to the Orient, and in the night of St. Bartholomew.[133]

Why bother with Bauer's fantastic absurdities except in a history of modern antisemitism? For three important reasons. First, to confirm in a second case a conclusion reached already in one— that no justice is done to Judaism once Hegel's image of Judaism is given a left-wing, atheistic interpretation. Second, to consider the first (though by no means the last) example of a left-wing account of Judaism concerned only with its own ideological consistency and totally indifferent to historical fact. Third, to supply the facts necessary for the understanding of what proved to be the most influential, and hence most disastrous, image of Judaism brought forth by the entire left-wing Hegelian tradition.

Karl Marx's writings on "the Jewish question" were provoked by those of Bauer, whom he calls a "theologian."[134] (One might prefer calling him a crypto-, pseudo-, or post-Christian ideologue who manages to avoid the disciplines of genuine theological and secularist thought alike.) Marx, no mere ideologue, breaks through Bauer's ideological constructs sufficiently to come upon a distinction crucial in historical reality. There is a difference between "political" and "human" emancipation, and the "political" emancipation of the Jews, he declares against Bauer, is both possible and necessary in the modern (albeit still bourgeois) state.[135] Indeed, he "takes the degree to which Jews enjoy political and civil rights as the criterion of the modernity of any particular state."[136]

Then why is the "non-theological" Marx drawn by Bauer into a discussion of Judaism at all? And what makes him affirm that Jews stand in greater need of "human" emancipation than Christians? It is often said that when Marx says "Judaism" he means "capitalism." If he means capitalism why doesn't he say it? And why does he ignore the fact that Judaism precedes capitalism by several millennia, and—so one must add in the age of orthodox kibbutzim—is quite capable of outliving it? Most important and painful of all, why does he withhold from oppressed Jews the compassion he extends so generously to the oppressed proletariat, and, indeed, in their case alone, systematically confuses oppressed and oppressors? Of Marx of all thinkers one might expect the obvious insight that any special Jewish involvement with money is both the result of, *and resistance to,* oppression in Christian society. Yet of this insight he shows not a trace.

Characteristically, Marx's views on the Jewish people and its religion are summed up perfectly in relatively few passages:

Let us consider the real Jew: not the Sabbath Jew, whom Bauer considers, but the everyday Jew.

Let us not seek the secret of the Jew in his religion, but let us seek the secret of his religion in the real Jew.

What is the profane basis of Judaism? Practical need, self-interest. What is the worldly cult of the Jew? Huckstering. What is his worldly god? Money.

Very well; then in emancipating itself from huckstering and money, and thus from real and practical Judaism, our age would emancipate itself.

An organization of society which would abolish the preconditions and thus the very possibility of huckstering, would make the Jew impossible. His religious consciousness would evaporate. . . . On the other hand, when the Jew recognizes his practical nature as invalid and endeavors to abolish it, he begins to deviate from his former path of development, works for general human emancipation and turns against the supreme practical expression of human self-estrangement.

We discern in Judaism, therefore, a communal antisocial element of the present time, whose historical development, zealously aided in its harmful aspects by the Jews, has now attained its culminating point, a point at which it must necessarily begin to disintegrate.

In the final analysis, the emancipation of the Jews is the emancipation of mankind from Judaism.

Judaism has maintained itself alongside Christianity, not only because it constituted the religious criticism of Christianity . . . but equally because the practical Jewish spirit—Judaism or commerce—has perpetuated itself in Christian society and has even attained its highest development. . . . It is from its own entrails that civil society ceaselessly engenders the Jew.

What was, in itself, the basis of the Jewish religion? Practical need, egoism. . . . Money is the zealous god of Israel. . . . The god of the Jews has been secularized and become the god of this world.

In its perfected practice the spiritual egoism of Christianity becomes the material egoism of the Jew. . . . The social emancipation of the Jew is the emancipation of society from Judaism.[137]

So much for Marx on the Jewish people and its religion. For the third time we ask: can this left-wing Hegelian image be taken seriously? For the third time we must answer: not for an instant. For it is too depressingly obvious that, no more than Feuerbach or Bauer before him, does Marx bother to inquire either into the "real" Jewish people or into its "real" religion. Like his predecessors, he merely adapts Hegel's image to the requirements of his own thought, and, moreover, in so doing uses elements not only of Feuerbach but also of the detested Bauer. We detect without difficulty Feuerbach's "Jewish egoism." We have no trouble whatever in rediscovering Bauer's "Christian perfection of Jewish egoism," or—what is possibly worse—Bauer's merely "chimerical" nationality of the Jewish people.[188] Any remaining doubt as to whether Marx deals with real Judaism is wholly dispelled by his attitude to the Talmud. Feuerbach's authority is Eisenmenger. Bauer blithely asserts that Eisenmenger is unrefuted.[189] Marx refers to the "Jewish [i.e., practical] Jesuitism . . . which Bauer discovers (sic!) in the Talmud"[140]—as if Bauer had ever read a single page in the Talmud itself.

Marx's defense, against Bauer, of Jewish "political" emancipation must therefore under no circumstances be permitted to obscure the fact that he rejects Bauer's version of Jewish egoism— demand for political privilege—only to replace it with another: the real Jew is the capitalist whose god is money. And this identification takes place—only contemporary propaganda has made it necessary to spell this out—not because the poor, persecuted Jewish masses of Poland and Russia are somehow in league with Rothschild, but solely and simply because within Marx's own ideological framework "real" egoism is capitalism.

It follows that the difference between the "theological" Bauer and the "non-" or "antitheological" Marx is not as absolute as is imagined by him or his followers. He rejects Bauer's inhuman demand that the "Sabbath Jew" must give up his Jewishness as the condition of political emancipation; he retains the expectation that the Jew—"real" and "Sabbath" alike—will automatically vanish once "human" emancipation is achieved.[141] He rejects Bauer's view that Judaism is a simple anachronism, and instead holds that it persists within Christendom as the "materialistic" nemesis of Christian spiritualization. He retains the view that the Christianization (i.e., universalization) of "Jewish materialism" is the necessary, albeit negative, condition of the future "human" emancipation. In that future, Christian universalism will survive, albeit dialectically transfigured. As for the Jew and his religion, they will simply have vanished. Thus the "nontheological" Marx remains, after all, the "last Lutheran."

It has emerged, then, that Marx, the most radical of the left-wing Hegelians, falls well within our two generalizations: his thought is postreligious, not simply non- or antireligious; and it is not simply postreligious-in-general but rather post-Christian, or, more precisely, post-Protestant. It is evident that in any encounter between Judaism and Marxism these two facts will be crucial—and that the second is both more important and more likely to be overlooked.

We begin with a protest against Marx's disposal of the "Sabbath Jew." This may seem to be an oddly indirect or even question-begging beginning. Is Marx's reduction of "Sabbath" to "real" Jew not simply one particular result of two general "criticisms"—the "criticism of religion," which is over and done with, and the "social criticism," which has begun? And should any challenge of Marx not be on behalf of "religion" and address itself to these two criticisms?

Yet such a response would leave Marx's "Lutheran" presuppositions unexposed and unchallenged. For his purported criticism of religion is in fact a criticism of Christianity only, and his view that the criticism of Christianity is ipso facto criticism of all religion depends on Hegel's view that the Christian religion is the absolute religion. Moreover, whereas in Hegel's own case this doctrine, crucial to his whole thought, is openly stated and defended (with the consequence that all other religions must be done dialectical "justice"), his left-wing followers, though no less in need of the doctrine, merely covertly assume it, with the consequence that the dialectical obligation of doing justice to other religions has largely if not altogether vanished. By the time we reach Marx —in whose view "criticism of religion" is over and done with— the consciousness that the "Sabbath Jew" may demand any sort of justice in his own right has totally disappeared: he is disposed of by what can only be called a new species of post-Christian propaganda. It is perhaps not coincidental that presently there exists a Christian-Marxist "dialogue" in which neither side finds it necessary to seek a Jewish presence. And it is in any case incontestable that it is the Marxist view of the relation between "Sabbath" and "real" Jew, not our protest, which begs the question.

> What, then, about "real" and "Sabbath" Jews?
> I will sing of a prince.
> His name is Israel.
> Witchcraft has transformed him
> Into a dog.

Dog with dog-like thoughts,
His workaday is spent
With life's dirt and garbage,
Mocked by urchins.

Yet each Friday,
As night falls,
Vanished is the witchcraft,
And the dog becomes anew
A human being.

A man with human feelings,
Head held high and heart exalted,
Clean and festively attired
Enters he his father's house.[142]

These are not the verses of an orthodox Jew, romantic reactionary, or sentimental apologist. Like Marx, Heinrich Heine was a nominal Christian, although, having been raised a Jew, he had some knowledge of Judaism. Both were atheist leftists, and Heine, who knew Marx personally, was attracted to much in his thought. Yet though he describes the "real" Jew much like Marx, what a difference in his image of the "Sabbath" Jew, and hence of the total Jewish reality! Marx's Sabbath Jew is an unreal shadow, that of Heine, a living man miraculously transformed. Marx's Jew—"real" and hence inevitably "Sabbath" as well—is at best the evil product of an evil society, and at worst its willing servant or even the prime villain; Heine's Sabbath Jew is a living protest against an oppressive society that, since it is successful one day of the week, has at least some effect on the other six.[143] Marx confuses oppressed and oppressors when he declares Jews to be more in need of "human" emancipation than Christians, and in this post-Christian propaganda he adds insult to injury when he describes Judaism as the source of the evil. Heine achieves a correct identification of oppressed and oppressors, and is able to perceive that the oppressed Jew has remained "human" at least one day out of seven. In Marx's scheme of things the oppressed proletariat is the paradigm par excellence of a free future Europe, and this despite the fact that he has yet to teach it to understand and rise above its "inhuman" condition.[144] The Marxist proletariat finds a rival in Heine's Jew who, as oppressed and "inhuman" during his workaday week, does not need any Marxist instruction during the Sabbath, for he is, at least then, already "human." Little philosophic insight is required for the conclusion that the Marxist scheme of things would have differed *in toto* had its author been prepared to consider the orthodox, persecuted Jew, as well as the alienated proletariat, as a paradigm of the future, liberated man.

Yet any such notion is patently ludicrous. Marx is said to have been deeply moved by the warmth and humanity he found in proletarian gatherings. Can one conceive of him sharing but a single Sabbath meal with a poor, orthodox Jewish family and being similarly moved?

Yet why *should* any such idea be ludicrous and altogether inconceivable? Because of Marx's ignorance of Judaism? The descendant of rabbis, he might have bridged this gulf as successfully as Heine, who knew little enough. Because of his antisemitism? Whether this charge is true or spurious, we do no justice to Marx as a serious thinker unless we understand even his failures philosophically. The true cause of the failure is no longer in doubt. Marx's atheism is the most radical and hence most serious form of left-wing Hegelian atheism; hence the injustice done to Judaism by all of left-wing Hegelian atheism is, in his case, most radical and most serious. Correspondingly to lodge a Jewish protest against that injustice—such as is done by the existence of even a single genuine "Sabbath Jew"—is to call into question, not just some accidental feature in Marxism or left-wing Hegelianism, but rather its very core, that is, its atheism.

These assertions are sweeping enough to require some expansion as well as careful limitation. Left-wing politics or economics, cut off from their religious (or antireligious) dimension, are not under discussion. Nor is positivistic atheism, which regards the Divine as having been all along the mere product of fear, ignorance and superstition, and which now removes this product by means of abstract "enlightenment." In question alone is a dialectical atheism for which the negation of the Divine is inseparable from a human self-affirmation; in short, the "transformation" of Hegel's "identity of the divine nature and the human" into an appropriation of the divine nature by the human.

We have seen that even Hegel (for whom the Christian Easter overcomes the otherness of the Divine) can do his partial justice to Judaism (the witness par excellence to the otherness of the Divine) only prior to the advent of Christianity, and is able to view Jewish survival within the Christian world, not as a free spiritual self-affirmation, but merely as a means used by the World Spirit to its own ends. If in contrast Feuerbach, Bauer, and Marx do no kind of justice to Judaism in any period—pre-Christian, Christian, or post-Christian—it is not by some kind of accidental fault but rather because they do not anywhere and in any sense *overcome* the otherness of the Divine but merely *deny* it. In consequence of this sheer, undialectical denial, Hegel's grandiose Jewish renunciation of renunciation necessarily shrivels into a tribal Jewish egoism—a conception that in turn forces each and every one of these left-wing Hegelians to affirm an utterly absurd "egoism" that is contrary to all self-interest, that is, voluntary Jewish survival against odds nearly always overwhelming, and at a cost not infrequently involving martyrdom. No wonder these thinkers all resort to absurd caricatures of Jewish religious existence, and systematically confuse oppressed and oppressors. No wonder Marx fails to recognize in the Sabbath Jew a resistance fighter against a hostile world. Yet for all such escapist devices the conclusion is unavoidable that all left-wing Hegelian atheism remains fraudulent so long as its image of Judaism is fraudulent; and that so long as even a single Jew stays freely covenanted to a God other-than-man the "criticism of religion" that Marx considers over and done with must be radically reopened.[145]

It need hardly be added that this conclusion has the most serious consequences for the destiny of all religion, and hence for that of the Christian religion. It is worth stressing, however, that, from the perspective in which we have viewed the issue, modern "post-Christian atheism" appears as the nemesis in this Christianity for its own betrayal of both the Jewish witness to the otherness of God, and of the Jewish element within Christianity itself. In any case, Hegel himself could hardly have seen the situation in any other light.

Yet we still shrink from deriving from one particular failure of left-wing Hegelianism so universal a conclusion. Might not the image of Judaism be radically revised and yet the atheism remain? By a most fortunate coincidence we need not rely on speculation, for the work of Ernst Bloch supplies the conclusive answer.

Bloch's image of Judaism not only differs from that of his predecessors. It is its exact antithesis. In one case, the God of Judaism is a jealous particularist, a law-giving tyrant who rules over slaves; in the other He is the first herald of freedom who strains toward universality, and the Jewish people are His first, prophetic witnesses. The image of the Jews as an eternal nonpeople, made so by an eternally reactionary God, is countered by the image of the Jews as *the* eternal people—eternal because they are geared to the future by the Exodus-God. In short, whereas for Feuerbach, Bauer, and Marx Judaism is egoism, for Bloch it is a visionary, ever self-sacrificing Messianism. The contrast could not be more complete.[146]

To be precise, Bloch's image of Judaism is the antithesis not of the image of his left-wing Hegelian predecessors, but rather of that of the master himself. For whereas Feuerbach, Bauer, and Marx do Judaism no kind of justice, Bloch, like Hegel himself, does it partial justice. And his partial justice is the exact opposite of Hegel's, so that the thought of each serves to expose the injustice done by the other.[147]

In doing justice to the otherness of the Divine in the divine-Jewish relationship Hegel is forced to make that relationship harsh, with the consequence that the concept of covenant is given no role and Jewish Messianism disappears altogether. Bloch's Judaism, in contrast, is Messianism—at the price, however, of so radical an elimination of the otherness of the Divine that atheism is inevitable.

This elimination is executed by Bloch with a reckless disregard for historical fact that matches that of his left-wing Hegelian predecessors, and certainly exceeds that of Hegel. (After more than a century of historical research, this has no excuse.) Why is the God of Sinai an alien intruder in Judaism? Because He is "contrary to the spirit of the Exodus." Why must the postexilic law of Esra be wiped off the map? Because it is "no part of the Mosaic impulse. Still less is this true of the God who is Lord, whose cult, adopted in Canaan, is in fact Baal."[148]

Assertions such as these abound in Bloch's writings, their common feature being that what is or is not part of the "Mosaic impulse" is determined, not by historical evidence, but rather by a presupposed standard. And the standard remains Hegel's Christian "identity of the divine nature and the human," given its atheistic left-wing "transformation." Hence while it is by no means insignificant that Bloch so revises the image of Judaism as to do some justice to Judaism, the main fact is that Jewish religious realities are merely interpreted to fit the left-wing Hegelian scheme; they are nowhere allowed to challenge that scheme. Thus it is a foregone conclusion that Jewish (i.e., religious) Messianism has a penultimate truth only—that "without atheism, Messianism has no place."[149]

To confront Bloch's partial justice with that of Hegel is to reach a conclusion concerning all Hegelianism. *Possibly this form of philosophic thought can do justice to the God of Sinai. Possibly it can do justice to the Messianic days. It cannot do justice to both, and the result is that the core of Jewish religious existence*

—the divine-Jewish covenant, which relates the incommensu-rables of a universal God and one particular family—is lost in every case.

Historically, this failure is expressed in the fact that no form of Hegelianism takes seriously the possibility of an authentically modern Jewish religious existence. That this is true of Feuerbach, Bauer, and Marx goes without saying. It is true, however, of Hegel and Bloch as well. Hegel does justice to the otherness of the Jewish God and to the particular Jewish family, but considers both safely past. Bloch makes Jews present as well as past, but since the singling-out God of Sinai never was, Jews are religiously significant only when they dissolve their Jewish particularity and emerge into a postreligious, Messianic mankind. Hence we conclude that any genuinely contemporary Jewish religious existence would serve to show that all forms of Hegelianism, Hegel's own included, dispose too cheaply of the otherness of the Divine.

However, the existence of such a form of Jewish religious existence has yet to prove itself in a climactic encounter, and this must necessarily be with the master himself. For not only does Hegel surpass all his followers in religious profundity. He surpasses them, vis-à-vis Judaism, in integrity as well. Though considering himself to have done justice to Jewish history he remains, nevertheless, with a riddle. His successors do not. Some (such as Feuerbach, Bauer, and Marx) dispose of it nastily; others (such as Bloch) dispose of it kindly and even flatteringly.[150] All manage to "solve" the "Jewish problem."

JUDAISM AND HEGELIANISM: A CONTEMPORARY ENCOUNTER

Would Hegel today be a Hegelian? Does Jewish religious existence today show radical, normative, self-mediating responses to Hegel's "modern world"—or what remains of it—such as we have sought hitherto, at least partly, in vain? It is in any case risky to speculate what a philosopher might think long after his time; no less risky is any judging among the religious commitments of one's own contemporaries. The risk is immense when both the philosophy and the religious commitment are radically self-exposed to history—and when history itself is as momentous as it is today. Yet to shun the risk would be, in this case, to opt out of an encounter at the point when it reaches its climax.

The encounter between Judaism and Hegelianism has been governed throughout by terms stated previously as follows: Hegel permits each historical self-understanding, the Jewish included, its own scope, and then mediates and resolves the conflicts between them. The Jewish religious self-understanding is world-historical from a Jewish point of view; the Hegelian philosophical comprehension is world-historical from a "world-historical" point of view, and it is its claim to "do justice" to all points of view which makes *its own* point of view world-historical. But can a Jewish thinker—or at any rate, a modern one—*himself* fail to ask how his own point of view stands related to others?[151]

As our encounter now moves into its present, contemporary phase, three possibilities come into view. Has the century and a half between us and Hegel left both Judaism and Hegelianism in essence unscathed? Then everything that needs to and can be said has already been said. Are either one or both principals destroyed? Then nothing of philosophical substance has been said, and our developing encounter has been a mere scholastic exercise. Or have the events been such as to affect the claims of both Judaism and Hegelianism deeply enough to require a *transformation* of the encounter between them? In that case, all that has thus far been said is vital and relevant—but the climactic phase of the encounter lies still ahead.

To put first things first, could Hegel today still write a "philosophical world-history," whose "spiritual principle" is "the totality of all points of view"—a history, that is, whose standpoint is "world-historical"?[152] Under no conceivable circumstances. Hegel's philosophy is *in* history and permits a contingent future. It is *above* history and rules out an essential future, for this latter is already present. Yet this Hegelian claim has been shattered by events that his philosophy not only fails to anticipate but maintains cannot happen. His "world-historical" standpoint suffers collapse not, as the vulgar textbook view has it, under the impact of subsequent philosophical criticism, but rather under the impact of subsequent history.

In order to judge what Hegel today could no longer claim we must restate precisely what, a century and a half ago, he in fact did claim. To encompass in thought the totality of any and all possible points of view is a manifestly absurd undertaking at any time; on his part, Hegel disclaims any such goal when he states that "philosophical contemplation has no other purpose than to remove the contingent."[153] Having refused long ago to invoke against Hegel the banal truth that in empirical history all things are possible, we cannot incongruously invoke against him now the no less banal truth that in empirical history all points of view are possible.

"The contingent," then, is "removed." What remains that, despite this removal, is a "totality"? A dialectically interwoven whole made possible by three basic affirmations: (1) history is not human but rather human-divine; (2) the modern world has realized the possibilities of this human-divine history at least in principle completely and unsurpassably, and the two aspects of this realization—modern secular freedom and modern Protestant faith—are themselves "implicitly" united; (3) the Hegelian philosophy explicates in thought what in life remains implicit, and in so doing not only completes the unsurpassability and unity of the modern world but also demonstrates both. These are the essential constituents of Hegel's "identity of the divine nature and the human." (*Mutatis mutandis*, they are also the constituents of the left-wing Hegelian "transformation" of the Hegelian "identity," that is, the appropriation of the divine nature by the human.)

This restatement suffices to distinguish between such historical realities as can, and such as cannot, threaten or destroy Hegel's world-historical standpoint. No threat is posed by the banalities of random chance, unforeseen or unforeseeable chaos, and relapses into anachronistic forms of religious or secular life. A threat *is* posed by events that render Hegel's identity of the divine nature and the human problematic. And the threat turns into catastrophe when events escalate to smash Hegel's identity beyond all repair. (Again *mutatis mutandis*, the foregoing applies quite precisely to the "transformed" world-historical standpoint necessarily claimed by every form of left-wing Hegelianism.)

We begin with a threat perceived at least marginally by Hegel himself even in his own time.[154] What if religious life had lost its substance, and secular self-activity, its confidence? We have already seen Hegel concede that from a world thus disrupted philosophers could only flee into a "separate sanctuary." They cannot rejuvenate the identity of the divine nature and the human in the sphere of life. And even in the sphere of thought they can preserve it only by means of flight from a world thus disrupted. Yet, if anything runs counter to Hegel's entire thought, it is precisely a flight by his *modern* thought from the modern world.[155] (How total would a "totality" remain if it were one of thought only?) For reasons that have yet to emerge, the theme of flight remains peripheral in Hegel's own thought. Yet were it to move to the center, could it fail to produce a radical crisis?

Nor is there much doubt that for any resurrected Hegelianism this theme would *have* to move into the center today. Hegel himself blames the decay of his age on the power of "the Understanding" to fragment, mechanize, dehumanize the life of the Spirit. In our own time this power has swollen so gigantically as to constitute a classic case (if ever there is such a case) of quantity turning into quality. To cite but a single example, Hegel could still believe that guns are better than spears inasmuch as they remove passion from human conflict. Such a harmony between spirit and technology has broken down radically when the weapons are megaton bombs; the victims, human persons indiscriminately quantified; and the ultimate warriors, machines that calculate the expendable percentage of the human species. Given this condition, Hegelian thought today would seem to have but two alternatives. It could stay with the contemporary fragmented world, and become itself infected by its fragmentation. Or it could flee from this world in an attempt to save its own unfragmented purity. It would, however, lose its world-historical standpoint in either case. In the first, it would explicitly renounce it. In the second, it would willy-nilly lose it through external assault. Once Neoplatonism, having fled from the Hellenistic world, was overwhelmed by post-Hellenistic history.[156] By Hegel's own standards, the same fate would befall his philosophy at the hands of an historical future yet unknown.

Yet in justice to Hegel, the fact of modern technology cannot be viewed as a mortal threat to his world-historical standpoint. This latter does require a matrix in history. It does not require a matrix that would pass the scrutiny of statisticians, or even of nonstatistically minded empirical historians and social scientists. Once the World Spirit could depend on a small band of Athenians. Hegel's philosophy does not rule out crisis situations in which, once again, its fate could depend on as minuscule a group. In the contemporary world there is no dearth of left-wing Hegelian vanguards of the absolute Future, with a built-in world-historical standpoint if only because the Future envisaged is absolute. One may doubt, criticize, reject some or all of these self-appointed vanguards. One cannot dismiss their claims on grounds of their microscopic size alone. Then why might not as small a group of men, so to speak, hold the fort in this age of crisis for Hegel's own absolute Present? It is clear that modern technology and all its works are an unprecedented test for Hegel's philosophy. That his philosophy and its world-historical standpoint is shattered by them is far from clear.

We turn to a qualitatively different threat when we shift attention from the theme of contemporary spiritual fragmentation to that of contemporary spiritual corruption. As conceived by Hegel, the modern world leaves room for the survival and revival of anachronistic forms of spirit. It leaves room, too, for the power of the unspiritual "Understanding" to cause spiritual fragmentation and decay. It leaves no room, however, for *radical anti-Spirit*. Hegel could not have viewed Nazi Germany as a lapse into "unfree" spirit uninformed by the modern identity of the divine nature and the human. (Of this more will be said.) Still less could he have seen it as the work of the unspiritual, fragmenting "Understanding," when in fact it was a protest of sorts against it. At work was an all-too-spiritual anti-Spirit that affirmed the modern identity of the divine nature and the human in an unprecedented, enthusiastic, self-sacrificing celebration of hatred, degradation, and murder. And the fragmenting power of the modern "Understanding" was "overcome" when every means at the disposal of modern technology was made subservient to the life—or, on the contrary, the living death—of what, in a moment of truth, was once called the Holocaust Kingdom.[157] No philosophy has yet dared to face the scandal that is the Nazi murder camp. However, while other philosophies have self-protective devices,[158] that of Hegel has none. Claiming to mediate all things, divine as well as human, it requires a world in which, except for the sphere of philosophical thought, so total a mediation is already actual. Yet in our time an absolute anti-Spirit has exploded precisely that mediation, in the heart of what once was Hegel's Europe.

Had Hegel lived through this hell in his native land his thought would have been forced into paradox. The anti-Spirit bound to be opposed by it proved itself to be a secular-Christian, human-divine identity when it united Nazi Christians and Nazi pagans in the common worship of Hitler. And the Spirit bound to be affirmed by it was manifest, if anywhere, not in the "German-Christian" church, which affirmed the divine-human identity, but rather in the Barthian "neo-orthodox" church—the most uncompromising Protestant rejection of the divine-human identity since the Reformation.

This paradox arises because the Barthian neo-orthodox and the "German-Christian" church testify, the one by stern and sometimes heroic opposition, the other by total and often enthusiastic surrender[159] to the reality of an absolute, yet undeniably modern idolatry—against a philosophy wedded to the thesis that there is no absolute idolatry anywhere, and none at all in the modern world.

This is not the place for an independent investigation into the unholy revelation of Nazism[160] but only for speculating how Hegel today might react to it. Serious about history, he would have scorned the current liberal pretense that nothing except a "relapse into tribalism" has occurred. Serious about religion, he would have scorned every form of secularist frivolity about idolatry, including above all the current left-wing Hegelian pretenses that Nazism is a mere species of "fascism," which in turn is but "the last stage of capitalism." For his part, this writer can imagine Hegel only as radically self-exposed to the realities—at the price that his "modern world" and his own philosophical comprehension of it both lie in shambles. His "modern world": constituted by the "identity of the divine nature and the human," it can survive anything except an idolatrous identification of the two. His own philosophy: requiring a "modern world" in which, except for comprehension, universal mediation is already actual, it cannot survive the demise of that world.

We began the present inquiry by considering the fate of Hegel's world-historical standpoint in the contemporary world. This inquiry has now inexorably led us to conclusions fatal to Hegel's system as a whole: after Auschwitz, the principle of the universal mediation of all things, divine as well as human, shattered in life, is shattered for philosophic thought as well. The animating principle of Hegel's entire philosophy has broken down.

It has not broken down, however, without traces or dialectical consequences: as yet unrecognized fragments of a post-Hegelian Hegelianism keep appearing on every side. That Hegel's claims for the modern world do not simply vanish with the loss of his *maximal* claims is made evident by the present state of secularity and religiosity. Thus Barthian neo-orthodoxy, inevitably lapsing into orthodoxy pure and simple, finds its nemesis in a "religionless Christianity" that rebels against such a "theological positivism," only in order itself to degenerate into secularism pure and simple.[161] On their part, all forms of secularism, the left-wing Hegelian included, deny their own denial of the Divine when they become pseudo-, crypto-, or would-be-religious. A return to the medieval divorce of heaven and earth is impossible, and the loss of Hegel's own claim for their modern union still leaves us with a world in which secular freedom and religious receptivity must be interrelated even as they are held apart.

The main consequence of this result for a post-Hegelian Hegelianism is that it must remain between these two spheres, capable and obliged, to be sure, to detach itself from both so as to reflect upon them, but incapable of rising above their duality. Vis-à-vis secular self-activity, such a chastened and fragmented role would require it to point beyond its own "comprehension" of the world back to secular self-activity itself, which alone can "change" the world.[162] Vis-à-vis religious receptivity, its role is described by Hegel himself in part as follows:

The experience . . . that I cannot help myself by means of reflection, that I cannot, in fact, take my stand upon myself at all, and the circumstance that I still crave something that stands firm—all this forces me back from reflection and leads me to adhere to the content in the form in which it is given.[163]

If this passage describes the new philosophical role only in part, it is because the reflection referred to *precedes* the Hegelian experiment of a rise of thought above finitude, hence transcends finitude only in recognizing the fact, and therefore leads to an adherence to the religious content in the form of submission to authority. The new philosophical "reflection," in contrast, has *passed through* the Hegelian experiment and is informed by its failure; and we shall discover that this has dialectical results which make it post-Hegelian in a more than merely temporal sense. Hegel writes:

I am to make myself fit for the indwelling of the Spirit. . . . This is my labor, the labor of man; but the same is also the labor of God, regarded from His side. He moves toward man and is in man through the act of raising him. What seems thus my act is thus God's, and, conversely, what seems His is mine. . . . In religion the Good and reconciliation are absolutely complete and existing on their own account. The divine unity of the spiritual and natural world is presupposed—the particular self-consciousness belongs to the latter—and the question is only, concerning me and over against me, that I should lay aside my subjectivity and take and have a share in the work which eternally completes itself. The Good is not something which merely ought to be but divine Power and eternal Truth. . . .

Grace enlightens the heart of man, it is the divine spirit in man so that man may be represented as passive in relation to its activity; i.e., it is not his own activity. In the Notion, however, this double activity must be grasped as single.[164]

We ask, first: in Hegel's own mind, whatever made the rise to an infinite, divine, complete Thought—"the Notion"—a possible enterprise for a finite, merely human thought? Our texts reply: the prior existence of a religious, divine-human relation that already is, not a relation of two activities—respectively, divine and human—but rather one double activity. Every religion is representational, i.e., it manifests the otherness *of* the Divine in its very relation *to* the human. The Christian religion is *doubly* representational because this otherness is here denied even as it is affirmed. An "antinomy"[165] exists between a divine Grace that, though overwhelming, yet needs to be humanly received, and a human reception that, though overwhelmed, can and must freely appropriate it. Pre-Hegelian philosophical reflection, if committed to Christianity, submits to this antinomy as a datum, on ecclesiastical authority; if not thus committed it rejects the authority and hence the datum as well. Left-wing Hegelianism overcomes the antinomy by destroying the divine side of the double activity. Hegel's own Notion too overcomes the antinomy; however, it preserves both sides of the double activity. Hegel's rebelling disciples *demythologize*. Hegel himself *transmythologizes*.

We ask, next: what results for philosophical reflection once Hegel's thought-experiment has failed? For anti-Christian (or perhaps more generally, for antireligious) reflection nothing results, for the whole experiment was all along chimerical; for a reflection committed to Christianity, a great deal. It cannot move either back to authority and its datum or forward to the destruction of the datum. Not to the first: for all its failure the Notion has discovered an inner logic in the supposedly sheer datum—the antinomy between divine Grace and human freedom. Not to the second: its "forward" is no forward at all, for the Notion has failed not because it has preserved too much but because it has preserved too little. In the camp of philosophers committed to Christianity, the true heir of Hegel's Notion is not the "nauseating triviality"[166] of Feuerbach and all his followers, but rather a philosophical reflection that points to the stance of human freedom over against divine Grace as one that cannot be transcended; a stance, that is, that is ultimate not only religiously but philosophically as well. Having tried to transmythologize and failed, philosophical thought remythologizes.

The "one double activity" of our text is, of course, Hegel's "identity of the divine nature and the human" in its religious, i.e., representational, form. It therefore comes as a considerable surprise that the exact stance just arrived at is adopted by the Jewish thinker Martin Buber. Buber writes:

I know that "I am given over for disposal" and know at the same time that "It depends on myself." . . . I am compelled to take both to myself, to be lived together, and in being lived together they are one.[167]

Is Buber influenced by Hegel? This is contradicted by all the evidence.[168] Has he accepted, overtly or covertly, Hegel's or any other Christian "one double activity"? The very core of his thought is that in every I-Thou relation, the divine-human included, the "Thou" is and remains other than the "I."[169] Does Hegel himself permit an antinomy between divine Grace and human freedom in a religion that expressly denies the identity of the divine nature and the human? Once again the answer is negative. Only where "the Good and reconciliation are *absolutely* complete" can the divine-human relation be *one double* activity; and only when this is the case is it possible either for the antinomy to be genuine or for a religion to be doubly representational. Hence there can be an "absolute religion" and *only one* such religion. That Christianity is that religion the Notion demonstrates.

At this late date it need not be stated that reasons far better than Constantinian imperialism or anti-Jewish prejudice are responsible for these Hegelian doctrines. The Christian antinomy between divine Grace and human freedom may be philosophically understood as manifesting Hegel's identity of the divine nature and the human. A corresponding Jewish antinomy cannot be so understood, but is, on the contrary, an unequivocal testimony against any such identity. For Hegel to concede that the divine-*Jewish* relation is not harsh but rather a covenantal mutuality would have meant nothing less than to concede that the Divine is and remains other than the human even in a dialectical togetherness of Grace and freedom; that therefore the Christian no less than the Jewish religion remains with this otherness; that there is not and cannot be an "absolute religion" in Hegel's sense of the term; and that a philosophical Thought at once human and divine —that is, Hegel's Notion—is impossible. Here is the ultimate reason why injustice to Judaism is so intrinsic a necessity in Hegel's thought that even his recognition of a remaining Jewish "dark riddle" is astonishing; and why left-wing Hegelians, impatient with religious riddles in a postreligious world, resort to slander.

If the Notion is the ultimate source of Hegel's injustice to Judaism, then, from the standpoint of Jewish testimony, it is ultimately a source of philosophical tyranny. Its breakdown, therefore, is a potential source of philosophical liberation. Could a Hegelian way of philosophical thought do justice to the Jewish covenantal reality that consistently and necessarily eludes Hegel himself? One would not, of course, wish to assert on the authority of one single Jewish thinker that Jewish religious existence is a togetherness of divine Grace and human freedom, the difference between the human and the Divine notwithstanding. The above Buberian Jewish text, however, was cited solely because it articulates age-old Jewish religious realities. Indeed, Midrashic thought—the most profound and normative thought ever produced within Judaism—is explicitly and consciously doubly representational if only because its key concept—that of covenant—can only be doubly representational. We have seen that the Notion makes it impossible for the Jewish concept of covenant to get so much as a hearing. Now we see, astonishingly enough, that with the Notion vanished, a Hegelian way of philosophical thought supplies the means—we are bold enough to assert, for the first time in the history of philosophy—of doing conceptual justice to the inner logic of Judaism.

If true, this assertion marks the beginnings of a venture wholly transcending the scope of this book. Hence a few strategically chosen examples must suffice for the present purpose.[170]

Rabbi Azariah and Rabbi Aha in the name of Rabbi Yohanan said: When the Israelites heard at Sinai the word "I" [i.e., the first word of the ten commandments], their souls left them, as it says, "If we hear the voice . . . any more, than we shall die" (Deut. 5:22). . . . The Word then returned to the Holy One, blessed be He, and said: "Sovereign of the universe, Thou art full of life, and Thy Law is full of life, and Thou hast sent me to the dead, for they are all dead." Thereupon the Holy One, blessed be He, sweetened [i.e., softened] the Word for them.[171]

Rabbi Shim'on bar Yohai said . . . "Only when Israel does God's will is his heavenly place secure." . . . Nevertheless, Rabbi Shim'on bar Yohai also quoted "This is my Lord, and I will praise Him" (Exod. 15:2), and he said: "When I praise Him, He is glorified, and when I do not praise Him, He is, as it were, glorified in Himself."[172]

"Ye are my witnesses, saith the Lord, and I am God." (Isa. 43:12) That is, when ye are My witnesses, I am God, and when ye are not My witnesses, I am, as it were, not God.[173]

The first Midrash shows why Hegel did not consider Judaism to be a doubly representational form of religious existence, and that in this judgment he did injustice to the Jewish religious self-understanding. Hegel accepts and philosophically transfigures the traditional Christian view that the Sinaitic revelation is Law without Grace. The Midrash tells the tale of this view, explores its implications as radically as any Christian ever did—and overcomes it. A divine commandment devoid of Grace would be humanly unperformable, and indeed, a divine Presence revealing itself as commanding is paradoxical. For qua present the divine Infinity destroys the human "family" in its humanity: "they are all dead." Qua commanding, however, it requires a response that is human and particular, and this is possible only if the family is humanly alive even in the moment of the divine Presence. This paradox is resolved by the Midrash in the second descent of the Divine, which, "sweetening the Word," makes a divine commandment capable of free human appropriation and performance. For Pelagius, divine Grace is merely an event subsequent to the human failure to perform the divine commandment. For Augustine, it redeems man from the commandment itself. In Judaism, Grace is manifest in the gift of the commandment itself, giving rise to an antinomy of divine Grace and human freedom in which God remains Lord of the Universe, and man, one human family. Thus the divine-Jewish covenant is born.

That the antinomy of divine Grace and human freedom that gives birth to this covenant does not vanish into the dead and irrelevant past is shown by the second and third Midrashim. On the one hand, the primordial divine commanding Grace has established a truly mutual relation, the incommensurability of the Divine and the human notwithstanding. Hence the bold words that the heavenly place is not secure, and indeed God not God, unless the Jewish family performs its labor, which (as Hegel has stressed) is the "labor of man." Yet since the pristine paradox and the Grace resolving it both remain, these affirmations are true only "as it were": they are stories that are *known* to be only stories and yet must not only be told but also expressed in action. And the divine-human incommensurability that remains even as the relation is mutual and real is fully explicated when Rabbi Shim'on bar Yoḥai affirms that, on the one hand, God needs human glorification, and, on the other, is "glorified in Himself."

The second Midrash thus seems to express a fuller and richer truth than the third. If nevertheless we cite this latter third, and indeed cite it at all, it is because it takes cognizance, if only implicitly, of a grim possibility inherent in Jewish religious existence, and perhaps unique to it. Both Midrashim take cognizance of Jewish infidelity to the covenant, and the second Midrash finds security against this cognizance in the knowledge that God, if not glorified by Israel, is as it were, glorified in Himself. But what if the Jewish family failed to witness, not because of infidelity but rather because of nonexistence? The cited Midrashim were all written after 70 C.E., the greatest catastrophe in all of Jewish history prior to the Nazi holocaust. The Christian covenant is with the individual and the church, and in extremis can fall back on the doctrines of the holy remnant, the holy Spirit, and the invisible church. (The Hegelian counterpart would be a small band of witnesses holding the fort for Hegel's absolute Present, referred to previously.) No such ultimate recourse is possible when the covenant keeps God and man apart even as it relates them, and is with an all-too-visible flesh-and-blood people. The rabbis who lived through the catastrophe of 70 C.E. had to reckon with the possibility that there would be no covenant because there would be no people—not because of Jewish infidelity but rather because of Roman massacres. Thus in extremis the last word cannot be that of the Midrash that makes God "glorified in Himself." Is He glorified in Himself if His people are dead? Such a pietistic smugness, not to say obscenity, is rejected in the third Midrash. Remaining, as it were, open-ended, it implicitly contains a whole host of religious possibilities, such as protest, defiance, and even despair.

Unlike anything possible within the limits of Hegel's *Grundidee* of Judaism, these Midrashim are all doubly representational. This is because their subject is not Hegel's "positive Law of Moses" but rather the covenantal mutuality of the Jewish religious self-understanding. This leads to a further crucial difference. The inner logic of Hegel's Law of Moses rules out every possible Messianic reference, for it "takes the place of reconciliation and redemption." The inner logic of the covenant, in contrast, requires such a reference and is unintelligible without it.

We have seen Hegel, unlike Kant, find a genuine (albeit limited) religious truth in the law of Moses by means of recourse to a renunciation of renunciation of which an absolutely submissive, yet absolutely confident Job is the supreme paradigm. This concept requires radical transformation if covenantal mutuality, not legal servitude, is the central religious reality. On the one hand, Jewish submission or renunciation must be less than absolute. (As we have stressed, the theme of protest, from Abraham to Job, has no place in Hegel's account of Judaism, and it might here be added that Moses himself—for Hegel a mere divine instrument—is quite other for the Jewish religious self-understanding when he stands not only over against his people in behalf of God but also over against God in behalf of his people.) On the other hand, Jewish "confidence" is and must remain absolute but becomes problem-

[164]

atical. Hegel quite rightly states that there must be "reconciliation and redemption" in Judaism unless (as is the case for Kant) it is to be totally devoid of religious reality. The covenantal mutuality, however, is shot through with a fragmentation in which "redemption" is not attained and "reconciliation" forever alternates with alienation and sin. Within this context redemption, if dependent unilaterally on God, would destroy the covenantal mutuality; if unilaterally dependent on the Jewish family, it would shatter on the rock of human sin. The Messianic future is clearly required.

The dialectical difficulties just referred to, however, do not vanish by the mere projection of the Jewish "confidence" into the future even if this latter is held to be ultimate, or Messianic. They disappear only, once the Messianic confidence has become as doubly representational as is the covenantal mutuality that gives rise to it. Here one might cite Midrashim whose name is legion. It suffices to sum up that the Jewish Messianic expectation is a dialectical togetherness of working and waiting, of action and prayer. The Midrash represents the Messiah as coming, on the one hand, when men are good enough to make his coming possible, and, on the other hand, when they are wicked enough to make it necessary. Midrashic Messianism requires this double representation. It is distorted alike by the absolutization of human action (whose radical expression is Bloch's Messianic atheism), and by the absolutization of divine action (whose radical expression would be Hegel's own Jewish "positivity without all human freedom," merely transferred from the Sinaitic past to the Messianic future.)

But a Messianic "confidence" that is absolute poses a problem additional to that of adequate conceptual comprehension. Characteristically enough, Hegel's own paradigm of the confident Jew is Job, a figure in a mere story. The subject of the Jewish covenant, in sharp contrast, is a flesh-and-blood people in actual history. And whereas the future, once liberated from the tyranny of the Notion (Hegelian or left-wing Hegelian), is the realm of surprise, its surprises are not for good alone. They include possible catastrophe. Moreover, enough catastrophic surprises have already become actual to disclose that Jewish Messianic confidence cannot rest, (and except for periods of religious decline never did rest), on historical probabilities. (This point is dramatized by one utter improbability that is already present—the bare survival of the Jewish family.) How then is an *absolute* confidence possible which does not flee from history but rather stays with it?

A confidence whose world-historical point of view is not above history, but rather remains a humble testimony within it? With this question, we are driven from the crisis of contemporary Hegelianism to the crisis of contemporary Judaism.[174] What has happened in the century and a half between Hegel and ourselves? We have asked this question of Hegelianism. We must now ask it of Judaism. And we shall find that whereas Hegelianism is threatened merely with intellectual fragmentation, Judaism is threatened with existential despair. After Auschwitz, must not all Jewish submission be overwhelmed by an *absolute* protest? And must not any confidence—not to speak of absolute confidence—yield to total disarray? The ancient rabbis had to reckon with the possibility that the people of the covenant might die. At Auschwitz this people did die. And the circumstances of its death transform even Jews still unborn into a people of survivors. The same absolute anti-Spirit that has shattered Hegel's identity of the divine nature and the human "had no other clear principle than murderous hatred of the Jews, for 'Aryan' had no clear meaning other than 'non-Jewish.' "[175] And when this principle was expressed in action, the Jewish people, singled out not by God but by the devil, was abandoned by God and man alike. We have expressed general caution as to the risk of judging among the religious commitments of one's own contemporaries. As we now face the present situation of Judaism, we can find no case in all recorded history, Jewish or other, in which the risk is similar.

Yet despite all caution and every self-restraint, one astonishing judgment at length forces itself on the contemporary Jewish thinker, no matter how long and tenaciously he may persist in doubt. We were unable to discover radical, normative Jewish responses to Hegel's "modern world." In contrast, there *is* a radical, normative Jewish response to the catastrophe that has destroyed that world. This response has yet to find articulation in the sphere of thought; however—a fact of far greater moment—in the life-commitment of a people it is already actual.

The response we speak of is not a mediating response, for the Holocaust Kingdom is incapable of any sort of mediation: it can be confronted only by uncompromising opposition. Such a radical opposition is offered by every Jewish survivor by his mere decision to remain a Jew; and this decision is normative because, by virtue of it, the survivor has become the paradigm of the whole Jewish people.

The Holocaust Kingdom murdered religious and secularist Jews alike. The decision just referred to requires philosophical thought to restructure the categories of religiosity and secularity. Only by virtue of a radical "secular" self-reliance that acts as though the God who once saved could save no more can even the most "religious" survivor hold fast either to the Sinaitic past or to the Messianic future. And only by virtue of a radical "religious" memory and hope can even the most "secularist" survivor rally either the courage or the motivation to decide to remain a Jew, when every natural impulse tempts him to seek forgetfulness and even bare safety elsewhere. A Jewish testimony is coming into being that is without precedent in all of history. After Auschwitz, the religious Jew still submits to the commanding Voice of Sinai, which bids him witness to the one true God. He is now joined, however, by the secular Jew, who, by the sheer act of remaining a Jew, submits to a commanding Voice heard from Auschwitz that bids him testify *that some gods are false.* No Jew can be and remain a Jew without ipso facto testifying that idolatry is real in the modern world.

To this new "submission" corresponds a new "confidence." No survivor could decide to expose his distant offspring to the threat of a second holocaust. To raise Jewish children, he therefore requires the hope and the determination that no second holocaust will occur. In a world that continues to harbor antisemites, however, it is only by dint of the most radical secular self-reliance that the religious survivor can hold fast to hope. And it is only by dint of an, as it were, religious hope that the secularist survivor can have the trust that his self-reliance will be sufficient or even effective.

This commingling of religiosity and secularity has found historical embodiment in the rebirth of a Jewish state. It has always been impossible to understand the Zionist movement either in purely religious or purely secularist categories, a fact obscured only by ideologies that have blindly taken these categories for granted. After the holocaust, the Israeli nation has become collectively what the survivor is individually. Except only for those who never became part of the modern world, all religious Israelis are willing, if required, to take up "secular" arms in defense of the state. And except for those who cannot extricate themselves from ideologies that do Jewish history no justice, all secular Israelis have the "religious" wish that the state be Jewish.

Hegel, were he alive today, would be far more open to this commingling of religious and secular realities than any contemporary philosopher.[176] In his *Early Theological Writings* he praises the ancient Jewish people for showing "the most enthusiastic courage" in their resistance to the Roman Empire, and goes on to assert that, after the state was destroyed,

... the scattered remnant of the Jews have not abandoned the idea of the Jewish state, but they have resorted not to the banners of their own courage but only to the standards of an ineffective Messianic hope.[177]

We ask: after the incomparably greater catastrophe of the Nazi holocaust, how would Hegel today respond to the restoration of a Jewish state? What *could* his response be except that the "religious" Messianic hope, not "ineffective" after all, has been transmuted into the "courage" of "secular" action? And that secular courage, in this case, is so bright a light after so total a darkness as to be "religious" by all except the narrowest standards?

If Hegel were alive today, he might risk an even bolder step. Without doubt he would view our present crisis in secular-religious terms. Without doubt he would see signs of hope only in a new life in which religiosity and secularity are intertwined. In looking for such signs, it is not impossible that he, like ourselves, might hazard that the reborn Jerusalem is overcoming the religious-secular split that his own premodern Jerusalem antedates. Freed of the tyranny of the Notion, he would in any case withdraw his sweeping assertion that no nation appears on the world-historical scene more than once. Jewish death at Auschwitz and rebirth at Jerusalem might make him wonder whether at least one people is not appearing on the scene for a second time, with world-historical consequences yet unknown.

EPILOGUE

Hegel fails to do justice to the divine-Jewish covenant. His failure is not without greatness. For the Jewish covenantal self-understanding, holding fast to the extremes of divine-human incommensurability and divine-human intimacy, is in a state of ceaseless tension. Hence it is tempted to flee either into a petrified past shrunk into a mere tribal memory or into an unreal future dissolved into an empty utopia. Only through resolute effort can it resist both these temptations, stay with history, and endure.

The Midrash recognizes this tension. And with characteristic realism it affirms that it will not end until the Messianic days. Only then will

... Moses ... come from the desert, and the Messiah from Rome, each at the head of his flock. [Then] ... the Word of God will mediate between them, causing them to walk in the same direction with one accord.[178]

Chapter 4

IDOLATRY AS A
MODERN POSSIBILITY

INTRODUCTION

The Jewish religious thinker is in and of the present. He cannot
be in and of the present alone. He is obliged to confront the
classical sources of Judaism—Bible, Talmud, Midrash—even if
he ends up with a modern dissent from the ancient wisdom. Nothing less than a genuine self-exposure to the past can lend Jewish
authentication to his own modern thought.

There are, however, a good many subjects on which it may
well seem a mere waste of effort to engage in an encounter or
confrontation of this kind. Foremost among these is surely the
subject of idolatry. Surely in this modern, technological, demythologized world ancient idol-worship is dead and buried, making
it romantic folly to expect any relevance in ancient wisdom.

Random examples from rabbinic literature seem to confirm this
judgment. The Talmud views idolatry as one of three deadly
sins that must be resisted even on pain of death.[1] Today, the
necessity for this particular martyrdom does not arise. According
to the Midrash, one who repudiates idolatry is as though he were
faithful to the whole Torah.[2] By this standard, any modern
Jew would be wholly faithful. Rabbinic law regards the worship
of graven images as so dangerous a temptation as to prohibit
ownership even when no worship is intended.[3] A modern man,
far from himself tempted, cannot understand how there could
ever have been an attraction. In fact, this apparently once desper-
ately serious business has become a mere joke, as in the story of
the parishioner who informs his minister that whereas he has
broken 9 of the 10 commandments, he has, he is proud to say,
never worshipped graven images. Can one doubt, then, that on
this subject at least any recourse to the classical sources of Judaism is mere folly? Is it to be denied that here at any rate the
whole truth is with the dogmatic modernist who asserts that the
past can at best only confirm what the present already knows,
and that in any conflict between past and present, the present is
ipso facto right? So it must seem, at least as long as one takes

idolatry in its literal ancient sense—as the worship of trees, rivers, statues, Roman Emperors and the like. And one must take it in this literal sense before one can argue the legitimacy of taking it in any other.

The impression of the irrelevance of the traditional Jewish teaching deepens as one considers contemporary Jewish religious life. The theme of a nineteenth-century East European story could still be the conflict between aesthetic appreciation of a statue and the traditional religious strictures. In the story the hero buys a statue but ends up in smashing it. In twentieth-century America this story has lost its poetic truth. Idol worship is no longer a real possibility, and a statue looked at, or even owned, tempts no one to worship it. This much is true even of orthodox Jews. Non-orthodox Jews go further. They have not hesitated to bring images if not statues into the house of worship itself. It occurs to nobody that a stained-glass window depicting Abraham or Moses might become an idol. The very idea is preposterous.

Equally important is the change in Jewish attitude toward non-Jewish religions. For millennia, this attitude was one of reserve and even suspicion. This was not motivated, as popular liberal Christian mythology has it, by particularism but, rather, by the fear of idolatry. That this fear has now vanished is evidenced by the modern Jewish willingness to participate in interreligious dialogue, which is widespread, and by the interest in interfaith cooperation, which is universal. No modern Jew would regard another religion as idolatrous simply because images or statues are part of it. So long as the one imageless God is the intended object of worship—and of what "higher religion" is that not true?—the images and statues are at worst symbols with which a Jew, even as visitor, cannot be comfortable. (He is not comfortable, but he can still be a visitor.) But "symbol" is a modern concept, and it reflects the fact that the old idolatry has become nonexistent, or at least quite harmless.

This harmlessness suggests that, when the old idolatry existed, it was nothing more serious than a species of superstition, and that this superstition, like all others, is destroyed by modern enlightenment. In the Jewish religious thinker, this suggestion is apt to produce a spirit of self-congratulation. The ancient rabbis had to wage war on idolatry. Their modern descendants can beat the swords of this particular warfare into plowshares. For, whereas the ancient superstitious world was full of "polytheists," in the enlightened modern world one is a "monotheist" if one believes in God or gods at all.[4]

This spirit of self-congratulation was widely current in the eighteenth and nineteenth centuries, and not among Jewish thinkers alone. In the twentieth century, however, it is wholly destroyed. No one detects a resurgence of ancient idolatry. Yet something obscurely related seems to survive in the modern world, erupting in the present age with such power as to compel universal notice. Thus a metaphorical use of "idol," "worship," "false god" has forced itself into the language of serious thinkers, both religious and secularist; even in popular usage money, success, sex, and the nation are all referred to as objects of "worship." Something therefore is wrong with the view that idolatry is a mere past superstition, now safely surpassed. Somehow, idolatry survives.

Yet, what *is* a modern idolatry? It is not, in the first place, actual worship, and its gods are not literal gods: it is a modern phennomenon. In the second place, it is somehow related to ancient idolatry, at least if the metaphors used have any meaning. And it surely is, in the third place, something more serious than a mere lapse into anachronism, and something more specific, as well as more serious, than sin in general. However, to judge by the evidence of thought both academic and popular, we do not yet understand modern idolatry. We define it either too narrowly, as a folly surpassed by modernity, or too widely, as a sin not in principle different from any other. But the effect of both errors is the same: the scandalous particularity of modern idolatry is lost.

For the Jew of this generation, this is no mere academic failure. For he has been the prime victim of the most horrendous idolatry of modern times and, perhaps, of all time. Yet Nazism might never have won its frightful victories had it not been belittled, on the one hand, by good enlightened liberals (who viewed it as a mere lapse into premodern "prejudice") and, on the other, by good Christians (who classed it with other sins, their own included). The Jew, if anyone, knows the frightful uniqueness of Nazi idolatry. He cannot escape into the false comfort that Nazism was a case either of prejudice in general or of sin in general. On him, if on anyone, weighs the heavy task of transforming unique suffering into unique testimony.

One cannot, however, bear witness without understanding. How must modern idolatry be marked off, on the one hand, from mere prejudice, which enlightenment is sufficient to destroy, and, on the other, from other sins, which, however grave, fall short of idolatry? This question raises the hope that ancient rabbinic wisdom may not, after all, be irrelevant to modern realities. For in their own age the rabbis did achieve a precise identification of ancient idolatry. They had surpassed idolatry, but they marked off idolatry from follies surpassed. They took a serious view of all sin, yet they set idolatry apart from every other sin. For the Jewish thinker of today, there is an experiment of thought, therefore, that is well worth attempting; its object is to discover whether ancient rabbinic wisdom can be made relevant to the idolatries of the present age.

CLASSICAL JUDAISM AND IDOLATRY

Why does classical Judaism take idolatry seriously? We shall ask this question of the rabbinic sources only. A Jew in any case reads the written Torah—the Hebrew Bible—in conjunction with the oral Torah—Talmud and Midrash. In addition, it is wise in the present case to abstract from the complicating fact that in biblical times Judaism was still in a state of genesis. There was then still serious competition with the cults native to Canaan, and for all a nonspecialist knows, those scholars are right who believe that the earlier parts of the Bible are not yet free of polytheism. In the rabbinic age, however, polytheistic remnants have wholly disappeared. The rabbis are in no doubt that the God of Israel is the one universal God, the Sovereign of all men, and that idolatry is the worship of nonexistent deities. Why then do they take seriously such foolish thraldom to empty phantoms? The Midrash states:

"Thou shalt have no other gods before Me" (Exod. 20:3). Why is this said? Because it says: "I am the Lord Thy God." To give a parable. A king of flesh and blood entered a province. His attendants said to Him: "Issue some decree for the people." He, however, told them: "No. When they shall have accepted My reign I shall issue decrees upon them." Likewise, God said to Israel: "I am the Lord Thy God, thou shalt have no other gods—I am He whose reign you have taken upon yourself in Egypt." And when they said, "Yes, yes," He continued: "Now that you have accepted My reign you must also accept My decrees. Thou shalt have no other gods before Me."[5]

We are faced, to begin with, with a startling connection between idolatry and divine jealousy. Whether or not idolatry would be possible if there were no God, or if He were not jealous, idolatry in any case achieves its full religious meaning only in the context of a covenant with a jealous God. The first commandment concerns Him who led Israel out of Egypt. It is because His is an exclusive lordship that the first commandment is followed by a second, which contains the prohibition of idols.

Divine jealousy is startling to modern man. We can understand that one particularistic god is jealous of others. Can we understand jealousy in a God who is universal and has no rivals? For Hegel, God is "not envious," that is, God is universally tolerant.[6] For Arnold Toynbee, Old Testament views on idolatry are mere abuse, heaped by the god of the in-group on the gods of the out-group.[7] Is the rabbinic notion of divine jealousy, then, a mere remnant of an outmoded particularism? Were the rabbis nothing better than chauvinists when they refused to place their God into the "universalistic" Roman pantheon?

But terms such as "particularism" and "universalism," in any case mere platitudes of Enlightenment-ideology, cannot do justice to rabbinic faith and thought. Under Vespasian, Rabbi Yoḥanan Ben Zakkai made his peace with Roman political universalism, became a traitor by the standards of zealot particularism, and saved Judaism. But when Hadrian tried to enforce idolatry, Rabbi Akiba died a martyr. Since earliest biblical origins, the God of Israel had been the all-important God. This importance remained when He had beyond all doubt become the only God. His universalism, in short, was not and never would be one of indifference. He still cared and always would.

But why care about idols? Why be jealous about idolatry, of all sins, when this is worship of "no-gods"? The question remains. It becomes still more puzzling when we proceed from the first element of rabbinic doctrine to the second, which asserts that the divine is a discriminating jealousy, which singles out idolatry alone. The Midrash already cited continues:

For I the Lord Thy God am a jealous God. Zealously do I exact punishment for idolatry, but in other matters I am merciful.[8]

We could understand an all-important, and hence totally committing, God who remained indiscriminately jealous even after He has become universal. We could certainly understand a God whose jealousy is focused on sins that are serious temptations. But can we understand a God who has become merciful of transgressions that remain serious realities and yet remains jealous of empty conceits?

The question becomes still more baffling when we add the third element in rabbinic teaching essential to our purpose: God's jealousy of idolatry extends to Gentiles as well as to Jews. Conceivably the rabbis might have taught that among Gentiles idolatry is either inevitable or impossible, inevitable in case the Sinaitic covenant alone saves men from idolatry, or impossible in case it alone raises men from an otherwise total religious ignorance. In fact, however, the rabbis firmly reject both these alternatives. Idolatry does not inevitably flow from the human condition, for whereas sin begins with Adam, idolatry begins only with Enoch.[9] Nor is man's native condition religious ignorance, if only because God made a covenant with Noah as well as with Israel, and Noah is the father of all men now living. But the very first commandment given to Noah concerns idolatry.[10]

The God of Israel, then, has become merciful about sins in Israel. He has, moreover, extended His love to Gentiles as well as to Jews, entering into a covenant with both. But He concentrates all the passion of an undiminished jealousy on the single sin of idolatry, in the case of Jews and Gentiles alike. Yet the object of idol worship is a mere nothingness, the figment of a foolish imagination! Here at last we have the whole enigmatic question.

The following passage (which contains the fourth and final element of rabbinic doctrine required for our purpose) is as if designed to answer the question:

When someone in his anger tears his clothes, breaks utensils, throws away money, this should be viewed as though he worshipped idols. For this is the cunning of the evil inclination: today it says "do this," tomorrow, "do that," until it finally says "go and worship idols," and he goes and does it. Rabbi Akin said: this is indicated in Ps. 81:10: "there shall be no alien god within you. . . ." What is the alien god that dwells in a man's body? The evil inclination.[11]

Here, we say, is the answer to our question. Idol-worship is a possibility implicit in the human condition. It is a possibility even though the idols are no-gods. It remains a possibility even when men know that they are no-gods. It is and remains possible because sinful passion can reach a point at which it becomes an independent power—as it were, an alien god within—a point at which the ordinary relation is reversed and passion no longer belongs to man but man to passion. This is why the rabbis refuse to belittle idolatry by defining it too narrowly, as a folly safely surpassed, or by defining it too widely, as indistinguishable from sin in general. This is why they more or less disregard the "fool who saith in his heart, there is no God" (Ps. 53:2) but build elaborate fences around the prohibition of idolatry. This is why the God of the rabbis has become merciful with respect to other sins but concentrates all the passion of His jealousy on the sin of idolatry.

But precisely the doctrine that reveals why the rabbis take ancient idolatry seriously also reveals the veritable abyss between them and us, for *we* cannot take ancient idolatry seriously. To a sin more widely or loosely defined we might find ourselves attracted; to idolatry in the exact ancient sense, not at all. That it should fascinate some benighted ancients we might understand; that its lure should extend to moderns as well as ancients seems simply laughable. Imagine the evil inclination says to a modern man, first, "Steal your neighbour's money!" then, "Seduce his pretty wife!" and, finally, "Prostrate yourself before a graven image!" What to the rabbis was the ultimate in evil fascination and the most devastating sin comes to us as a ludicrous anticlimax.

PROTESTANT CONCEPTS OF IDOLATRY

What is this abyss between ancient and modern experience, and what is its cause? The ancient world is "full of gods" (Thales). The modern world, as the current expression puts it, is "demythologized." In the ancient world finite external objects can be higher than man, so much so as to demand and receive worship. In the modern world, these objects have all tumbled from their exalted position. Rivers and hills are lifeless objects, and trees, monkeys, and cows are forms of life lower than the human; as for statues, they are the mere work of human hands. Even the stars are not, as Aristotle thought, divine in themselves but at best only, as Kant believes, "sublime" in relation to us. Not even the universe as a whole is divine, for the myth of a World-Soul, a "likely story" to ancient philosophers,[12] is now only a poetic conceit. This much is plain and indisputable fact.

What is the cause of this abyss between ancient and modern experience? One must not think of modern science only, but, rather, of the "modern, enlightened" way of life as a whole, for one way of life can be replaced or destroyed only by another. It will be useful to compare this modern way of life with two ways of life in the ancient world, which, each in its own way, demythologized the idols. Ancient Rome turns Greek poetry into prose; in the pantheon the gods are all assembled and, because made subservient to human use, all destroyed. The Hebrew Bible too empties the earth of gods, and here too human use enters, for the earth is placed at the disposal of man. But whereas in Rome the gods are destroyed by a human empire, in the Bible their destruction is by the presence of God.

These two forms of ancient "enlightenment" differ greatly from each other. How does modern enlightenment differ from both? Rome destroys the gods but makes human emperors into gods. The Hebrew Bible destroys false gods in praise of the true God and, having done so, must live with the persisting danger of idolatry. Modern enlightenment alone is radical. To be sure, there is disagreement on the meaning of this radicalism. To some it means the demythologization of both God and the gods. To others it means that God is expelled from the world, into the irrelevance of a sheer, deistic transcendence. To others again it means that, whatever the effect, God can enter into the modern no less than into the premodern world. All agree that in the modern, secular, demythologized world literal worship of finite external objects—idolatry in its ancient sense—is impossible.

What, then, is idolatry in modern eyes? Is it a mere superstition confined to the ancient world and safely surpassed in this day and age? But we have seen that this long-popular view is no longer tenable in the twentieth century—that while the old idolatry is safely dead, something different, and yet obscurely related, is terrifyingly alive. Even those who deny reality to all literal gods admit that metaphorical ones are all too real. Even those for whom no true worship exists see "false worship" on every side. These facts suggest that ancient idolatry was more than mere superstition when it was alive, as well as that ancient rabbinic wisdom may possibly be relevant to modern as well as ancient experience. Can the concept of idolatry be so expanded as to make the God of Israel as jealous of the modern metaphorical "gods" now as He once was of graven images?

In pursuit of this question, we must first consult modern Protestant rather than ancient Jewish thinkers. Of all forms of Biblical faith, Protestantism alone is exclusively modern, and Protestant thinkers may well spare us labor since they will deal with modern idolatry if they deal with idolatry at all. It will turn out, however, that, unlike the rabbis, these thinkers are apt to define idolatry either too narrowly or too widely, and in the end we shall have no choice but to resort to the ancient rabbis. Thus we will have to try so to bridge the gap between the ancient and modern worlds as to make them speak to modern realities.

We begin, as we must, with Martin Luther. Luther writes:

Idolatry consists not only of the worship of idols but above all exists in the heart which looks elsewhere for help and comfort, to creatures, saints and devils. . . . It is also the kind of worship which seeks help, comfort and blessedness in one's own works, and is arrogant enough to wish to force God to yield His heaven.[18]

Luther expands the concept of idolatry. He rejects the view that idolatry is a folly surpassed in the modern world. Indeed, he does so before that view has made an explicit appearance in man's thinking. This great virtue, however, is bought at a price fatal by any standard, and altogether unacceptable by the standard set by the ancient rabbis. Luther so expands the concept of idolatry as, in effect, to make all sin idolatrous. For the rabbis, idolatry begins with Enoch; for Luther, it begins with Adam's pride. The rabbis single out idolatry as one of three sins that must be resisted unto death. Luther singles out all sin and no sin at all. Luther's virtue, his radicalism, becomes a vice when he elevates all sin to the status of idolatry and thus trivializes actual idolatry.

A Jewish thinker may well wonder whether this vice in Luther's doctrine is not responsible for fatal consequences. It would be absurd to blame Luther for a contemporary "German-Christian" church that did not hesitate to accept Hitler's word as the word of God. But is it absurd to connect Luther with a strange and fatal contemporary Christian impotence (by no means all Protestant or all German) that, while opposed to Nazism, failed to identify it as idolatry, classifying it instead with such sins as nationalism (not confined to Nazism), dictatorship (not limited to Hitlerism), and, indeed, with the normal failings of good Christians?

We turn next from the first Protestant to contemporary Protestants, confining ourselves to Karl Barth and Paul Tillich. Both are great theologians, and representative because they are at opposite poles of the spectrum. Both have shed liberal illusions and face the fact of modern idolatry. Both are opposed to Nazism and indeed bear brave personal witness against it. Yet neither is able to match personal testimony with theological comprehension. Barth writes:

In the Old Testament the reference to the unfathomable wisdom of God is adduced as a proof of the impossibility, and therefore of the utter folly, of all idolatry. If the wisdom of God and therefore God Himself could be known by man in the created world . . . there would be no real reason why the adoration of God in images of all kinds should not be a justifiable and even necessary result of this natural knowledge of God. But the Old Testament says, quite rightly from its standpoint, that all idolatry is folly. It is not [sic!][14] of course sin, but only sin in the sense of folly.[15]

This is not how the rabbis read the Hebrew Bible. In Barth's understanding, those within the covenant—old or new—cannot relapse into idolatry, for it is a folly surpassed. Those outside the covenant either know God through nature (in which case idolatry is inevitable) or not at all (in which case it is impossible). In each case what remains, in the view of the rabbis, as a deadly, yet resistible, temptation has reduced itself in Barth to a bagatelle. Is this because, like Luther, Barth defines idolatry too widely, as sin in general? Or too narrowly, as a folly surpassed with the advent of the Christ?

We find no clear answer to this question, for we can detect in Barth's theological work no sense of urgent need for expanding the concept of ancient idolatry so as to make it encompass modern realities. Thus-one passage startles us by classing German church proclamations of Hitlerian "revelations" with American church tolerance of racial discrimination, but of course, the subject of the passage is not idolatry but rather sins against the universality of the church.[16] Another passage confuses and shocks us by listing "Nero, Caligula . . . , Nietzsche, Hitler" among the "monstrous caricatures produced by world history." We are confused because to class Hitler with Nero and Caligula is to obscure the difference between modern and ancient idolatry, and we are shocked because Nietzsche is included in the list at all. But, then, we have little right to be shocked, and none to be confused, for the subject is not idolatry but rather man's self-alienation from God.[17] We are thus forced to conclude that on the subject of modern idolatry, we are failed by Barth the theologian. This failure is all the more poignant in a theologian who did not fail us as a witness and a man. In 1949 Barth wrote:

National Socialism . . . was a spell which notoriously revealed its power to overwhelm our souls, to persuade us to believe in its lies and to join in its evil-doings. . . . We were hypnotized by it as a rabbit by a giant snake. We were in danger of bringing, first incense, and then the complete sacrifice to it as a false god. . . . We had to object with all our protestantism as though against the evil. It was not a matter of declaiming against some mischief, distant and easily seen through. It was a matter of life and death, of resistance against a godlessness which was in fact attacking body and soul, and was therefore effectively masked to many thousands of Christian eyes.[18]

We turn next to the opposite end of the theological spectrum. Paul Tillich writes:

Idolatry is the elevation of a preliminary concern to ultimacy. Something essentially conditioned is taken as unconditional, something essentially partial is boosted to universality, and something essentially finite is given infinite significance (the best example of contemporary idolatry is religious nationalism).[19]

This definition for the first time opens up real possibilities. As it stands, however, it has serious difficulties, of which some reflect mere conceptual obscurity whereas others concern doctrine—a doctrine that, at least to a thinker inspired by rabbinic wisdom, will turn out to be unacceptable.

To understand the definition at all, one must bear in mind two well-known Tillichian doctrines: religion is man's ultimate concern, and all men necessarily have an ultimate concern. In the light of these two doctrines, what is idolatry? One cannot ascribe to Tillich the foolish view that whatever is in fact made an ultimate concern is truly ultimate, for then idolatry—the elevation of a preliminary concern to ultimacy—is by definition impossible. What, then, is the standard of true ultimacy? If it is exclusively Christian, all non-Christians—Jews, Mohammedans, Marxists, agnostics—are ipso facto helpless idolaters. Is it, then, religious-in-general? But this makes nonreligious humanism idolatrous and idolatrous religion, not. Is it the standard of an "authenticity" that may take both religious and nonreligious forms? But this makes the terms "conditioned" and "unconditional," "partial" and "universal," "finite" and "infinite" so fluid as to raise doubt whether they can still serve as standards. Moreover, it provokes legitimate protests from atheists and agnostics who will wish to be classified, neither as religious despite themselves, nor as idolatrous despite themselves. Must a theologian embrace this dichotomy, which, to put it plainly, smacks of misguided religious apologetics? The rabbis in their day did not. They certainly did not make professed unbelievers into believers. But—and this is the crux—neither did they make them inevitable idolaters, and for the doctrine that each man must have an ultimate concern—either genuine or idolatrous—one can find no rabbinic warrant. Has Luther's fatal error crept into Tillich's thinking? Is this what induces him, in the case of modern idolatry, to make the God of Israel too indiscriminate in His jealousy?

If too indiscriminately jealous in the modern world, Tillich's God is, of ancient idolatry, not jealous enough. Tillich writes: "Apollo has no revelatory significance for Christians."[20] It appears that, so long as Apollo speaks at all, his voice is, however, inadequately, the voice of the true God, and that, when he speaks no more, he has become a harmless work of art. Between these two alternatives, has the possibility even of *ancient* idolatry disappeared?[21]

Protestant thinkers, then, have failed to provide an acceptable conception in which ancient and modern idolatry are both comprehended. (This is true at least if the representative examples given are representative enough.[22]) From a Jewish standpoint, is this failure due to some quality in their Protestantism? Or in their Christianity? Perhaps it is as much due to the gap between ancient and modern idolatry, which requires bridging, for this is suggested by the fact that Jewish thinkers too have their difficulties. Thus Will Herberg makes all pride idolatrous.[23] This is closer to Luther than to the rabbinic sources. A. J. Heschel abandons the rabbis, and makes divine jealousy indiscriminate, when he writes that "man cannot live without [an ultimate object of worship, and that this is either] God or an idol."[24] Yet Heschel is an outstanding student of the rabbinic sources. His example shows, as eloquently as any other, the need for the Jewish thinker to make every effort to bridge the gap between the ancient and modern worlds, in the hope that rabbinic wisdom might then speak to the present day.

THE PROCESS OF DEMYTHOLOGIZING

In order to do justice to both ancient and modern idolatry we must frame a concept of demythologizing more subtle than thus far used. The required concept must satisfy three conditions: it must allow that the old idols are now dead; it must allow that they once had a terrifying power; and it must make possible the assertion that this power has now not simply vanished but rather passed into something else. These three conditions must all be satisfied: the first, unless we are to ignore the qualitative difference between ancient and modern idolatry; the second, if we are to assume that the rabbis in their ancient day had any genuine wisdom; the third, if we are to assume that their ancient wisdom is capable of modern application. It is true that the second and in particular the third may well be unfounded assumptions; indeed, they suggest that we shall be presupposing what we shall try to establish. Against this, however, we can stake the fact that our proposed concept of demythologizing is no mere ad hoc invention. It is more or less common property of modern philosophers, among them Hegel,

Feuerbach, Marx, and Nietzsche. This does not, to be sure, solve all methodological unclarity, and, in particular, raises questions of priorities, such as between faith and reason or between ancient tradition and modern thought. But these questions can here only be mentioned, and must otherwise be left aside.[25]

We begin with the great stumbling block that we can no longer hope to understand ancient idolatry. More is involved than the fact that it is long past. The crux is that it ceases to be intelligible the moment it is demythologized. One no longer really knows what it is like. Hence even the Bible no longer fully understands the ancient idols, which is why it can speak of them as mere "silver and gold, the work of men's hands." (Ps. 115:4) Surely only fools would worship such things, and there is thus some truth to Barth's previously criticized view that, for the Bible, idolatry is folly. This is not, however, either the whole truth or the most important truth. To the idolater himself, the idol is no mere work of men's hands, and the Bible, while failing to understand, is aware of its own failure to understand. Why otherwise take idolatry seriously? In the Bible it is the atheist who is the fool, which is why he hardly appears on the biblical scene. Idolatry, in contrast, is a constant temptation in the Bible, all the more terrifying because it is un-intelligible. The temptation remains even when it has lost all traces of intelligibility, that is, in rabbinic times, when the truth that there is no god but God has been established beyond all possible doubt.

If then neither Bible nor Talmud understands ancient idolatry how can modern men hope to understand it? The idolater actually believes that the idol can hear, speak and act. More, he actually hears it speak, sees it act, and responds to what he hears and sees with a degree of passion and sacrifice that leaves no doubt as to his sincerity. All this is unintelligible to us, and we are therefore apt to regard ancient idolatry as mere superstition, that is, as a phenom-enon without rhyme or reason, which the light of reason destroys without leaving a trace.

But ancient idolatry is not without a rhyme and reason of its own, and it need not remain totally unintelligible. We cannot understand it, if by this we mean entering into the experience. We *can* understand it if all we seek is abstract concepts that enable us to reconstruct what is now dead but was once alive.

Such a concept is the familiar one of projection. The ancient idolater projects a feeling—fear, hope, pleasure, pain—upon an external object, and he then worships the object. The object, on its part, remains no mere object; the projected feeling gives it a life of its own, and there may be, or even must be, a special rite of consecration during which this life is conjured into it. There is, then, *worship* because the object is *other* and *higher* than the worshipper, and the worship is *idolatrous* because the object is *finite*—if only because it *is* an object. (The idolater does not, of course, recognize his projections in the worshipped object. If he did, he would withdraw the projections, demythologize the object, and cease to worship it.)

However—and this is why Freud does not appear in the previously listed sources of inspiration—the concept of projection is not by itself adequate for the present purpose. What is to be grasped is the *religious* nature of idolatrous worship. This cannot be done so long as the feelings we understand are no more than animal fear, limited hope, a pleasure and a pain that are mere "need." For so long as nothing more than these is projected there is no such thing as genuine worship. Moreover, the idolatry in question being in fact mere superstition, the withdrawal of the projected feelings, if and when it occurs, leaves no trace. A doctrine, however, that in effect regards all religious idolatry as only pseudoreligious is guilty of reductionism, and fails in its explanations. (Thus Freud never manages to explain why the frustrated need for nothing more than a human father should produce the projected image of something more than a substitute human, that is, a Father who is divine.) And what must actually be reckoned with is fear that is numinous terror, a hope that is geared to infinite bliss, a pleasure and a pain transported into total sacrifice—and an idol with a life explosive enough to inspire such terror, bliss, and sacrifice.

If we are to reckon with these, we must bestow on the concept of projection a dimension of infinity: what is projected by the idolater upon the finite object is an *infinite* fear, hope, pleasure, or pain. Only because the feeling is infinite is there a religious— not a pseudoreligious—relation to the finite object. Only because the finite object is made infinite is the object endowed with its shattering powers, and the idolatrous worship of it, qualitatively distinct from mere superstition. And only because the finite object is both other than the worshipper and made infinite does the idolatry take the form of worship. Here at last we have grasped ancient idolatry, to the extent to which abstract thought can grasp it.

But we have also grasped something else, crucial for our entire purpose. The withdrawal of finite feelings leaves no trace; the withdrawal of infinite feelings produces a dialectical transformation. The demythologization of ancient idolatry, to be sure, destroys the possibility of idolatrous worship. But only the form of idolatrous worship is destroyed, and this very process of destruction creates the possibility of idolatry in a new form, hitherto without precedent.

Demythologization withdraws the infinite feeling; thus the object is reduced to its proper finitude and loses the power to command worship. But, because the withdrawn feeling is infinite, it does not vanish but rather is transformed in the inner realm into which it is withdrawn. It thus acquires the power of generating what may be called *internalized idolatry*. This is a thraldom to no alien other, but rather to what is within, remains within, and is *known* to be and remain within. It does not and cannot take the form of worship. Yet, though Hitler did not and could not demand religious worship, the passion of Nazi idolatry matches any ancient idol worship.

The new, internalized idolatry is dialectically related to the old. It is wholly like the old in that it is composed of the same essential elements; wholly unlike the old in that these elements are totally reorganized. The new idolatry is, further, more "mature" than the old in that it presupposes and arises from its demythologization. Common speech notes all these characteristics but fails to relate and thus to understand them. As regards the first two characteristics, we speak of the new idolatry as the "worship" of "gods" and "idols," indicating likeness by the terms used, and unlikeness by the fact that their employment is consciously metaphorical. As for the third characteristic, this is recognized in part by the speech of the new idolater. He does not, of course, recognize his own idolatry. His "worship" of *Volk* and *Führer* is in his mind no idolatrous thraldom but rather a new freedom, for his very self is part of the *Volk* and the *Führer* embodies the *Volk*.[26] But the truth in this new false "freedom" is that, negating all worship, it negates all idolatry in the form of worship. This new idolater takes himself as an enlightened modern. (He does so even when he hankers after long-dead pagan myths. For he does not return to the old myths but rather resorts to concocted myths —myths that spell the final death of the old, genuine ones if only because they are deliberately, "creatively" invented.) And, shocking though this is to Enlightenment-liberals, there is truth in this self-appraisal. The new idolater is not enlightened, but he is most decidedly modern. The new idolatry is not a relapse into premodern superstitions. It is a bastard-child of the Age of Enlightenment.

So much for the concepts needed for the present purpose. Before we try to apply them a word of caution must be addressed to theologians. In addition to a new, internalized idolatry, the dialectical process sketched in the preceding pages has given rise to a variety of internalized religions, all of them rivals to the biblical God. Idealistic faith in a higher Self, humanistic hope for a mankind potentially infinite in perfection, the Nietzschean and Marxist dreams for a superior Man and Society, these all internalize or deny the biblical God who remains other than human, and this fact tempts Jewish and Christian thinkers to respond to them with an indiscriminate charge of idolatry. There is, however, no warrant for such a response in rabbinic wisdom. In their day, the rabbis refused to brand all sin against or ignorance of God as idolatry, and in the light of this restraint a modern doctrine of "either God or idol" is a clear case of misguided apologetics. The concepts developed in the present section entitle the modern Jewish thinker to assert the *possibility* of a modern, internalized idolatry. They do not justify the view that wherever God is not worshipped there is *actual* idolatry. Indeed, such a view is fatal in the light of rabbinic wisdom. Making idolatrous what is in fact at most sin, ignorance, error, or indeed partial truth, it reduces actual idolatry to a mere bagatelle.

MODERN IDOLATRY

What, then, is actual idolatry? In the light of the concepts furnished in the preceding section, how shall we identify the qualitative leap that occurs when the evil inclination no longer says "Do this" or "Do that," but "Go and worship idols," and a man goes and does it?

With regard to ancient idolatry, we shall fail totally if we mistake the idol for a mere religious symbol. A religious symbol, if and when it points to Divinity itself, expresses inadequately the inexpressible, and this inadequacy is part of the religious consciousness. There is, for this reason, no idolatry where this gap both exists and is known to exist, which is why the Hebrew Bible, while absolutely opposed to idolatry, is nevertheless full of religious symbols. A burning bush can reveal the divine Presence, for it is not itself that Presence. A divine Voice can be heard even though the divine Face cannot be seen, for it but points to the divine Speaker. Then why can revelatory significance attach to symbols such as these but not to the statue of Apollo? Why is the statue not a partial truth but, rather, an absolute falsehood?

Because it is not a "symbol" at all. The ancient idol is not a finite object that distinguishes itself from the divine Infinity even as it points to it. The idol is itself divine. The idolatrous projection of infinite feeling upon the finite object is such as to produce not a symbolic but rather a *literal* and hence *total* identification of finiteness and infinitude. Only thus can we explain the otherwise inexplicable facts that the idolater believes that the idol can literally hear, speak, and act; that he actually hears it speak and sees its actions; and that, rather than merely toy with the fantasies of worship and sacrifice, he in fact sacrifices to Moloch, not this or that, but his all. This is the behavior that the rabbis knew to be possible, and indeed to be a terrible temptation, although they did not pretend to understand it. This is why, to them, the ancient idol was not an irrelevance but rather the demonic rival of the One of Israel, and radically intolerable.

But we in our modern tolerance balk at this ancient intolerance, especially when it is directed, not against Moloch, but against dear beloved Apollo. Hence, like Tillich, we read modern harmlessness back into the ancient idol, and reduce it to a mere symbol, that is, to a partial albeit no longer relevant revelation of truth. This tolerance, however, has its bitter nemesis. We deny God's ancient jealousy of idols that no longer hurt or threaten, and we become impotent adequately to identify modern "idols" whose threat is all too real. We become then inclined to assert an ultimate and hence religious concern where none is in consciousness, and/or to brand as idolatry what is in fact mere dissent, error, or sin— all of which fall short of idolatry. Having become not jealous enough of ancient idolatry, the God of Israel becomes too indiscriminate or too uncertain in His jealousy of modern idolatry. To avoid this danger, we shall use the criterion that we established in the exposition of ancient idolatry as we make an attempt to identify its modern heir and successor: idolatry is the *literal* identification of finiteness and infinitude.

Is the modern scientific agnostic an idolater? In his own self-understanding, he suspends all infinites and confines himself to finite affirmations. May the religious thinker go behind the back of this suspension and assert an infinite affirmation, or ultimate concern, where none is in consciousness? The rabbis give no warrant for such a procedure. There is in any case little sense in affirming a commitment where there is explicit suspension. As for affirming an unconscious idolatrous commitment, this would appear to be contrary to anything found in rabbinic wisdom. Not until there was actual worship of idols in the ancient world was the evil inclination, though potentially idolatrous, in fact idolatrous. Not until finiteness and infinity are actually identified is there modern idolatry. Yet this identity is explicitly denied by the agnostic's suspension. To the believer, agnosticism is doubtless error; but not all error is idolatry.

What, next, of the atheist? He is a more likely candidate, if only because he ends the agnostic suspension. There are, however, two kinds of modern atheists, at least one of whom is not an idolater. The true God known to religious faith and experience is infinite, and shows His infinity by His all-importance, by His demand for a total commitment, and by His capacity for saving Presence. The God denied by the atheist presently under consideration, however, is a mere God-hypothesis, unable to demand commitment, incapable of saving Presence, and important only for the limited purpose of scientific or pseudoscientific explanation. He is, in short, a mere finite postulate, and to deny this postulate is to make a merely finite denial. To be sure, the atheist fails to distinguish between God and God-hypothesis, believes himself to be denying the one when in fact he is merely denying the other, and in this shows, to the believer, religious ignorance. But ignorance is not idolatry.

But what if the divine Infinity is *knowingly* denied, by a self that is raising itself to infinity in this very act of denial? With this question we come at once upon two modern phenomena: internalized "religion" and internalized idolatry. It would be, however, a fatal error to confuse the two. A Jewish or Christian believer may have to disagree with both, but whereas the one is an authentic challenge likely to bring out the best, the other is a demonic perversion that tempts to the worst. Jewish or Christian faith may have dialogue with modern internalized religion, and indeed must have it unless it is to shut itself off from the modern world. Internalized idolatry, in contrast, represents, not the modern world, but rather its specific possibilities for radical evil.

In order to recognize this distinction we turn briefly to six modern philosophers—Fichte, Schelling, Hegel, Feuerbach, Marx, and Nietzsche. These thinkers all explore the modern theme of internalized religion and are thus exposed to the danger of modern internalized idolatry. Yet not one of their philosophies is in fact idolatrous. Indeed, one may say that what makes these philosophies great is precisely the care with which the possibility of idolatry is both recognized and avoided.

This is certainly true of the first group of thinkers. These are idealists because their denial of divine otherness issues, not in an atheistic rejection of the Divine, but rather in its internalization. Divinity comes to dwell, as it were, in the same inner space as the human self, and this is enough to raise the specter of a modern, internalized idolatry. It is therefore all the more significant that finiteness and infinitude are nevertheless kept firmly apart in the internal space that they jointly occupy. Fichte's moral self becomes divine only in infinity—forever aimed at but never reached. Hegel reaches the Fichtean goal, but does so in the realm of thought only; existentially man and God remain apart.[27] Schelling alone yields to the romantic temptation to fuse the finite and the infinite—but only, after a brief period of yielding, in order to set them the more firmly apart.

Idolatry is as firmly (if not as obviously) rejected by the second group of thinkers. These are humanistic atheists, made so by the fact that Divinity vanishes in the process of internalization, to be replaced by a humanity potentially infinite in its modern "freedom." Yet despite so Promethean an atheism they are not idolaters, for the potentiality never seems to become quite actual. Feuerbach's man is not yet quite free, Marx's society, as yet far from classless. Even Nietzsche, for all his recklessness, does not declare himself to be Overman but merely to be Overman's fragmented prophet. And the blessed vision he beholds but accentuates the anguish to which he remains confined. In short, just as the first group of thinkers holds fast to the ideal divine infinity, so the second holds fast to real human finitude, prepared, if they must, to project infinity into a mere elusive future. With thinkers such as these, the religious thinker can have dialogue, and he must have it if he is to expose himself to the profoundest challenge of modernity. With idolatrous ideologies, in contrast, dialogue is impossible.

We face this ineluctable fact as we turn, next, from genuine modern philosophies to ideologies that are their idolatrous parodies. Among the grimmer facts of modern intellectual history is that almost all the philosophies mentioned (and a good many others) have become prey to ideological perversion. Fichte's thought became rabid Teutonic nationalism when his risky proposition became inverted, and goodness was no longer the standard of the true German but true "Germanness" the standard of goodness. Hegel's thought became statism when the Prussian state became divine. Marxism became totalitarianism with the apotheosis of the present party line in place of the future society. Nietzsche's dream of a future innocence was defiled when it became a present barbarism "beyond good and evil." All the ideologies have two things in common: they are not philosophies at all, for they lack all honest rationality; and they are idolatrous.

These two characteristics are not unrelated. These ideologies are all the product, not of reason, but of passion, and the passion at work in them is idolatrous. (This is true at least if the ideologies themselves may be taken as accurate reflections of realities.) For these ideologies are blueprints for nothing less than the actual, literal identification, within the inward space of the individual or collective self, of finiteness and infinity. Through them speaks unmistakably, albeit, in modern terms, the evil inclination when, tearing off its mask, it makes the ultimate, unspeakable, idolatrous demand.

THE LEAP FROM IDEOLOGY TO EXECUTION

But one can toy with idolatrous feelings and fantasies. One can play with ideologies about God being dead and everything being permitted, about the need to exterminate lower races, and about a charismatic *Führer* who can do no wrong. This, to be sure, is a game both evil and dangerous. Yet there is a qualitative leap between idle feeling and the passion of actual belief, between fantasy and serious plan, between what remains "theory" and actual, literal, total execution.

Such an execution boggles the mind.[28] One can somehow still grasp idolatrous ideology, and indeed a certain bogus rationality can attach to works such as *Mein Kampf*, making possible at least the parody of a serious discussion. But can one understand that anyone might seriously believe the fantasies of that work? Or that they might be executed with the utmost literalness? If Hitler was not believed by the world, the best excuse is that he was incredible.

He is incredible still. Before Nazism happened we thought it could not happen. Now that it has happened, we resort to explanations that explain it away. We take it, in the style of Enlightenment liberalism, as a mere lapse into atavistic prejudice, superstition, or neurosis, ills that should not happen in this day and age and for which—soon if not now—there will be a cure. Or we take it, in neo-Lutheran style, as a mere case of national pride, lust for power or xenophobia, sins will always happen because we are all sinners. Possibly we take it as a mixture of the two. In any case we resist confronting it as a modern idolatry—

one might say, as *the* modern idolatry because, being unsurpassable, it reveals all that idolatry can be in the modern world.

Nazism was not nationalism or imperialism: these have limited goals. Nor was it a plausible reaction to defeat and depression, if only because no other nation ever reacted like Nazi Germany to these traumas. Nazism was more like pan-nationalism, totalitarianism, and antisemitism, for these are all nurtured by a groundless hate, have unlimited goals, and hence are insatiable. Nazism, in fact, could look like all these things before it happened. After the event, we may not ignore the difference between Nazism and pan-Germanism or other forms of totalitarianism,[29] nor the fact that no other antisemitism ever made the murder of every available Jewish man, woman, and child on earth into an unshakable principle.

To come anywhere near grasping the scandalous particularity of Nazi idolatry we must take the incredible leap from mere ideology to literal execution. The historian Allan Bullock writes of Hitler:

Every single one of his ideas, from the exaltation of the heroic leader, the racial myth, anti-Semitism, the community of the *Volk*, and the attack on the intellect, to the idea of a ruling elite, the subordination of the individual and the doctrine that might is right, is to be found in the anti-rational and racist writers (not only in Germany but also in France and other European countries) during the hundred years which separate the Romantic movement from the Foundations of the Third Reich. By 1914 they had become the common-places of radical anti-Semitic and pan-German journalism and cafe-talk in every city in Central Europe. . . . *Hitler's originality lay not in his ideas, but in the terrifyingly literal way in which he set to work to translate fantasy into reality, and his unequaled grasp of the means to do this.*[30]

How can we understand this translation of fantasy into reality —by no means the work of one individual only but implicating, for 12 years, a whole people and much of Europe? Notions arising in connection with ancient idolatry crowd back into the mind: the "alien god within" who becomes an independent force when idolatrous passion and fantasy, toyed with too long and too seriously, have undermined the power of both the understanding and the will; the serious belief, immune to all evidence, that the idol can hear, speak, and act; the final act of worship that no longer toys and plays but does not shrink from overt, total sacrifice. Yet a gulf separates Nazi from ancient idolatry. It is no worship and indeed denies and destroys all forms of worship. The *Führer* is no Roman emperor-god, and there are no gods beside or above him.[31] As for the "myth of the twentieth century," this is no genuine myth at all but rather a "creative" invention, known to be so by inventors and believers alike.[32] Belief, therefore, is not belief at all. There is, on the contrary, a total lack of all serious belief, and in its place there is make-believe. Yet this make-believe commands infinite passion and has the power to exact unlimited sacrifice!

All this is because Nazism has internalized the idolatrous identification of finiteness and infinitude. The *Führer*, no emperor-god, embodies the *Volk*, and the *Volk*, no worshipping community, realizes its selfhood in blind obedience and total sacrifice. Because Nazism internalizes divinity, it is an idealism. Yet since it idolatrously identifies finiteness and infinitude, it is an idealism *totally without ideals*. As for finite ideals—family love, vocation, the relation between finite but real men—these are all dissolved in an infinite, "idealistic" passion. As for infinite ideals—the True, the Good, the Holy—these are defiled and destroyed by subjection to the will of a *Führer* that obeys no principle but is rather the extreme in finitude—namely, absolute whim. Indeed, destroyed are even those idolatrous ideals to which Nazism pretends so long as it is mere ideology—when the point is reached at which fantasy no longer controls reality but the passion of reality overwhelms all "theory." Hence there is a grim logic in the fact that, when all was finished and the Third Reich was ashes and ruins, Hitler expressed ghoulish satisfaction at the apparently imminent demise, not of his enemies, but of the "master race."

Yet, as has been said, the *Führer* whose whims demand all and receive all is neither god nor object of worship. He is, in fact, a nothing who becomes something only at the *Sieg Heil* of the *Volk*, and then he becomes everything. The *Volk*, on its part, is no ordinary mob. It is a mob that has destroyed every vestige of private reserve, every remaining trace of individual personality in order to become an actual infinity through the shout of *Sieg Heil*. A demonic circularity thus exists between *Volk* and *Führer*. Ancient idol-worship, too, showed this circularity, for the idol owed its divinity to the worshipper, yet held him in thrall. In the modern Nazi idolatry, however, this circularity is a conscious compact. For there is no otherness between *Volk* and *Führer*. Theirs is a relation of mutual self-realization; in deadly fear of the finite—something each might be—they are both nothings that seek to become everything in their relation.

For this reason, this demonic compact between *Volk* and *Führer* —two nothings—can express itself only in a passion for infinite destruction. In its own fantasies, to be sure, the lived unity of *Volk* and *Führer* is an exorcism of nothingness and, indeed, the *creatio ex nihilo* of divinity. In fact, however, it can occasion no surprise that even by the standards of its own idolatrous ideology, Nazism left behind not a single positive accomplishment. In the end, Nazism achieved but one specific goal, and that was negative: the murder of six million Jews.

IDOLATRY IN AMERICA

The "idealistic" idolatry that is unsurpassably manifested in Nazism is alien to the spirit of America. America, and indeed the "empirical" West as a whole, suspects all absolutes and is thus largely immune to all false absolutes—the deified nation, the totalitarian state, the cult of personality, the pseudomessianic goal, and the romantic longing for long-lost gods. Its goals are finite, naturalistic, and pragmatic, not infinite, romantic and idealistic, and the thinkers looked to are not Marx and Nietzsche but Dewey and Freud. Even the theologian in America is apt to ignore existentialist anxiety, guilt, and despair and to give proximate answers to ultimate questions.

This contrast between "empirical" America and "metaphysical" Europe has given rise to a spirit of triumphalism among recent American theologians.[33] The modern world has demythologized ancient idolatry. The modern American world has demythologized modern idolatry as well. The original Age of Enlightenment withdrew the infinite feelings projected upon the finite objects. The present American age of enlightenment is reducing these infinite feelings to their proper finite size. American democracy already has done away with the worship of nation, state, and charismatic leaders; and American psychiatry is doing away now with those neuroses that all along have been the true ultimate cause of all idolatry everywhere. God may or may not be dead in America. In any case, dead are all grounds for His jealousy, except in such dark pockets in which either ancient or modern European superstition still survives.

It would be a mistake to respond to "empirical" America with an indiscriminate charge of idolatry. As we have seen, there are no grounds for asserting the inevitability of an infinite affirmation or an ultimate concern where none exists in consciousness. Much less are there grounds for asserting that the affirmation or concern are idolatrous. The formula "either God or idol" being a case of misguided religious apologetics, Freud and Dewey are no more idolaters than Hegel, Nietzsche, or Marx. To deny the inevitability of idolatry, however, is by no means to concede its impossibility. An American triumphalism—theological or other—must be rejected.

Why is "empirical" or "pragmatic" America not invulnerable to idolatry? Because elevation of the finite individual or collective self is only one of two forms that idolatry may take in the modern world. The other is degradation of the infinite aspect of selfhood to a false finitude. A society that has achieved a degree of immunity from the one has done so at the price of greater vulnerability to the other. Freud's thought is not idolatrous; the ideology summed up with the slogan "Freud is a fink" certainly is.

Why is Freud a fink? He demands no "idealistic" sacrifice, no worship—literal or metaphorical—of true or false gods. He sets before us no more than finite, "naturalistic" goals, and the pursuit of these is counseled by enlightened self-interest. Yet Freud *is* a fink. (So presumably would be Dewey, if his thought still aroused passion and interest.) He becomes the target of attack not because of the nature of his goals but, rather, because he has any goals at all. Even the most naturalistic of philosophies still remains with the one imperative that man should make himself into the natural being he is. A type of idolater currently at large in the secular city wants simply to *be*.

A haunting portrayal of this ideology-become-actuality is given in a recent work, *Last Exit to Brooklyn*.[34] The heroes, or rather antiheroes, of this work are all slum-victims; hence their idolatry implicates the society that creates, perpetuates, or permits the slum. What makes them idolaters, however, is that they are not mere victims but rather willing and indeed passionate participants in their own degradation. No love exists between husband and wife or parent and child, no religion except for a grim farce, and the single attempt at poetry is pathetic by virtue of its very solitariness. Thus no "higher purpose" ever appears. As for natural purposes, all energy is spent not on their pursuit but on their defilement. For just as "idealistic" idolatry is an idealism without ideals so this "naturalistic" idolatry is a naturalism without nature. No desire remains innocent, no animal lust clean. For, whereas sex is all-pervasive, it is permeated by a universal pleasurelessness, joylessness, and, above all, by a groundless hate. Infinite despair lurks everywhere, yet no one ever screams the infinite scream that would make it human. So totally and completely does the antihero of *Last Exit to Brooklyn* use his human powers to deny every trace of his own humanity.

So complete a negation would not be possible for an individual in his solitariness. There is, therefore, a society or rather anti-society. Each is related to the other in a compact of mutual destructiveness. Negro is object of white contempt and himself despises Jew. There is rage between husband and wife, whether the cause is vital or trivial. Father starves child to lavish his plenty on illicit sexual conquest, yet the conquest is no affirmation of self but negation of the other. Need does not seek fulfillment but is rather a club with which men and women beat each other, with children reduced to mere objects in the struggle. This need, in short, forms a circle of mutual hate, and the circle is unbreakable because the hate is groundless. The rabbis teach that the first Temple was destroyed because of idolatry. Why then, they ask, was the second Temple destroyed, when at that time no idolatry existed? Because of groundless hate, is the reply, for groundless hate is equivalent to the worship of idols.[35]

The possibility of idolatry does not vanish in a society that suspects or spurns all absolutes, true or false. A "secularism" may arise for which the Divine is absent, irrelevant or dead: man still must come to terms with what the Bible describes as the divine image. The idolatry still possible is the desecration of that image.

COVENANT WITH A JEALOUS GOD

Opposition to the idolatries of the present age is not confined to Jewish faith or to religious faith as a whole. Yet it remains true that within Judaism such opposition can achieve its full significance only in the context of a covenant with a jealous God.

The Jewish thinker therefore does well to have recourse to ancient rabbinic wisdom. In so doing, however, he must take care lest he mistake the modern object of the divine jealousy. Like ancient idolatry, its modern successor is the work of "the strange god within." Unlike ancient idolatry, it *remains* within. There is nothing to fear from literal worship of literal gods. There is everything to fear from metaphorical worship of metaphorical gods.

The ancient battle must therefore be fought on a different front and with different means. With the false gods of old, the true God once shared the form of worship. Since this form is possible only where the Divine seems to speak, the true God therefore disclosed His own truth and their falsehood by His *actual* speech: *their* speech—works of gold and silver—was but a vain human conceit. The new false "gods" in contrast, are not gold and silver. They are in the heart and remain of it. And, far from illusory, their speech is real. Against false gods such as these, the testimony must be otherwise. It must stress that the true God may speak to the heart but is not in it or of it.

For this reason a strange irrelevance attaches to a current self-styled theology of relevance that would empty church and synagogue, dissolve religious tradition into secularity, and transmute the Divine into a wholly internalized, metaphorical "God." An older group of religious thinkers—Buber, Rosenzweig, Niebuhr, Barth, to name but a few—was wiser in its generation. It understood that the testimony against modern idolatry derives its religious inspiration from literal worship, not from "worship"; and that this worship is not of "God" but of God.

Chapter 5

EXISTENTIALIST
FINALE—
AND BEGINNING

In the mid-nineteenth century Søren Kierkegaard expressed the insight, at once philosophical and antiphilosophical, that there are areas in which thought may not "abstract from existence" if it is to get at the truth. Such a philosophical procedure, he conceded, has a serious motive, for a thinker must abstract from his own existence in order to become objective, and from that of his object in order to find universality in it. He went on to insist, however, that in some regions, this stratagem is foredoomed to failure. Here the thinker must not flee from but rather stay with *his own* existence in all its uniqueness if the Other is not to escape him. And he must be open to the Other in *its* (or *his*) existential uniqueness even if his goal is universality.

In all its many forms twentieth-century existentialism has stayed with this Kierkegaardian insight. Given this fact, we are led to expect that the encounter between Judaism and modern philosophy that earlier in this book we were required to bring about is, in this case, already a full-blown reality. Even Hegel already has an encounter with Judaism in his own right, so that all that remained for us was to confront his image of Jewish history with actual Jewish history. In the present case, we are disposed to find an existentialism open to Jewish existence, a Jewish existentialism that takes its stand on Jewish existence, and a dialogue between the two already so fruitful that our own task is merely to look on.

Even an existentialist, to be sure, can hardly be open to all forms of existence, however unique. Thus Kierkegaard himself is so wholly geared to the one task of becoming a Christian that the Jew at his highest (that is, Abraham) becomes a proto-Christian and nothing else. However, to expect existentialist openness to Jewish existence in this century is hardly to expect the impossible, when events have occurred in it of which Kierkegaard could not have dreamt.

To look for a Jewish existentialism is nothing more than to take Kierkegaard's insight seriously. Unlike the spectator of detached thought, the existential thinker is not man-in-general but rather a particular man. If he is a Jew, he is therefore a Jewish particular man. And one must then demand that he will not evade this particularity whenever and wherever it is at stake; indeed, that he will heed the general existentialist maxim, and test in the light of his Jewish particularity any universal that might come on the scene and challenge it. Such a testing might well spell the end of that long tutelage of modern Jewish to modern philosophical thought that has necessitated the present work. Its effect might be to liberate Jewish thought for a task awaiting it in the modern world.

That the second of these expectations has been partly fulfilled has been evident throughout the present work. (Indeed, without the inspiration and the pioneering accomplishments of Martin Buber and Franz Rosenzweig it could not have been written.) The same, however, cannot be said of the first expectation. In the age in which all existentialism should have become open to Jewish existence, its morally most involved representative has failed to do it justice, while its philosophically most profound representative has ignored it altogether. Though itself far from abstractly universalistic, existentialism here and elsewhere suddenly becomes so when Jewish existence is at stake; and the result is that, superficial impressions to the contrary notwithstanding, we are left, in the decisive points, not with the expected dialogical mutuality but rather with two solitudes. Jean Paul Sartre and Martin Heidegger have been on one side, Martin Buber and Franz Rosenzweig, on the other, and attempts to bridge the gulf have all been on one side.[1]

Thus this book cannot end with the hoped-for accord but only on a note of discord. The expected climax will become an anti-climax. Our series of encounters has followed an order of increasing depth and fruitfulness. It ought to culminate with existentialism. Committed to openness to existential uniqueness, this philosophy should be open to Jewish uniqueness. It has therefore a rare opportunity, and hence the obligation, to make an end of the anti-Judaic bias that has vitiated modern philosophy too deeply and too long. One may hope that it may yet grasp this opportunity. One must judge that thus far it has failed. To use an existentialist phrase, it has been, of a sorry tale, the tragic finale.

SARTRE

In 1944 some of the French-Jewish survivors who returned yearned to tell the tale. They experienced difficulty in finding publishers. "There has been too much hate," they were told. "Let's have a love story."² In this situation *Anti-Semite and Jew* was written and published. The mere act of writing and publishing this book was thus an act of courage, decency and friendship for a remnant much in need of friendship. The book appeared in 1946. As early as 1944 J. P. Sartre wrote:

Today those Jews whom the Germans did not deport or murder are coming back to their homes. Many were among the first members of the Resistance; others had sons or cousins in Leclerc's army. Now all France rejoices and fraternizes in the streets; social conflicts seem temporarily forgotten; the newspapers devote whole columns to stories of prisoners of war and deportees. *Do we say anything about the Jews? Do we give a thought to those who died in the gas chambers of Lublin? Not a word. Not a line in the newspapers. That is because we must not irritate the anti-Semites;* more than ever, we need unity. Well-meaning journalists will tell you: "In the interest of the Jews themselves, it would not do to talk too much about them just now." For four years French society has lived without them; it is just as well not to emphasize too vigorously the fact that they have reappeared.³

The first goal of the book, then, is to expose the Jewish situation in postwar France, a situation that, as the author grimly discovers, is the joint work of relentless antisemitic enemies and half-hearted "democratic" friends.

What is antisemitism? It "does not fall into the category of ideas protected by the right of free opinion." A "passion" rather than an "opinion," it is the passion of hate. The passion in question, moreover, is not geared to an object—in this case, real or imagined Jewish faults. It is a passion that the antisemite has chosen, which is why "we are forced to conclude that it is the *state* of passion that he loves." And of this particular state it must be said that it permeates its possessor's entire being.

What if . . . [the antisemite] is like that only with regard to Jews? What if otherwise he conducts himself with good sense? I reply that this is impossible. There is the case of a fishmonger who, in 1942, annoyed by the competition of two Jewish fishmongers who were concealing their race, one fine day took pen in hand and denounced them. I have been assured that this fishmonger was in other respects a mild and jovial man, the best of sons. But I don't believe it. A man who finds it entirely natural to denounce other men cannot have our conception of humanity; he does not see even those he aids in the same light as we do. His generosity, his kindness are not like our kindness, our generosity. You cannot confine passion to one sphere.[4]

An example such as this will provoke protests from all sides. What of genteel antisemitism? What of antisemitism that does not deserve this title at all but rather is sound criticism of real Jewish faults? Sartre disposes of all such protests. He has already shown that antisemitism loves hate itself and is quite unrelated to Jewish faults, real or imagined. He adds that there is no such thing as "genteel" antisemitism, for though well aware that antisemitism has degrees, he insists that, here as elsewhere, extremity discloses truth. Hence this portrayal:

A destroyer in function, a sadist with a pure heart, the anti-Semite is, in the very depth of his heart, a criminal. What he wishes, what he prepared, is the *death* of the Jew.[5]

But why should a man choose passion for passion's sake? How can he make the state of passion—that of hate!—into a total way of being? Finally, why should and how can this state, its lack of object notwithstanding, nevertheless single out the Jew as its victim? Questions such as these are ultimately philosophical, and in Sartre's own answers well-known Sartrean philosophical notions are unmistakable. Human existence is not a given fact but rather a situated "project." The project is that of a situated nobody who may choose to make himself an "authentic" somebody, but who may also have recourse to "unauthentic" flight. To choose the first is to choose a fragile and uncertain humanity. The antisemite, however, "in fear of the human condition," shrinks from this choice of uncertain affirmation and instead flees into the choice of certain negation. Choosing the nonhuman, which may be denied absolutely instead of the human, which can be affirmed only relatively, fragmentarily, and dangerously, he reveals himself as a Manichean who would destroy evil and indeed *is* this act of destruction, in order that good may come of itself. To realize his own negativity, he only needs a victim. This he finds in the Jew. Why the Jew? He "only serves . . . as a pretext; elsewhere his counterpart will make use of the Negro or the man with the yellow skin."[6] The French antisemite, then, is an antisemite only because none but the Jewish victim is available. And if even this victim were not available, he would have to invent one. Indeed, in a sense he *in fact* invents one. For this mythical Jew and the actual Jew have nothing in common.

So much for one component of the French Jewish situation in 1946—the Jew's implacable enemy. The other is his half-hearted "democratic" friend. Whereas "the antisemite has only one enemy, and he can think of him all the time," the "democrat has much to do; he concerns himself with the Jew when he has the time." Having "passionate enemies," the Jew has only "defenders lacking in passion," a lack ultimately due to the fact that, while the antisemite hates the Jew as Jew, the "democrat" defends him only as a man. Joining the two together, Sartre comes to define the French Jewish situation as follows:

[The antisemite] wishes to destroy [the Jew] . . . as a man and leave nothing in him but the Jew, the pariah, the untouchable. [The "democrat"] . . . wishes to destroy him as a Jew and leave nothing in him but the man, the abstract and universal subject of the rights of man and the rights of the citizen.

The anti-Semite reproaches the Jew with *being* Jewish; the democrat reproaches him with wilfully *considering himself a Jew.*[7]

What the Jew might do and be within this situation remains to be seen. (This is the second goal of Sartre's book.) The situation itself, in any case, has no exit.

Without doubt this account succeeds in exposing prevalent myths about antisemite and "democrat" alike. (To name but the two most important: the myth that antisemitism is either caused by Jewish vices or curable by Jewish virtues, and the myth that "democratic" friendship for the Jew merely as a man is an adequate response to antisemitism.) At the same time, it is evident without any further inquiry that Sartre fails to identify the uniqueness both of antisemitism and the half-heartedness of the "democratic" opposition. The racist, projecting his hate on the black man or the yellow man, wants to keep his victims in a permanent state of subjection. The antisemite, projecting *his* hate on the Jew, aims at murder, and has reached his aim unsurpassably in our own time.[8] The "democrat," defending black men or yellow men "as men," will surrender this half-heartedness (albeit reluctantly) when confronted by militancy in his victims. However, no amount of Jewish militancy will persuade Sartre's "democrat" to stop reproaching the Jew "with wilfully considering himself a Jew." When the chips are down, the Jew, and no one else, is required by him to be and remain a man-in-general.[9]

To account for these failures, it is not enough to point to the obvious and freely admitted French parochialism in Sartre's account. (Even in the France of 1946 potential victims other than Jews were surely available. Moreover, if the French antisemite then, like his English counterpart in the Middle Ages when no Jews lived in England, requires actual Jews no more than actual Jewish vices to realize his hate, why not invent a mythical enemy, such as nameless conspirators against· *la patrie?*) A recourse to philosophical notions is clearly required, moving somewhat beyond those already given. Condemned to be free, Sartrean man is condemned because situated by forces *absolutely outside* his control, and free because forced to choose *absolutely inside* the conditions of his situatedness. A radical dualism thus manifests itself: for his situation a man is wholly nonresponsible, for he can neither alter it nor escape from it; for his own *very being* within the situation he is wholly responsible, for what he is and will be is wholly his own "project." This dualism has its ground in a Cartesian individualism in Sartre's existentialism whose extremity is matched by no other existentialist.[10]

One might consider the virtues and vices of this dualism in general philosophical terms. (Among the more obvious virtues: the emphasis on decision within the situation and the rejection of escape either into abstract universality or into the utopian future; among the more obvious vices: the refusal to accept any responsibility whatever for a situation that may well be alterable by collective if not individual action, and the ascription of total responsibility for his own being to the human individual who was a child before he attained adult freedom.) For the present purpose, it is more telling (as well as more economical) to test these concepts at once by the facts to which they are applied. Is Sartre open to the reality of antisemitism and "democratic" half-heartedness? Or does he commit the sin, cardinal in an existentialist, of letting abstract concepts come between him and the reality which is to be confronted?

The answer is hardly in doubt. Sartre's notions do come between him and the reality, if only because they cut off the existential present from its historical past.[11] Sartre's antisemite is antisemitic only accidentally, and the passion of hate is his total being. The actual French antisemite is antisemitic essentially, and hate is not necessarily his whole being if only because he is heir to a tradition that was able to combine Jew-hatred with genuine Christian piety. Sartre's French "democrat" is merely lacking in passion. The actual French "democrat" is an antisemite of a different kind

—the kind who was prepared, ever since the French Revolution, to give Jews as men everything only on condition of giving to them, as Jews, nothing.

Reality is thus distorted. So is the moral perspective. On the one hand, Sartre holds antisemites and "democrats" *wholly* responsible, as if there were no antisemitic children. On the other hand, he implies that a tradition that has produced passionate antisemites and half-hearted "democrats" is a "situation" that must be, and in the end can only be, accepted. Of Sartre's failures, the last-named is the most serious. For the only possible moral response to the Nazi holocaust is to call for a revolutionary end to any and all antisemitism.[12]

Sartre thus fails at least partly to confront the actual Jewish situation, even if it is narrowed down to the France of 1946. His failure to confront the Jew himself is complete. Having exposed the anti-Semite's "Jew" as a myth, we shall now find him replace that myth with a myth of his own. And the cause, as before, is that concepts come between him and reality.

Who is the Sartrean Jew? A man *defined* as Jew by a situation created by passionate enemies and half-hearted friends. This is true of "unauthentic" and "authentic" Jew alike. All that the first is or tries to be—something general such as rationalist, lover of mankind, or the like, or something specific such as mathematician, musician, or dedicated social worker—is *nothing but* an unauthentic flight from the singled out Jewish condition as defined by his enemies. As for the authentic Jew, he

. . . knows himself and wills himself into history as a historic and damned creature. . . . He knows that he is one who stands apart, scorned, proscribed—and it is *as such* that he asserts his being.[13]

Not only is he unable to alter or escape from his situation. (This is presumably the reason why Jewish militancy, Zionist or other, has no important role in this book.) To go a vast step further, even within the limits of his situation the Jew, however authentic, has no freedom beyond proud and defiant acceptance of his own "damnation." His Jewishness has and can have no other content.

This definition of Jewish existence is so extraordinary that no serious author could offer it without factual support. What is offered in this case as factual support, however, are assertions themselves so extraordinary that one must ask why they should be considered factual. The Jewish people is not "a concrete historical community [which] is basically *national* and *religious*." On the contrary, are not the Jews the only community still extant in the

West in which these characteristics are authentically intertwined? "If it is true, as Hegel says, that a community is historical to the degree that it remembers its history, then the Jewish community is the least historical of all, for it keeps a memory of nothing but martyrdom, that is, of a long passivity." By Hegel's standard, is the Jewish community not the most historical? For two millennia it has existed on nothing but memory (and a hope nourished by it), and the memory has included so many things beside "passivity" as in the end to make possible the unprecedented feat of a resurrected nation. "Jews cannot take pride in any collective work that is specifically Jewish, or in any civilization properly Jewish, or in a common mysticism."[14] Of all the assertions cited, this is the most extraordinary. Where else in the West could one find a history of "collective work," "civilization," or "mysticism" that, despite adversity, has been so long, so unbroken, so unique, so alive?

To explain these assertions we must, as before, go beyond Sartre's French parochialism, and this despite the fact that it is his recourse to thorough-going French-Jewish assimilationists that lends them a semblance of plausibility. For how could random references to these lead to a definition of Jewish existence that renders marginal the militant Jew who takes up arms against his enemies, that rules out the Yiddishist Jew who takes notice of his enemies for his safety but not for his identity, and that rules out most of all the religious Jew who knows that the "damned," if anyone, are the murderers and would-be murderers and not their victims?

In a staunch friend of the Jewish people and a staunch foe of their enemies, only a philosophical failure can furnish the answer. And we have, in fact, no difficulty rediscovering concepts already discovered. Once again there is the situation that defines and is unalterable and inescapable. Once again there is the individual defined, radically free vis-à-vis his situation but otherwise empty. Above all there is once again the divorce from history. If in Sartre's scheme, the Jew is cut off from *his* history (just as antisemite and "democrat" are cut off from *theirs*), it is not as a matter of empirical fact but rather as a matter of philosophical fiat. However, whereas the antisemite would turn racist if there were no Jews, the Jew, were there no antisemites, would simply vanish.

To these concepts already mentioned another must now be added. Unlike most other history, Jewish history has been for two millennia an unequivocally *religious* history, and for Sartre religiosity and authenticity are incompatible. In his well-known view, an individual's freedom is limited by the human other; it would be destroyed by a *divine* Other; and atheism is necessary if authentic freedom is to be possible. His authentic individual, to be sure, is cut off from history. He would have to turn against religious history even if he had otherwise access to history.[15] Here may well lie the ultimate reason why Sartre would have to cut off the Jew from his history even if black men and yellow men can remain with theirs. We are not told in this context what authentic choices are open for black men and yellow men. The authentic choices open to the Jew, at any rate, are but two. In case antisemitism persists, he can only "will himself into history," as "damned." In case for some cause antisemitism will vanish, he will, to be sure, accept himself as damned no more. (No authentic man is a masochist.) The price paid for such authenticity, however, is that he then *wills himself out of history*. Such are the lamentable consequences of an existentialism that permits preconceived notions to come between the confronting thinker and the reality that is to be confronted.

So much for the Sartre of 1946. Much has happened between then and now in Sartre's thought. Considerably more has happened in the course of Jewish events. It is necessary to ask whether detachment from the grim days of 1946, subsequent philosophical reflection, the events in Jewish history, or a combination of all these factors has led to an authentic confrontation with Jewish existence on Sartre's part.

In March 1967 Sartre visited Israel and subsequently gave a remarkable interview. Most remarkable of all is what he himself, presumably not accidentally, refers to as his "first impression."

The first impression, I may say, is that Israel is the only country where one can say of someone that he is a Jew without being an anti-Semite. Back home, when I am told that a certain professor, for instance, is a Jew, I say to myself: Well, the man who says that must be something of an anti-Semite. Now here, someone may say: You've known Jean Kelevich at the Sorbonne, haven't you? Well, he's a Jew—and that is not anti-Semitism any more. By the way, this may spoil me. When I'm home again, I will perhaps say that Jean Kelevich is a Jew, and then it will be my turn to be called an anti-Semite.

But that, at any rate, is the first impression, and I must tell you that it is something of a liberation—not only evidence of your liberation, but a liberation for the non-Jew himself.[16]

What a shocking admission, 20 years after, if not about the world, at any rate about France! And what an altogether extraordinary tribute to Israel! It is certainly extraordinary from Sartre's

lips, for it says nothing less than that the "Jewish situation," considered virtually immutable in 1946, has been swept
aside by the fact of Israel. Indeed, all the other preconceptions are
swept aside as well. Gone is the Jew who is defined as Jew by
other people. Gone is the man who is without tradition, history,
and a common collective work in the past, for without all of these
the fact of Israel would be an incomprehensible *creatio ex nihilo*.
Gone is a fatal alternative for the non-Jew as well. The French
gentile of 1946 seemed to have little choice except passionate hate
for the Jew as Jew or "democratic" defense of him as a man, and
it will be recalled that the antisemite then was a "criminal," while
the "democrat" was not much of a man. Now we find the French
Gentile "liberated" from this fatal alternative—in Israel if nowhere
else. Thus all the previous preconceptions have disappeared without a trace. Or so it seems.

Later in the interview Sartre himself makes some of the points
which we have just made in his behalf. Thus whereas the Jew
of 1946 was a man without history, there is now in many Jews
"a depth which is historical," and, indeed, "a will to preserve the
historical tradition in its deepest sense" which exceeds that of
Frenchmen. Of Jewish tradition, Sartre has this to say:

When I came away, I did not know what Jewish tradition was, but I
did know that most of the Jews who came here were deeply attached
to something—we would have needed much longer to bring out what
that something was, but all the same it was a tradition.[17]

Only at a single point in the entire interview preconceptions
seem to come to the surface, and even here it is not clear where
the trouble lies. As a moralist, Sartre recognizes the "tragic" conflict between two rights, the "recognition of Israel's sovereignty"
and "the right of the Palestinian refugees to return to Israel." As
an existentialist, he recognizes that "neutrality is something that is
not really possible in a problem of this kind." Yet though himself
forced to list no less than four reasons that make the recognition
of both rights a political impossibility, he nevertheless claims the
right, as an "intellectual" (i.e., a moralist), to endorse both rights,
leaving to "the politicians" the task of making the impossible possible.[18] It is not clear, we say, exactly where the trouble lies. Unfortunately it will become clear soon enough.

The interview just cited preceded the Six-Day War. Soon after-
wards former friends were to turn into enemies overnight. Sartre,
though far from joining their number, was too weak in his newly
won insight to be sustained in the novel situation. Back in 1946

he had written that it would be a lazy solution to wait for the future revolution to take care of the "Jewish question." Reminding him of this earlier admission, a new interviewer asked him whether he now espoused Zionism.[19] Sartre answered in the negative. The right of Israel to exist was one thing, and the right of Jews to move to that country was part of it. Zionism, however, was another thing. It was the active encouragement of Jewish immigration to Israel. In France and the United States (where all Jews wishing to go to Israel had already done so) this encouragement was bound to fail. In the "socialist" countries, "jealous" as they were of their "sovereignty," it might create "communities of dual affiliation," and this in turn meant nothing less than "encouraging anti-Semitism." Soviet or Rumanian citizens, "even now only too much tempted by anti-Semitism," were bound to feel that Jews of dual affiliation were "non-loyal." What is more, their respective governments would "look on them with hostility, saying that from the moment they choose or can choose Israel, they are not socialists." Whether these governments were "wrong or right" in showing such hostility, Sartre professed not to know.[20]

What a depressing lapse from the insights of March 1967, and, indeed, even from those of 1946! (Were the insights of March 1967 ever real?) Sartre would not deny black men or yellow men or Algerians the right to liberate their brethren from a colonial or slave mentality. Why does he deny "Zionists" the right to liberate fellow Jews from a false peace with an environment in which, if Sartre himself is to be believed, "Jew" is a dirty word?

This double standard might be excusable on the grounds of "political" necessity, and indeed we find Sartre argue that large scale Jewish immigration into Israel would require "territorial annexations."[21] He cannot, however, both prior to the Six-Day War demand on "intellectual" (i.e., moral) grounds the "politically" impossible, and, thereafter, deny on "political" grounds what experience has proved to be far from impossible. (The argument from the "absorptive capacity of Palestine," as advanced at the cost of countless Jewish lives by the antisemites of the British colonial office in the 1930s, lies in the dustbin of history.) Sartre's case, if advanced on "political" grounds, would be a clear case of mauvaise foi.

We must therefore seek its "intellectual" grounds, which in any case are its essence. Why is Jewish "dual affiliation" wrong in countries "tempted by anti-Semitism"? Sartre states that "violent anti-Semitism which would make the situation of the Jews intolerable cannot exist in the foreseeable future."[22] The validity of this prediction aside (and, for that matter, what is and is not "violent" antisemitism) why is any Jew anywhere morally required to tolerate any antisemitism whatever? Sartre relapses into his definition of 1946 with his declaration that "if someone is a Zionist, he isn't a leftist, because he wants a state built on race."[23] Indeed, he forgets what he knew in 1946—that antisemitism has no cause in Jewish behavior. For now it seems that—in "socialist" countries at least—Jews can "encourage" it.

One is tempted to associate these moral confusions and double standards with current ideologies. It is preferable to give a philosopher his due and seek out his own philosophical conceptions. Concerning the earlier Sartre one may say, in sum, that just as the man of *Being and Nothingness* is defined by the hostile glance of others, so the Jew of *Antisemite and Jew* is defined by the hostility of the antisemites.[24] (That Jews do not define themselves in this way, and that Sartre's Jewish fellow-existentialist Buber does not define man in this way, are facts disregarded.) Concerning the later Sartre we may say that, having converted his Cartesian into a Marxist existentialism, he is now open to community, and also that the State of Israel has left its mark, but that to *Jewish* community he is as closed as he ever was. To be sure, on account of Israel Jews are no longer a nonpeople. They are now, however, what may be called a half-people, that is, a people when inside Israel and, outside Israel, as much a nonpeople as ever. Frenchmen can be both French and socialist, and the same is true of Russians, Algerians, black men, and yellow men. Then why is a "Zionist" guilty of "wanting a state built on race" when he wants no more than to liberate his fellow-Jews from antisemitism? Ultimately, it seems, because outside Israel the "authentic" Jew still has two choices only. Given antisemitism, he must "will himself into history," as "damned." Given the absence of antisemitism, he must reject "damnation"—and vanish. Where does this leave Jean Kelevich? And where does it leave his colleague Sartre, who must consider him either a Jew or a man?

Why does even the later Sartrean scheme of things have no room for Jewish community? Perhaps we can find a clue in an admission of his cited earlier. In March 1967 Sartre said that he knew a Jewish tradition existed, but did not know what it was. This admission, while admirably frank, should not be taken at face value. After all, no scholarly expertise but only imagination was required. Sartre, not lacking in imagination, expressed bafflement rather than ignorance. And what baffled him was a tradition that is religious in nature, yet so far from being mere "passivity" as to have made possible the survival of the Jewish people against over-whelming odds and, in the end, to have had an indispensable share in its liberation. Sartre, in short, is baffled by Judaism.

This turn of the argument may seem to call for a move into the religious dimension of Sartre's thought. For three reasons, however, it is wise to pursue a different course. First, it is never entirely clear just how close a connection exists between Sartre's philosophy and his sociopolitical judgments, the above attempt to connect the two notwithstanding. Second, Sartre's atheism fails to pass beyond, and in some respects falls below, left-wing Hegelian atheism, and the argument of the present work would not be advanced by considering it.[25] Third, if we wish to confront Judaism with an existentialist concern with the Divine, we are obliged to seek out that concern where it has proved to be most profound.

HEIDEGGER

Without doubt the deepest and most compelling account of the human condition offered by a twentieth-century existential philosopher is Martin Heidegger's *Being and Time*[26]—deepest because uniting the most relentless rejection of any (philosophical or religious) escape into "eternity" with the most radical emphasis on human "temporality," that is, its being-toward-death; most compelling because disposing most convincingly of the possibility that, rather than describe "the" human condition, it might describe only *one particular* human condition. Long before Heidegger, a variety of philosophies were forced to deal with "historicism," that is, with the doctrine that human existence has historical limitations so radical that philosophy itself can only reflect and not transcend them. *Being and Time* confronts that doctrine radically and—so it seems—refutes it.[27] Hence if any existentialist work can ever tempt a Jewish thinker to inquire first into "the" human condition, in order only thereafter and in the light of that first inquiry to consider the Jewish condition, that work is *Being and Time*.[28]

Nor is that temptation diminished greatly, or even at all, by the insight, fairly obvious and arrived at independently in many quarters, that the human condition as described in *Being and Time* bears an extraordinary resemblance to Christian descriptions such as those given by St. Paul, St. Augustine, Martin Luther, and Søren Kierkegaard.[29] The work does not of course focus on the truism that man must die. It focuses on his *knowledge* that he must die, or, more accurately, on the distinction between two kinds of "knowledge," i.e., the "unauthentic," which vainly seeks escape from the truth, and the "authentic," which confronts it. To be more precise still, both kinds of "knowledge" are "existential" instead of merely detached and "objective." And it is this existential characteristic that lends "authentic" knowledge—care, anxiety, guilt and the *memento mori* itself—its resemblance to Christian descriptions. But does this description resemble Christian descriptions alone? (It is, in any case, not Christian proper because man as described in *Being and Time* remains without access to God.) It was, after all, a Jewish sage who observed that a man should repent a day before his death and, not knowing its date, every day.[30]

A more than ordinary persistence (philosophical, Jewish, or both) is therefore required if the universality of the account given in *Being and Time* is nevertheless to be called into question. Beginning with philosophical persistence if only because it antedates Jewish persistence in our own development,[31] we ask: what are the grounds on which the possibility of an "authentic" pagan-Stoic suicide is ruled out?[32] A sweeping denial of either the honesty or the courage of each and every Stoic is clearly impossible; yet far from remaining with existential anxiety, the Stoic rejects and in his own eyes overcomes it. By what standards is his "overcoming," nevertheless, an "unauthentic" escape?

The author of *Being and Time* is too reflective a thinker to give the inconsistent reply: by the standards of a philosophical thought that transcends the limitations of the human condition. "Ontology" —within the limited context of *Being and Time*, the interpretation of human existence as a whole—is itself rooted "ontically," that is, in a particular and limited human existence. And if nevertheless an "ontological" grasp of the totality of authentic human possibilities is an achievement of which human existence is capable, it is only because all "ontic" human existence already has an "ontological" dimension. To call its own being-in-the-world-as-a-whole into question is an intrinsic part of it. This, to be sure, involves a "circle," for the "ontological" interpretation given in *Being and Time* already rests on an "ontic" understanding that is "authentic," while at the same time only that interpretation can provide the criteria for a possible distinction between authenticity and unauthenticity. However, Heidegger denies that this circle is fatal and goes to great lengths and into intricate distinctions to corroborate his denial.[33]

Yet, intricate distinctions or no distinctions at all, why should the Stoic surrender to the Heideggerian circle? There exists a German philosophical tradition of disposing lightly of Stoicism. Unlike at least some of his predecessors, the Heidegger of *Being and Time* would appear to have no legitimate grounds for any such disposal.[34] And this one case suffices to give rise to the possibility that the human condition as described in *Being and Time*, the description itself included, is not, after all, "the" human condition, but rather at best only one human condition among others.

The ancient Greek example having been cited for purely philosophical reasons, it would appear to be not illegitimate to cite an ancient Jewish example for reasons that are no longer philosophical alone. When Abraham died, Scripture tells us, he was of "good ripe age, old and contented," and his contentment was due to the knowledge that Isaac would live (Gen. 25:8). To be sure, it might be objected that this Abraham, unlike the Stoic, is a mere myth, and, moreover, that the knowledge that gives him contentment derives from a God who, so far as *Being and Time* is concerned, is either absent or nonexistent. However, the biblical Abraham has had many Jewish successors who were not mythical; and, at least since the Nazi holocaust, we must include in their number some Jews who do not or cannot believe in God. By what right do we deny authenticity to individuals who are individuated (and thus rendered authentic) not by their own being-toward-death, but rather (if a singling out call of God must be ruled out) by a concern for others, the concern for a son or daughter being, perhaps, the most individuating of all?

To this question the author of *Being and Time* (who, unlike the author of *Being and Nothingness*, shows enough existential openness to recognize an original *Mitsein*, or being-with-others) would doubtless reply that an authentic being-toward-death is the paramount condition without which an authentic concern for others is impossible. This reply, however, rather than allay our suspicion that "the" human condition of *Being and Time* is but one particular human condition, would only lead us to suspect further that this particular human condition is in fact what may be called a post-Christian condition. Assuredly it is not Christian, for a recourse to God is ruled out. But could it be that it is post-Christian because, like Paul and Christians who follow his example, its authentic man *is* authentic toward others because he faces authentically his own death, whereas Abraham faces his own death authentically because he stands in an authentic relation to Isaac? (It must be stressed that this remains true even if Abraham stands related to God, for this God promises only life for Isaac, not immortality for Abraham himself.) Should this question require an affirmative answer, we would be required to conclude that "the" human condition of *Being and Time* has even limited (i.e., modern Western) universality only on the assumption that the post-Christian condition is a universal modern Western condition or, to be more specific, that Heidegger's post-Christian condition is ipso facto also a post-Jewish condition. And if we should be unprepared to accept this assumption without a murmur of protest it would then follow that even the posture of *Being and Time* toward the Divine becomes radically questionable if it were to advance universal claims.[35]

In view of the admitted philosophical rigor of *Being and Time*, we are well advised to remain tentative with doubts that would call the work radically and *in toto* into question. By the same token, however, we must inquire closely into possible lapses from philosophical rigor. We detect at least one such lapse, and shall single it out for inspection because subsequent events proved it to be of catastrophic consequence.

We have already noted that the Heidegger of *Being and Time*, unlike the Sartre of *Being and Nothingness*, is no abstract individualist. Thus, turning from abstract "temporality" to concrete "historicity," he comes upon the notions of a shared anticipated future and a shared past that must be recovered if it is to become an authentic heritage.[36] It is in this context, otherwise full of immensely fruitful insights, that the lapse occurs that we must single out for inspection. Without doubt authentic historicity can only belong to a "community." This community, however, is at once identified with the *Volk*. No justification is offered for this identification. There is not even a single word explaining the meaning of the term. Nor does the word seem to occur anywhere else in the entire work. The identification, in short, is entirely unexamined, and accepted as if it were self-evident.[37]

Being and Time was completed in 1926. Seven years later Heidegger not only became a Nazi but gave Nazism his philosophical endorsement. The controversy that resulted over these events has not yet ended and may never be resolved. No serious critic or defender can leave the philosophy untouched by the device of blaming the man alone. And the possible positions in the controversy lie between the extremes that something in Heidegger's philosophy "compelled" a surrender to Nazism and that it was "unable to prevent" that surrender.[38]

On our part, we have no wish to contribute to the controversy.

To the extent to which involvement is inescapable, we shall exercise restraint, on the one hand, in order not to dismiss *in toto* what after all, remains one of the profoundest philosophies of this century and, on the other hand, in order to identify as exactly as may be possible a philosophical failure that can *only* be rejected *in toto*. In attempting to reach such exactitude, we shall move from the extremes of the controversy into the middle.

"The *Führer* himself and alone is the present and future German reality and its law."[39] Even the stoutest defender must concede that this statement, explicitly and deliberately given a philosophical formulation, reflects a failing in Heidegger's philosophy more serious than an "inability to prevent" a surrender to Nazism, It is a statement that was made "to the shame of philosophy"[40]—indeed, if one takes Heidegger to be a great figure in philosophy, to its everlasting shame. Yet one would like to believe the defenders when they assert that Heidegger's Nazism was short-lived, that his break with the Nazi regime occurred over antisemitism, and indeed that his "first official act as Rector . . . [was] to ban anti-Semitic propaganda from the campus."[41] We ask: if this is true, how could a Heidegger principled and courageous enough to perform the acts with which his defenders credit him ever make a statement for which there was no sort of external compulsion, and which means nothing less than that *no* principle, apart from the *Führer*'s will, has any kind of validity?[42]

If we take Heidegger seriously philosophically we must seek a philosophical answer, and it is not impossible that it lies in the lapse to which we have referred. A "community" geared to a common future and recovering a common heritage might take a variety of forms. To give one example, it might, among Jews between 70 C.E. and the rise of the State of Israel, take the form of a Diaspora without a common language or geography. To give another, it might, among Germans under the Hitler regime, take the form of a resistance movement with a common geography only of concentration camp and the world outside Germany. A *Volk*, in contrast, lacks this capacity for variety, and if the term remains totally undefined it is prey to all the perversions that had been common among Heidegger's countrymen long before Nazism ever came into power. We therefore tentatively conclude that a single philosophical lapse in *Being and Time* sufficed to produce two cardinal philosophical sins. It ruled out in principle the possibility that Jews constitute any sort of authentic community. And it produced philosophical surrender when the shout reverberated throughout Germany: *"Ein Volk, ein Reich, ein Führer."*

If the conclusion just reached must remain tentative and is offered only for what it is worth, it is not only because we must avoid a fuller discussion of the subject "Heidegger and Nazism," as leading us astray from our own task. A further reason must be adduced. We have thus far treated *Being and Time* as an account of the human condition. In Heidegger's own intention, however, this account was all along preparatory to a renewal of the ancient philosophical inquiry into Being, and in 1933 he had already passed beyond that preparatory stage. Whether this description of the state of affairs is accurate is debatable, for a controversy exists as to whether the famous *Kehre* from the earlier author of *Being and Time* and the later *Denker*-on-the-road-to-Being represents an abandonment, not to say betrayal, of the earlier project or rather, as the author himself would have us believe, its proper fulfillment. This controversy, like that referred to earlier in this account, must be left for those to settle whose goal is Heidegger scholarship. Our own present task emerges with the insight that, whatever the relation between the early and the late Heidegger, the power of the work of the later *Denker* to captivate the Jewish thinker far exceeds that even of *Being and Time*.

Earlier in this book the theme "Athens and Jerusalem" was described as being well-nigh inexhaustible.[43] As an existentialist version of that theme one might offer the view, occasionally expressed by Martin Buber, that whereas ever since Plato philosophers "see," ever since Moses Jews "hear." With this view in mind, one may well consider the later Heidegger to be engaged in no less startling an enterprise than the Judaization of the entire history of Western philosophy. For that whole history, we are now told, is a lapse from an original "hearing" into a derivative "seeing." At least from Plato to Nietzsche there has been a fateful yet inevitable falling away from an original *Denken*-of-Being—fateful because it manifests a *Seinsvergessenheit* and inevitable because it manifests a *Seinsverlassenheit*. As for the recognition of that condition, this is possible only for one who himself is in the process of transcending it. Thus the later Heidegger is turning from a philosopher into a *Denker*.

This turning is the sole, albeit many-sided, theme of Heidegger's entire later work. Our present purpose permits a brief summary. Being is not Water, the Good, Matter, Spirit, or the like. It is a *Presence*. This Presence does not dwell in timelessness but rather manifests itself in history. Truth, therefore, is primordially unconcealedness. (Only derivatively is truth a characteristic of statements made by subjects about objects; originally it precedes or

[218]

overcomes the subject-object dichotomy, and thus also the truth proper to that dichotomy.) This unconcealedness is accessible to an original "thinking," which is a "hearing" rather than a "seeing," and which, include as it does the whole being of the thinker, is a "thanking" as well. So much for the necessary summary. It suffices to give prima facie evidence to the view that the later Heidegger Judaizes philosophy, and hence also to the view that the Jewish thinker is justified in being attracted to his later thought.

Whether this Judaization is actual and the attraction in fact justified remains to be seen. Two things, in any case, are not in doubt. Heidegger's assertions are startling and unheard of from the lips of the philosopher; however, provided one may change the vocabulary, they are neither startling nor unheard of from the lips of a biblical theologian. May one change the vocabulary? Or must, perhaps, theology in this time change its own vocabulary? Much contemporary Christian thought finds it necessary to free itself from traditional Greek modes of thought. In this effort it has not failed to note that Heidegger far transcends the superficialities of Sartre's atheism. Hence, however the question of the vocabulary may have to be answered, it is not surprising that a whole school of Christian theology has arisen that looks to the later Heidegger as the source from which its own salvation comes.

Under these circumstances, it was an historic event, at once ironical and appropriate, when a Jew and admitted "mere child of the world" appeared before a group of Christian Heideggerians in order to expose the radically pagan character of Heidegger's later thought. (The irony is obvious. The appropriateness will become so shortly.) Admitting at once the Judeo-Christian relevance of Heidegger's later "nonobjectifying" thinking (that is, its commitment to "primal hearing" rather than "primal seeing"), the speaker pointed out Christian elements that Heideggerian thought, both early and later, had appropriated from Christian theology from the start, and that any Christian theologian who now wished to reappropriate what Heidegger's thought had appropriated could not avoid the question: "what have you done with my little ones?"[44] On his part, the speaker was in no doubt as to the correct answer. Heidegger's primal thinking is not neutral to Christianity. It is not an atheistic enemy. It is a pagan rival.

How can we tell the one from the other? It is not a matter of vocabulary only when it is "Being" that "speaks" to Heideggerian thought. The God of the Judeo-Christian tradition is other than the world and speaks into it. The Heideggerian Being—the so-called "ontological difference" notwithstanding—is in and of the world *only*. To theologians in any case dubious about "transcendence," this may be a matter of small moment. The speaker showed, however, just how momentous this matter is even for a mere child of the world. Where Heidegger's Being speaks, "the gods," considered long dead, necessarily reappear, and "where the gods are, God cannot be." Why not? For one crucial reason if no other. Where "the gods" are, a *radical* "No" to *false* gods is in principle impossible.[45] In Heidegger's later and possibly also in his earlier thought, between the possibilities of "presence" and "absence" of "the Divine," the very possibility of idolatry has in principle disappeared. This may well be the ultimate ground for Heidegger's surrender to Nazism. It is in any case what makes a Jewish warning to Christian Heideggerians appropriate. For what open-minded Jew, however "worldly," does not in this age know of idolatry?

For our present purpose, it is to go a step further to move from the criticism issued by Hans Jonas to that issued by Martin Buber. Speaking to Christians, Jonas, presumably for the purpose at hand, effaced his own Jewishness—so totally, however, as to commit at least one major blunder about Judaism.[46] Writing on behalf of what Jews and Christians have in common, Martin Buber made an additional discovery on our present behalf. It should in any case have given pause to anyone that, in support of his own primal thinking, Heidegger cites pre-Socratic philosophers (dubiously interpreted) and modern poets (arbitrarily selected), while any reference to Jewish if not Christian sources is virtually nonexistent. Buber discovers for us that the few references there are reflect nothing but hostility and obtuseness. Interpreting the poet Hölderlin, Heidegger asserts that the true poet, radically insecure between a past which is no more and a future is not yet, is a prophet, "in the strict sense of the term." *Which term?* The Greek term given in the original! Of the Jewish prophets he has this to say:

The "prophets" of these religions [i.e., Judaism and Christianity] do not begin by foretelling the word of the Holy. They announce immediately the God upon whom the certainty of salvation in a supernatural blessedness reckons.[47]

Buber comments as follows:

I have never in our time encountered on a high philosophical plane such a far-reaching misunderstanding of the prophets of Israel. The prophets of Israel have never announced a God upon whom their hearers' striving for security reckoned. They have always aimed to shatter all security and to proclaim in the opened abyss the final insecurity of the unwished for God who demands that His human creatures become real, they become human, and confounds all who imagine that they can take refuge in the certainty that the temple of God is in their midst. This is the God of the historical demand as the prophets of Israel beheld Him. The primal reality of these prophecies does not allow itself to be tossed into the attic of "religions": it is as living and actual in this historical hour as ever. [48]

In order to appreciate the full power of these critical remarks, one must in one respect go beyond Buber himself and speak, not on behalf of what Judaism and Christianity have in common, but rather on behalf of Judaism alone. Christian readers of the Jewish prophets have not been uninclined to understand their message in the light of a salvation already complete. (One might observe in passing that if it is now Christians rather than Jews who seek a Heideggerian absolute insecurity toward a future God as yet wholly unknown, it may be in reaction to a spurious Christianity that, secure in its salvation, escapes the risks of worldly existence.) No Jew could ever read the Jewish prophets except in expectation of a salvation as yet incomplete, and so anticipated as to inspire terror even as it inspires hope. For this reason, it may be true enough that "the controversy [between Heidegger and Buber] can easily degenerate into a race in which he wins who offers the smallest security and the greatest risk."[49] This danger, however, is nonexistent if we abstract from the dilemmas of current Christian thought and draw the lines between Heidegger's paganism and Buber's unexpurgated and uncompromised prophetic Judaism. Each has a radical insecurity and a radical terror. The two insecurities and terrors, however, are not the same. Heidegger's pagan insecurity is total because the future is wholly open to all possible gods. Buber's Judaism does not share this total insecurity because, knowing that some gods will always be false, it refuses to be wholly open even now.[50] On its part, however, this Judaism has a total insecurity of its own. This is the possibility that it might itself mistake false gods for the true God, and of *this* insecurity Heidegger's paganism shows not a trace.[51] Which of these two insecurities inspires the greater terror? This question, today, divides the religious world.

Buber is self-exposed to Heidegger's paganism. That Heidegger does not *in fact* expose himself to Judaism (or to Buber's articulation of Judaism) we have already stated. It remains only to be shown that he cannot do so; that, were it to risk such a self-exposure, his whole later thought would be questionable in its entirety. For this purpose the brief examination of a single but characteristic essay is quite sufficient. "The poet names the gods and names all things in that which they are."[52] In Genesis, to be sure, man names "all things"; he does not name God.[53] "The speech of the poet is establishment not only in the sense of the free act of giving, but at the same time in the sense of the firm basing of human existence on its foundations." In Judaism this office belongs only partly to speaking, and still less so to a human speaking. "Poetry is the primitive language of a historical people." It is the primitive language of a pagan people only, and the possibility that Jews are a historical people is here ruled out by a pagan fiat. "The poetic word only acquires its power of naming, when the gods themselves bring us language. How do the gods speak?" With the question thus formulated, the possibility is a priori ruled out that He who is said to have spoken at Sinai ever did speak, or ever had the power to speak. [This] "is the time *of need*, because it lies under a double lack and a double Not: the No-more of the gods that have fled and the Not-yet of the god that is coming."[54] Thus the pagan poet is given the authority to legislate even now that the god who will come is not God.

The possibility still remains that Heidegger's primal thinking, though incapable of any "no" to idolatry resembling that given within Judaism and Christianity, is capable of a "no" of its own. This possibility needs investigation the more urgently since, if his defenders are to be believed, Heidegger did in fact come to say "no" to Nazism, and the question arises whether this "no" was as philosophical as his "yes" had once been. This investigation is best connected with Heidegger's judgments on technology, which, it is not insignificant to add, bear a certain resemblance to those made by Martin Buber. He writes:

The "world wars" and their "totality" already are consequences of a prior loss of being. They aim at securing a permanent form of use. Man himself is drawn into this use, and the fact that he has become the most important raw material of all is no longer concealed. . . . The moral indignation of those who do not yet know what is the case often concentrates on the arbitrariness and claim-to-power made by *Führers*, and this is the most fatal form of lending them dignity. . . . In truth they are but the necessary consequence of the fact that that-which-is has gone astray.[55]

Much credit is due to the insight shown here and elsewhere into the dehumanizing effects of modern technology; more credit still, to the implied critique of those of his countrymen prone to exculpate themselves by blaming a single mad individual. What continues to escape Heidegger is that, while technology and *Seinsverlassenheit* may produce "world wars," there has been no war like that which Hitler unleashed on the world. Even in 1946[56]—after the truth of the death camps had been fully revealed—Heidegger's "no," unlike his earlier "yes," fails to face up to the fact that in this century there have not been *"Führers"*; there has only been one *Führer*.

Why do the death camps appear nowhere in Heidegger's writings? In view of a record that is not unimpeccable, it might be replied that this is due to tactful restraint. Then why is this quality missing when great pain is expressed about the "many Germans [who] have lost their *Heimat*, had to leave their villages and towns, were driven from their *heimatlichen Boden*"?[57] It is hard not to be nauseated by this combination of silence about murdered Jews with eloquence about Germans who, though expelled—it might be added, not always without just cause—are otherwise well and alive. Repressing nausea, one still finds it hard not to suspect traces of Nazism when one sees the virtues of the German *Heimat* contrasted with the vices of an atomic *riesenhaftes Geschäft*, carried on, of all countries, by England.[58] Exercising every ounce of self-restraint, one still remains with the minimum judgment that the later as much as the earlier Heidegger remains incapable of recognizing radical evil. Is his later "no" to Nazism as philosophical as his "yes" had once been? Having refused to say no to Apollo,[59] his thought has rendered itself impotent to say no to Baal, including and above all the modern Baal who devoured the souls of his countrymen and to whom these countrymen sacrificed the bodies of one-third of the world's Jewish population.

CONCLUSION

Authentic Jewish existence today begins with the "no" Heidegger has not spoken.

Genocide, whatever its extent, never succeeds completely. That perpetrated by the Nazis failed more than any other, because it provided the main reasons for the creation of the State of Israel. Encouraged by the way Hitler practiced genocide without encountering resistance, the Arabs surged in upon the nascent Israeli nation to exterminate it and make themselves its immediate heirs. The military and political leaders of the Arab states, along with Foreign Minister Bevin and his advisors in the Colonial Office, did not understand that the *millennial epoch* of the Jews' sanctifying of God and themselves by their submitting to violent death *had just come to an end with the Warsaw Ghetto uprising.* With this conclusive experience of European Jewry there also came to an end the illusion that they could count on other men to defend them. The Arab armies were cut to pieces and thrown beyond the borders by men who, in going to battle with no thought of retreat, meant also to avenge a people murdered and not buried, whose brothers, sons or nephews they were. They meant to teach the world that the long hunting season was over forever, and that one could no longer kill Jews easily or with impunity. To be sure, the soldiers of this new Hebrew army, Zionists for the most part, were fighting for the land that their labor had redeemed, for the villages, towns and kibbutzim that they had brought into being out of nothingness, and for the lives of all of them. But they were fighting above all—particularly since 1945 and beyond the spring of 1948—to deliver their people from a degradation that encouraged exterminators, their sons and grandsons, as well as their innumerable silent accomplices the world over.

For the greatest boon that can be brought to peoples tempted by aggressive anti-Semitism is to make the crime that it inspires dangerous to the instigators and the executors themselves. Between 1933 and 1945 the whole world provided Hitler—who moved only step-by-step at first—with proof that he could undertake anything he pleased against the Jews, with nothing to fear but verbal protestations never followed up with the slightest reprisal. This is why the abduction of Eichmann by agents of the State of Israel and his trial in Jerusalem are events of *major significance.* . . .

One can certainly take Israel to task for some pretensions and omissions, but certainly not for its decision to assume the heritage of the exterminated and, along with it, the right and duty to pursue the authors, executors and active accomplices of the *hurban.* Wherever they are, "let them tremble and let the rustling of a leaf in the wind pursue them!" . . .

It is considered natural that Polish tribunals judge the executioners who had tortured and killed Poles by the tens of thousands. Is the case of Adolf Eichmann captured in Argentina different then? In fact, that country opened its doors to the whole genocidal gang. Our torturers and murderers are among us on this earth, in Argentina, Germany, Austria, everywhere. Sometimes, a few are arrested and brought before judges; their sentences scarcely exceed those doled out to swindlers and counterfeiters. And some are even acquitted.

"Wo kein Kläger, ist kein Richter"—without an accuser there is no judge, it is said in German. Now, Israel alone wants to accuse—can and must accuse. And judge also? Of course! But, if the victims were Jews . . . ? Precisely because of that! But the genocide perpetrated

against the Jews was a crime against humanity—isn't that a reason for having it judged by an international tribunal? Every real crime is a crime against humanity, or, in the eyes of the believer, against God Himself. This is true in a general sense, but the crime committed is always particular, just as its victim is.[60]

These words were written when the world, more concerned with the Jewish "crimes" of abducting Adolf Eichmann and taking him for trial to Jerusalem, proved itself to be still largely composed of antisemites, "democrats," and unauthentic Jews. The passage speaks of the first two of these groups. Of the third, the author writes as follows:

Some Jewish voices were raised against all action of this sort. Among Jews, particularly their middle classes and intellectuals, one sometimes encounters the self-indulgence of a certain submissiveness. They are obsessed with the problem of finding out what the Gentiles will think of this or that Jewish gesture, or what impression has been or will be made upon them. . . . In their eyes, *the subject*—he who judges— is always *the other man*, the non-Jew. *The object*—he who must never forget that he is being looked at and judged—is the Jew.[61]

The Sartrean authentic Jew "wills himself into history" as "damned." Ever since the Warsaw Ghetto uprising, the *actual* authentic Jew takes up arms against this Jewish "damnation," vis- ited upon his people by the world. Indeed, he is *obliged* not to rest in this war, which Hitler brought to its climax but did not start, until the millennial, murderous combination of antisemitic hate, "democratic" indifference, and Jewish powerlessness comes to an end. Manès Sperber, a survivor, a resident of Sartre's own country, and a part of his philosophical milieu, uses recognizably Sartrean terms but revolutionizes Sartre's own application of these terms to the Jewish people. We ask: why does Sartre himself fail to bring about this revolution?[62] Why does he to this day apply one standard to Algerians fighting against colonialism and another to Jews fighting against antisemitism?[63] "The heirs of Belzec, Maidenek and Auschwitz *have no right* to be lambs."[64] Might an existentialist not be expected to be open to *this* moral imperative?

In the case of Sartre, such lack of openness may affect only his sociopolitical and moral judgments. In the case of Heidegger, it flaws an entire philosophy that, impressive in any case, might otherwise have been great. The ontic-ontological "circle" of *Being and Time* (1926), taken by its author as nonvicious "all-too- lightly," but considered sufficient for the total destruction of all

(Christian or Greek) claims to Eternity, would have been either tested or broken had there been any self-exposure on his part to the "ontic" testimony of the *Star of Redemption* (1921), whose Jewish author found it possible to affirm the "Davidic star of eternal Truth" because of, not in spite of, his insistence on the temporal, creaturely, existential limitations of his "new thinking."[65] As for the surrender to Nazism (May 1933), this, brief or not so brief, could not have occurred at all had Heidegger been open to Jewish as well as German community—or at any rate to his Jewish fellow-existentialist Martin Buber, who had already written (April 1933) that the Jew was the most exposed man of the age, that in testing him the tensions of the age were testing all humanity, and that, though well-nigh torn asunder, the authentic Jew was he who would overcome.[66] The author of *Being and Time* was then turning into the hearing *Denker* on the road to Being. His *Denken*, however, could not have degenerated into a vacuously open neopaganism had the *Denker* not been deaf to epoch-making events then occurring to and within the Jewish community.[67] Any confrontation of the murder camps would perforce have led to the knowledge that *some* gods—past, present or future—are *absolutely* false. A confrontation of authentic Jewish responses would have led to the recognition that—it is true, astonishingly enough—the Western biblical past possesses a truly present life in one authentic community if in no others. As early as 1939—that is, when the apocalypse was as yet only a threat and not a reality—Martin Buber had made a crucial distinction between "dismembered" and "dispersed" Jews—the former, uprooted from their religious traditions and lacking a living center—the latter an authentic community because their center was Zion.[68] After the apocalypse, to be sure, Buber's crucial distinction has assumed an ever-sharper, clearer, and more painful reality. But it has also become ever more unmistakable that authentic Jewish community today, whether "at home" or "dispersed," escapes the categories of the earlier and later Heidegger alike. Neither of the anachronistic past nor of the godless future nor yet waiting for unknown gods still to come, the "being-toward-the-future" of the religious Jew is secular in that Auschwitz has destroyed all "religious" illusions; and the secular Jew is "recovering" a religious heritage in his search for a present identity. This relation to "anticipated" future and "recovered" past, however, is no more and no less true than its opposite. For in order to take up arms against possible future catastrophe the present authentic Jewish community must have recovering recourse to the "secular"

Existentialist Finale—and Beginning

Bar Kochba. And in order to confront *absolutely* all false gods yet ahead it must have recovering recourse to the "religious" Rabbi Akiba, who hoped against all hope in the midst of catastrophe.[69] It is in so unprecedented, so paradoxical a way that authentic Jewish community today bears witness unto the nations, to Eternity in the midst of time. But alas, the "hearing" *Denker* Heidegger to this day shows no signs of listening.

B E G I N N I N G

Twenty-five years after. A quarter-century. . . . A metamorphosis was taking place. On many levels and affecting all humanity: executioners and victims alike. The first too anxious to become executioners, the latter too ready to assume the role of victims. How long did it take? One night, one week. Or more. A year, perhaps three. Time is a lesser factor than man's ability to discard his inner self. To a victim of the "concentrationary" system, it no longer mattered that he had been an intellectual, laborer, angry student or devoted husband. A few beatings, a few screams turned him into a blank, his loss of identity complete. He no longer thought as before, nor did he look men straight in the eyes; his own eyes were no longer the same. Camp law and camp truth transcended all laws and all truth, and the prisoner could not help but submit. When he was hungry, he thought of soup and not immortality. After a long night's march, he yearned for rest and not for mercy. Was this all there was to man?

People wanted to understand: the executioner's fascination with crime, the victim's with death, and what had paved the way for Auschwitz. . . .

So we turned to the victims, the survivors. They were asked to bare themselves, to delve into the innermost recesses of their being, and tell, and tell again, to the point of exhaustion and beyond; to the delirium that follows. How it had been. Had the killers really been so many and so conscientious in their task? And the machinery so efficient? Had it really been a universe with its own gods and priests, its own princes with their laws, its philosophers with their disciples? And you, how did you manage to survive? Had you known the art of survival from before? And how were you able to keep your sanity? And today: how can you sleep, work, go to restaurants and movies, how can you mingle with people and share their meals? People wanted to know everything, resolve all questions, leave nothing in the dark. What frightened them was the mystery.

The survivors were reticent, their answers vague. The subject: taboo. They remained silent. At first out of reserve; there are wounds and sorrows one prefers to conceal. And out of fear as well. Fear

[227]

above all. Fear of arousing disbelief, of being told: Your imagination is sick, what you describe could not possibly have happened. Or: You are counting on our pity, you are exploiting your suffering. Worse: they feared being inadequate to the task, betraying a unique experience by burying it in worn-out phrases and images. . . .

Sooner or later, every one of them was tempted to seal his lips and maintain absolute silence. So as to transmit a vision of the holocaust, in the manner of certain mystics, by withdrawing from words. Had all of them remained mute, their accumulated silences would have become unbearable: the impact would have deafened the world.

When they agreed to lift the veil, many obstacles and inhibitions had to be overcome. They reassured themselves: This is but a difficult first step. In any event, we are only messengers. With some luck, other men will benefit from our experience. And learn what the individual is capable of under a totalitarian regime, when the line between humanity and inhumanity becomes blurred. And what wars are made of and where they lead. They will discover the link between words and the ashes forever.

How guileless they were, those surviving tellers of tales. They sought to confer a retroactive meaning upon a trial which had none. They thought: Who knows, if we can make ourselves heard, man will change. His very vision of himself will be altered. Thanks to illustrations provided by us, he will henceforth be able to distinguish between what he may and may not do, what goals to pursue and forego. He could then forge for himself a reality made of desire rather than necessity, a freedom commensurate with his creative impulse rather than with his destructive instinct.

Twenty-five years later, after the reckoning, one feels discouragement and shame. The balance sheet is disheartening. . . . A French politician—and member of Parliament—publicly accuses the Jews of peddling their suffering. Robbed of their property and rights, the Jews in Arab countries live in constant fear. They are slandered in the Soviet Union, persecuted in Poland. And, a fact without precedent, antisemitism has finally reached China.

Which raises the question for the survivors: Was it not a mistake to testify, and by that very act, affirm their faith in man and word?[70]

Can any existentialism (or, for that matter, any kind of philosophical comprehension) do ultimate justice to an existence so unprecedented and paradoxical? Hegel holds that philosophic thought, the owl of Minerva, can comprehend existence only after it *is*. Opposing the master, his left-wing disciples reverse this relation, transfigure Hegel's owl into a cock, and attribute to it the power to anticipate and help shape future existence. Jewish existence today overwhelms existentialist and indeed all philosophical thought. Confronting Auschwitz, all such thought is fragmented if not shattered[71] by a many-sided, endless mystery. Confronting Jerusalem, thought too is fragmented if not shattered by a mystery. Those who have heard her long-stilled voice speak of her with awe and wonder, knowing that the ground on which they stand is holy.

I did not enter on my own the city of Jerusalem. Streams of endless craving, clinging, dreaming, flowing day and night, midnights, years, decades, centuries, millennia, streams of tears, pledging, waiting— from all over the world, from all corners of the earth—carried us of this generation to the Wall.[72]

Notes

Chapter 1

ELIJAH AND THE EMPIRICISTS:
THE POSSIBILITY OF DIVINE PRESENCE

1. Reprinted in Antony Flew, ed., *Logic and Language* (Garden City: Doubleday Anchor Books, 1965), pp. 194–214. Originally published in the *Proceedings of the Aristotelian Society*, 1944–1945.

2. R. B. Braithwaite, "An Empiricist's View of the Nature of Religious Belief," in John Hick, ed., *The Existence of God* (New York: Macmillan, 1964), p. 233. Originally published separately as the Eddington Memorial Lecture, Cambridge (England and New York: Cambridge University Press, 1955).

3. Antony Flew, "Theology and Falsification," in Antony Flew and Alasdaire MacIntyre, eds., *New Essays in Philosophical Theology* (London: SCM Press, 1966), p. 97. Henceforth cited as *NE*.

4. According to Jewish tradition, YHVH (the divine name) is not pronounced in ordinary discourse but is replaced with *Adonai* ("My Lord"). I see no reason for departing from that tradition.

5. R. M. Hare, "Theology and Falsification," *NE*, pp. 99–103.

6. Braithwaite, "Nature of Religious Belief."

7. Ibid., p. 213.

8. A brief account of the fate of logical positivism, geared to its theological implications, is M. L. Diamond, "Contemporary Analysis: The Metaphysical Target and the Theological Victim," *The Journal of Religion*, July 1967, pp. 210–232.

9. See the section "Faith and the Limits of Empiricism" in this chapter, where it is argued that for biblical faith (Jewish or Christian) a divine Presence is manifest only to a faith open to it.

10. See for example, Jehuda Halevi, *Kuzari*, I:§§87ff.

11. See the masterful exposition given by R. G. Collingwood, *The Idea of History*, (Oxford: Clarendon, 1946), part 5, especially §3.

12. See David Hume, *An Inquiry Concerning Human Understanding*, section 10.

13. A. J. Ayer, *Language, Truth and Logic*, 2nd ed. (London: Victor Gollancz, 1949).

14. Ibid., p. 120.

15. Braithwaite, "Nature of Religious Belief."

16. *The Advancement of Learning*, part 2.

17. The sources referred to are all given in Louis Ginzberg, *The Legends of the Jews* (Philadelphia: Jewish Publication Society, 1912–1928) vol. 4, pp. 197–199; vol. 6, pp. 319–321.

18. Antony Flew, "Theology and Falsification," *NE*, pp. 99, 97.

19. R. M. Hare, "Theology and Falsification," *NE*, pp. 99–103.

20. Ibid., p. 99.

21. *On Religion* (New York: Harper Torchbooks, 1958), e.g., pp. 213–214, 252. Unlike Schleiermacher, Hegel attempts to *demonstrate* that Christianity is the comprehensive religion, which is the reason he cannot be charged with imperialism. See Emil L. Fackenheim, *The Religious Dimension in Hegel's Thought* (Bloomington: Indiana University Press, 1968; Boston: Beacon, 1970). Also see Chapter 3 of this book.

Notes

22. Basil Mitchell, "Theology and Falsification," *NE*, pp. 103-105.
23. Ibid., p. 103
24. C. B. Martin, "The Perfect Good," *NE*, p. 215.
25. Frederick Ferré rightly comments: "Faith may be sorely tested by great disasters or personal tragedy. In such circumstances it is not linguistically absurd to say: 'Is God good after all? Is His Love towards me perfect? Still less is it an empty tautology to affirm with renewed faith: 'Yes, God *is* good! His will *is* perfect!' " (*Language, Logic and God* [New York: Harper & Row, 1961], p. 115)
26. Mitchell, "Theology and Falsification," *NE*, p. 105.
27. I. M. Crombie, "Theology and Falsification," *NE*, pp. 109-130.
28. Ibid., p. 124.
29. John Hick writes:

    Judaic-Christian theism postulates an ultimate unambiguous existence *in patria*, as well as our present ambiguous existence *in via*. There is a state of having arrived as well as a state of journeying, an eternal heavenly life as well as an earthly pilgrimage. The alleged future experience cannot, of course, be appealed to as evidence for theism as a present interpretation of our experience; but it does suffice to render the choice between theism and atheism a real and not merely an empty or verbal choice. [*Philosophy of Religion* (Englewood Cliffs, N.J.: Prentice-Hall, 1962), p. 102.]

    Hick's either/or (which leaves Judaism no choice but to be classified with Christian theism or with atheism) renders virtually meaningless the admission, made earlier in the book (p. 3), to the effect that the "immense range of religious phenomena" deserves careful philosophical attention.

    It should be stressed that the Jewish Messianic expectation has, in addition to the "left-wing" tendency dealt with in the following pages, also a "right-wing," apocalyptic tendency. We here deal with the first because the logic of the second would not substantially differ from that of Christian eschatology—and because no form of the Jewish faith can embrace the second so thoroughly as to produce a total dichotomy between "earthly pilgrimage" and "eternal heavenly life."

    We have suggested that the expression "Judeo-Christian tradition," as currently employed by the philosophic establishment, is a mere case of tokenism. This is nicely illustrated in the following passage from Ninian Smart, *The Philosophy of Religion* (New York: Random House, 1970), p. 115.

    Another necessary condition of the acceptability of revelation is a mixture of the ethical and the historical. Still confining our examples to the Judeo-Christian tradition: suppose that tomorrow a new document were turned up in the sands of the Negev, which was seen to be an account of the life of Jesus (or Moses), but by usual historical criteria was much more reliable biographically than the Gospels (or the Old Testament). Suppose that it showed conclusively that Jesus wantonly murdered one or two people (or that Moses did). Would it be easy to think of Jesus (or Moses) in the way in which orthodox believers do? Would it still be possible to treat this real (not just technical) criminal *as Son of God?* (Italics added.)

    No comment is necessary.
30. See Elie Wiesel, *The Gates of the Forest* (New York: Holt, Rinehart & Winston, 1966), p. 225.
31. Braithwaite, "Nature of Religious Belief."
32. Mitchell, "Theology and Falsification, *NE*, p. 105.
33. In the following I confine myself to Martin Buber as an exponent of the doctrine, largely in order to emphasize its Jewish inspiration, but without imply-

ing either that Buber is the sole sound exponent of the doctrine or that his own exposition is sound in every respect.

34. Martin Buber, *I and Thou*, 2nd ed (New York: Scribner's 1958), p. 81.

35. Martin Buber, *Between Man and Man* (Boston: Beacon, 1955), pp. 22ff.

36. An earlier statement of the conflict between subjectivist reductionism and a faith understanding itself as openness to the Divine may be found in "On the Eclipse of God," ch. 15 of Emil L. Fackenheim, *Quest for Past and Future* (Bloomington: Indiana University Press, 1968; Boston: Beacon, 1970). In some respects my earlier statement is more comprehensive. It is not, however, specifically focused on the problems of an empiricist philosophy of religion.

37. R. W. Hepburn, *Christianity and Paradox* (London: Watts, 1958), pp. 47ff. In the following criticisms I confine myself to this book, since it is an unusually sympathetic and competent treatment of the doctrine of encounter by an empirically minded linguistic philosopher. For the most part, the criticisms applicable to this book would a fortiori apply to less sympathetic and competent treatments of the doctrine of encounter coming from the same philosophical quarter.

38. C. B. Martin, "Religious Way of Knowing," *NE*, p. 80.

39. Hepburn, *Christianity and Paradox*, p. 25; italics added.

40. Hepburn nowhere asks whether Buber himself shares the claim to self-authenticating experiences made by his Protestant disciples.

41. If Buber ever intimates the existence of self-authenticating experiences, this would appear to me under undue Protestant-subjectivist-individualist influence, and, as it were, against his better Jewish judgment. For this reason more stress is laid in the following on his interpretations of Jewish sources than on his very individualistic *I and Thou*, a work I consider to mark the major turning point in his thought, but not to represent the most mature statement of his teaching.

42. Martin Buber, *The Prophetic Faith* (New York: MacMillan, 1949), p. 179.

43. Hepburn, *Christianity and Paradox*, p. 44.

44. See Martin Buber, *Eclipse of God* (New York: Harper Torchbooks, 1957), p. 23 and especially p. 66:

> Let us ask whether it may not be literally true that God formerly spoke to us and is now silent, and whether this is not to be understood as the Hebrew Bible understands it, namely, that the living God is not only a self-revealing but also a self-concealing God.

45. For a less limited context, see chs. 2, 3, and 5.

46. Hepburn, *Christianity and Paradox*, p. 44.

47. Hepburn, *Christianity and Paradox*, pp. 47–48.

48. Ibid.

49. Hepburn misunderstands Buber when he classifies him among those imposing an "embargo on philosophizing about the religious encounter," and when he castigates the "misleadingness of . . . [his] either/or of the philosophical God-idea and the living God of Abraham." Buber's actual teaching is a dialectical relation between the God-idea of reflective thought and the living God, the God-idea "dissolving" at the point when the living God is confronted (*Eclipse of God*, p. 50). Hepburn is misled by Buber's avowed practice of philosophizing "no more than necessary." (For a systematic account of Buber's doctrine, see Emil L. Fackenheim, "Martin Buber's Concept of Revelation," in P. A. Schilpp and Maurice Friedman, eds., *The Philosophy of Martin Buber*, [La Salle, Ill.: Open Court, 1967], pp. 273–296.)

50. Ginzberg, *The Legends of the Jews*, vol. 4, p. 233; vol. 6, p. 33.

Chapter 2

ABRAHAM AND THE KANTIANS:
MORAL DUTIES AND DIVINE COMMANDMENTS

1. See Louis Ginzberg, *The Legends of the Jews* (Philadelphia: Jewish Publication Society, 1961), vol. 1, p. 218.

2. Literally, "the binding"—the traditional Jewish term for the events narrated in Gen. 22.

3. See Ginzberg, *The Legends of the Jews*, p. 283.

4. See ch. 1, pp. 12ff.

5. See ch. 1, pp. 16ff., 22ff.

6. See Ginzberg, *The Legends of the Jews*, p. 277.

7. *Streit der Fakultäten* (Prussian Academy edition, 1900–1956) vol. 7, p. 63. (In the following pages readily available English translations of Kant are used when possible. Otherwise the Academy edition is the source, and the translation is mine.)

8. Søren Kierkegaard, *Fear and Trembling* (New York: Doubleday Anchor Books), 1954.

9. *Ibid.*, p. 129.

10. *Ibid.*, p. 66.

11. According to rabbinic theology God gave 7 laws to Noah, thus making a covenant with the whole human race. See this chapter, "Pre-Kantian Philosophy and the Revealed Morality of Judaism" and "The Revolutionary Kantian Thesis of Moral Self-legislation."

12. Kierkegaard, *Fear and Trembling*, p. 78.

13. *Ibid.*, p. 89.

14. *Ibid.*, p. 90.

15. The following section was the original nucleus of this entire essay, and was first conceived and published (in somewhat different form) independently, under the title "The Revealed Morality of Judaism and Modern Thought: A Confrontation with Kant" in Arnold Wolf, ed., *Rediscovering Judaism* (Chicago: Quadrangle, 1965), pp. 51–75. (See also "Kant and Judaism," *Commentary*, December 1963, pp. 460–467.) The essay is reprinted in *Quest for Past and Future* (Bloomington: Indiana University Press, 1968; Boston: Beacon, 1970).

16. *Pirke Abot*, I:3.

17. *Bab. Talmud*, Yoma 67b.

18. Kant, *Groundwork of the Metaphysics of Morals*, H. J. Paton, trans. (London: Hutchinson, 1958), pp. 98–100.

19. The "creative morality" interpretation of Kant, given by thinkers from Fichte to Hermann Cohen, has affected quite un-Kantian philosophies, such as those of Nietzsche and Dewey, as well as much popular moral and psychological thinking. I cannot here pause to document my own interpretation, but only refer, as to one with which I am in substantial agreement, to G. Krüger's *Philosophie und Moral in der Kantischen Kritik* (Tübingen: Mohr, 1931). On Hegel, who wholly transforms the issues here under discussion, ch. 3.

20. Ch. 3 will do so within the limits of its own concerns.

21. A remarkable nineteenth-century Jewish thinker neatly illustrates this dilemma. Samuel Hirsch subscribed to Kantian autonomous morality. Yet he also

quite literally believed in revelation. Aware of the possibility of conflict, he sought to resolve it by interpreting revelation (following Lessing) as divine education toward moral autonomy. Hirsch's ingenuity in developing this doctrine does not save it from ultimate failure. Revelation here is divine guidance the sole purpose of which is to emancipate man from the need for guidance, and hence from revelation itself. See Emil L. Fackenheim, "Samuel Hirsch and Hegel" in A. Altmann, ed., *Studies in Nineteenth Century Jewish Intellectual History* (Cambridge, Mass.: Harvard University Press, 1964), pp. 171–201. On Hirsch, see in Ch. 3, "Jewish Existence in the Bourgeois-Protestant World."

22. Kant returns to this theme on countless occasions. We confine ourselves to one representative passage: "So far as practical reason has the right to guide us, we shall not regard actions as obligatory because they are divine commandments. We shall regard them as divine commandments because we are inwardly obligated to them." [*Critique of Pure Reason*, B 847.]

23. This definition appears too often in Kant's writings to make a reference to sources either possible or necessary, except in an analysis devoted to its meaning in its own right, a task we hope to perform elsewhere.

24. See *Op. Post.*, *Werke*, vol. 21, p. 145: "God is moral-practical reason legislating to itself."

25. See for example, *The Metaphysical Principles of Virtue*, James Ellington, trans. (Indianapolis-New York: Library of Liberal Arts, 1964), pp. 100ff.; (hereafter cited as *MPV*).

26. This view, reflected throughout the *Critique of Practical Reason*, as well as in the important Preface to the first edition of *Religion Within the Limits of Reason Alone*, is also implied in Kant's thesis that among the three celebrated Kantian questions in which all "interests of reason are summed up," the third ("What may I hope?") is irreducible to the other two ("What can I know?" and "What ought I to do?") [*Critique of Pure Reason* B 832–833].

27. Kierkegaard, *Fear and Trembling*, p. 78.

28. *Werke*, vol. 8, p. 405.

29. See for example, Gen. 12:1ff.; Exod. 3:4ff. and 19:5ff.; Isa. 6:1ff.; Jer. 1:1ff. When bidden to become a holy nation (Exod. 19:5-6), Israel is, of course, already in possession of *some* commandments in terms of which the content of holiness may be specified. Still, it is of the greatest importance that the bulk of revealed commandments is yet to come. On the divine-human historical context of pristine moments of divine commanding Presence, see this chapter, the section "On Human Sacrifice, or the *Akedah* as Perpetually Reenacted and Superseded Past."

30. Isa. 6:8; Exod. 24:7. We follow the traditional interpretation of the second passage. A consideration of the Sinaitic revelation will be possible only in an encounter with Hegel. See ch. 3.

31. See for example, Isa. 6:4; Jer. 1:6.

32. Whether or not all the six hundred and thirteen commandments of traditional Judaism may be regarded as having permanence and intrinsic value is a large question, and one ultimately transcending the scope not only of this chapter but of this entire work. It appears in ch. 3 to the extent that history (here abstracted form) is essential in it.

33. Jer. 27.

34. See "On Human Sacrifice, or the *Akedah* as Perpetually Reenacted and Superseded Past," in this chapter.

Notes

35. See for example, *Midrash Tanḥuma*, Yitro, and many other passages, in Ḥasidic as well as rabbinic literature.

36. Mic. 6:8. For further discussion of the Micah passage see, in this chapter, the *Introduction* to "On the *Akedah*, or Sacrifice and Martyrdom," and *Midr. Genesis Rabbah, 55.5*.

37. *Bab. Talmud*, Berakhot 61b.

38. Kant, *Critique of Judgment*, trans. J. C. Meredith (Oxford: Clarendon 1952), p. 110. The translation is mine.

39. According to one Midrash (*Tanḥuma*, Ḥukkat), the righteous do not cease to fear God even though they have received His assurance. According to another (*Sifre Deut.*, Va'etḥanan, No. 32), while elsewhere love drives out fear, this is not true of the love and fear of God.

40. In *Tanḥuma*, Beḥukkotai, God is made to reject the offer of the angels to observe the Torah, on the ground that the Torah is appropriate only for human observance.

41. See for example, *Bab. Talmud*, Berakhot 31a; Shabbat 30b.

42. Isa. 6:6–7; Jer. 1:7–8.

43. As already indicated in "Judaism between Autonomy and Heteronomy," for reasons beyond the scope of this essay, Kant does not regard the divine will as an *absolute* redundancy. He does, however, regard it as redundant within an exclusively moral context.

44. *Pesikta Kahana*, 15.

45. II Kings 3:27. See for example, *Midr. Genesis Rabbah, 55.5*.

46. See "The Torah as Bridge between Divine Giver and Human Recipient," in this chapter.

47. *Midr. Genesis Rabbah, 55.5*.

48. See the introduction to this chapter.

49. *Streit der Fakultäten, Werke*, vol. 7, p. 63.

50. For the epistemological aspect of the question, see ch. 1.

51. *Streit der Fakultäten, Werke*, vol. 7, p. 63.

52. See, in this chapter, "Pre-Kantian Philosophy and the Revealed Morality of Judaism," and *Bab. Talmud*, Yoma 67b.

53. Maimonides, *The Guide of the Perplexed*, trans. Shlomo Pines (Chicago: University of Chicago Press, 1964), 3:24, p. 501.

54. See *Midr. Genesis Rabbah*, Noah, 34:8. In this Midrash it is asserted that Deut. 18:10, which forbids child sacrifice, is applicable to the Noaḥides.

55. *Ibid.*, 3:24, p. 501.

56. See, in this chapter, "The Revolutionary Kantian Thesis of Moral Self-legislation" and "Kant's Moral Theology."

57. See *Religion Within the Limits of Reason Alone*, T. M. Greene and H. H. Hudson, trans. (New York: Harper Torchbooks, 1960), p. 95: ". . . pure moral legislation, through which the divine will is primordially engraved in our hearts, is not only the ineluctable condition of all true religion whatsoever but is also that which constitutes such religion. . . ."

58. Ibid., p. 157.

59. For example, *Werke*, *Op. Post.*, vol. 21, p. 12; vol. 22, p. 120.

60. Kant's *Groundwork of the Metaphysic of Morals*, p. 95.

61. Ibid., p. 96.

62. Ibid., p. 97.

63. *MPV*, pp. 83–84.

Notes

64. Kant, *Lectures on Ethics*, trans. Louis Infield (London: Methuen, 1930), p. 149 (hereafter cited as *LE*).

65. *MPV*, p. 84.

66. Ibid.

67. Ibid.

68. Kant makes a distinction between *Selbstentleibung* and *Selbstmord* and writes: "The deliberate killing of oneself (*Entleibung seiner selbst*) can be called self-murder (*Selbstmord*) . . . only when it can be shown that the killing is really a crime committed either against one's own person, or against another person. . . ." (*MPV*, pp. 82–83).

69. In *MPV* Kant merely states those "casuistical questions" some of which we have cited, but leaves them unanswered (pp. 84–85). In his *Anthropologie* he praises the courage of a Seneca who, being a free man, preferred inflicting death upon himself to unjustly suffering it, yet will not defend the morality of his action (*Werke*, vol. 7, p. 259). In *LE* he writes that "had Cato faced any torments which Caesar might have inflicted on him with a resolute mind and remained steadfast, it would have been noble of him; to violate himself was not so" (p. 153). In the same work he also writes that "the rule of morality does not permit [suicide] . . . under any condition because it degrades human nature below the level of animal nature and so destroys it" (p. 152).

70. *LE*, pp. 153–154.

71. *LE*, p. 154.

72. Ibid.

73. Kant, *Religion Within the Limits of Reason Alone*, p. 158. (Italics in text added.)

74. Kierkegaard, *Fear and Trembling*, p. 80.

75. Ibid.

76. Ibid., p. 59: "By faith Abraham did not renounce his claim upon Isaac, but by faith he got Isaac."

77. Ibid., p. 70.

78. Ibid.

79. Ibid., p. 82.

80. Ibid., p. 89.

81. Ibid., p. 90.

82. Ibid., p. 82ff. It goes without saying that this is an arbitrary interpretation of the Luke passage, although it does seem that Kierkegaard is closer to the text than, for example, H. J. Paton, who interprets it along the lines of the Kierke-gaardian category of the tragic hero. (*The Good Will* [London: Allen and Unwin, 1927], p. 402.)

83. Ginzberg, *The Legends of the Jews*, p. 281.

84. Kierkegaard, *Fear and Trembling*, p. 70.

85. Ginzberg, *The Legends of the Jews*, pp. 283–284.

86. Kierkegaard, *Fear and Trembling*, pp. 91–129.

87. Ginzberg, *The Legends of the Jews*, p. 279.

88. See, in this chapter, "On *Kiddush Hashem* or Martyrdom, or the *Akedah* as Present Reality."

89. *Midr. Genesis Rabbah* 55.5. See the end of the present section.

90. See the introduction to this chapter and Ginzberg, *The Legends of the Jews*, p. 283.

91. Ginzberg, *The Legends of the Jews*, p. 285.

92. Ginzberg, *The Legends of the Jews*, p. 284.

93. Kierkegaard, *Fear and Trembling*, p. 57.

94. While the Bible as well as Greek philosophy tolerates slavery it would find the Greek term for slave—"animated tool"—wholly intolerable.

95. See Emil L. Fackenheim, "The Historicity and Transcendence of Philosophical Truth," *Proceedings of the Seventh InterAmerican Congress of Philosophy* (Quebec: Laval, 1967), pp. 77–92. Also see, in this book, ch. 5, "Heidegger."

96. See ch. 1 of this book.

97. See, in this chapter, "The Torah as Bridge between Divine Giver and Human Recipient."

98. See, in this chapter, "On the *Akedah*, or Sacrifice and Martyrdom."

99. See especially the already frequently referred to passage, *Midr. Genesis Rabbah* 55.5, and, in this chapter, the end of "On the *Akedah*, or Sacrifice and Martyrdom."

100. Kierkegaard, *Fear and Trembling*, p. 39.

101. See the characteristic passage already cited, at the end of "Kant's Moral Theology," in this chapter.

102. The philosopher Hans Jonas reports that a former German teacher of his who had remained an unwavering anti-Nazi confessed to him that without Kant he could not have done it. Jonas contrasts his attitude with that of the most famous contemporary German philosopher of the time who declared in 1933 that "the *Führer* himself and alone is the present and future German reality and its law." See in ch. 5 of this book, the section, "Heidegger."

103. The various versions of the story are related, and the sources listed, in Shalom Spiegel, *The Last Trial* (New York: Pantheon, 1967), pp. 13ff. Spiegel's work is a masterpiece and, indeed, the present section of this essay could hardly have been written without its inspiration.

104. Ibid., p. 15.

105: Ibid., p. 25.

106. Ibid., pp. 24–25.

107. This is a recurrent theme in Spiegel's work. The exegetes begin with the puzzling fact that Gen. 22:19 states that after the *Akedah* "Abraham returned unto his young men." Where was Isaac?

108. In a celebrated *Responsum on Martyrdom*. Maimonides does not cope adequately with Jewish realities from the Crusades to Hitler when he writes: "If a man is forced to transgress the commandments, he is forbidden to remain in that place but must emigrate, leave everything behind, wander by day and by night, until he has found a place where a man can observe the commandments. *The world is large and wide*." (Italics added.) The text is conveniently available in N. N. Glatzer, *Rabbi Moshe Ben Maimon* (Berlin: Schocken, 1935), pp. 136ff. The translation is mine.

109. *LE*, p. 154.

110. In Maimonides, *Responsum on Martyrdom*, p. 135.

111. Spiegel, *The Last Trial*, pp. 13ff.

112. Ginzberg, *The Legends of the Jews*, pp. 285.

113. Cited in S. Y. Agnon, *Days of Awe* (New York: Schocken, 1965), p. 72.

114. Spiegel, *The Last Trial*, p. 103; Ginzberg, *The Legends of the Jews*, p. 280.

115. In Jewish literature the question is asked, who is superior, "Abraham who with his own hands was prepared to slaughter his son, or . . . Isaac who cast all thoughts of himself to the winds and offered himself to be slaughtered,"

Notes

and the answer is not always in favor of Abraham. (Spiegel, *The Last Trial*, pp. 102–103.)

116. *MPV*, p. 84.

117. Kant, *Religion*, p. 76.

118. "Hat ein Mensch das Recht, sich für die Wahrheit totschlagen zu lassen?" *Der Gesichtspunkt für Meine Wirksamkeit als Schriftsteller*, trans. A. Dorner and Chr. Schrempf. (Jena: Diederichs, 1922), pp. 103–137.

119. Ibid., p. 135. James Parkes writes. "It is significant that the victims of the persecution of Antiochus Epiphanes are the first ordinary men and women to become religious martyrs, so far as we know, in the history of mankind." Parkes comments further: "This is not to belittle the death of Socrates, or to deny that in even earlier centuries unknown men may have died for their convictions. But the special claim for the martyrs of Antiochus lies in the fact that they were found among ordinary men and women. They were not outstanding personalities, like Socrates, who could appear to endanger the 'powers that be'" [*The Foundations of Judaism and Christianity* (London: Valentine-Mitchell, 1960), p. 95.]

120. Kierkegaard, "Hat ein Mensch das Recht," pp. 108, 110, 115.

121. Ibid., p. 114.

122. Ibid., p. 115.

123. Ibid., p. 118.

124. Ibid., p. 121.

125. Ibid., p. 135.

126. Ibid., p. 115.

127. Maimonides, *Responsum on Martyrdom*, p. 135.

128. See for example, Spiegel, *The Last Trial*, p. 21.

129. A theme that, inevitably, recurs through Spiegel's work.

130. See for example, *Midr. Song of Songs*, I:15, 2: "As the dove puts forth her neck for slaughter, so does Israel, as it says, 'For Thy sake are we killed all the day' (Ps. 44:23). As the dove atones for iniquities, so Israel atones for the other nations. . . ."

131. *Midr. Song of Songs*, 7:8.1.

132. Ibid.

133. Leon Poliakov, *Harvest of Hate* (London: Elek, 1956), p. 125. The translation from the original German is mine.

Chapter 3

MOSES AND THE HEGELIANS:
JEWISH EXISTENCE IN THE MODERN WORLD

1. This chapter reflects (and in some respects extends) the Hegel-interpretation given and documented in Emil L. Fackenheim, *The Religious Dimension in Hegel's Thought* (Bloomington: Indiana University Press, 1967; Boston: Beacon, 1970); henceforth cited as *RD*). Documentation in the present essay is therefore confined to its specific contentions. A much briefer version, confined to Hegel's interpretation of Judaism alone, is scheduled to appear in the *Proceedings* of the 1970 Marquette University Hegel Conference.

2. See *Guide for the Perplexed*, III, chs. 35, 39; *Yessode Ha-Torah*, ch. 7.

3. Hegel, *Vorlesungen über die Philosophie der Religion*, ed. Georg Lasson (Hamburg: Meiner, 1966), vol. 2, 1, pp. 96–97. Italics added. (Henceforth cited as *PhRel.*) Here and subsequently our citations are for the most part from the section entitled "The Religion of Sublimity." The reader will have no difficulty locating these in the E. B. Speirs and J. B. Sanderson translation (London: Kegan, Paul, Trench, Trübner and Co. 1895), vol. 2, pp. 170–219.

4. See for example, N. Rotenstreich, "Hegel's Image of Judaism," *Jewish Social Studies*, vol. 15 (1953), pp. 33–52.

5. The reference is, of course, to Heinrich Heine. Any Jewish history may be consulted for what the historian S. Dubnov referred to as "the baptismal epidemic."

6. For a brief exposition of Hegel's distinction between "actuality" and mere "existence," see Emil L. Fackenheim, "On the Actuality of the Rational and the Rationality of the Actual," *The Review of Metaphysics*, vol. 23, 1970, pp. 690–698.

7. *Hegels Leben* (Berlin: Duncker & Humblot, 1844), p. 49.

8. Hegel writes that his own comprehension of history "must be the result of history itself." Of this "result" he asserts that, in order to be philosophical, it cannot be one viewpoint among others but must rather be such that "its spiritual principle is the totality of all viewpoints." [Hegel, *Vorlesungen über die Philosophie der Gechichte*, ed. George Lasson (Leipzig: Meiner, 1919–1920), vol. 1, pp. 6, 7, 9. Subsequently cited as *PhG*.] The importance of this assertion for all that follows cannot be exaggerated. See, in this chapter, "Judaism and Hegelianism: A Contemporary Encounter."

9. For this reason Kant's image of Judaism is ignored in ch. 2, whose purpose was philosophical rather than historical. It will be seen that whereas our philosophical purpose requires the exclusion of Kant's image of Judaism it requires the inclusion of the Hegelian image. For the most recent historical account of the image of Judaism in Hegelian and post-Hegelian thought, see Hans Liebeschütz, *Das Judentum im Deutschen Geschichtsbild von Hegel bis Max Weber* (Tübingen: Mohr, 1967).

10. Hegel, *Philosophy of Right*, trans. T. M. Knox (Oxford: Clarendon, 1942), § 358 (subsequently cited as *PhR*).

11. *PhR*, § 270.

12. See his *Rome and Jerusalem*, trans. M. Waxman (New York: Bloch, 1945). For more on Hess, see, in this chapter, "Jewish Existence in the Bourgeois-Protestant World."

Notes

13. Here Liebeschütz's otherwise excellent account shows the limitation that, the work of a historian rather than a philosopher, it lays too much stress on the "continuity in concept formation," and not enough on the philosopher's ability radically to rethink and alter his own earlier ideas.

14. *Early Theological Writings*, trans. T. M. Knox and Richard Kroner (Chicago: University of Chicago Press, 1948), p. 312. Kroner rightly calls this formula Hegel's "future philosophic system in a nutshell" (p. 14). He fails to add that it also expresses Hegel's mature view of Christianity, considered by him the "true content" necessarily preceding his own philosophy which gives that content its "true form."

15. *PhRel.*, II, I: 82.

16. Ibid., II, I: 81.

17. Ibid., II, I: 55–59.

18. Ibid., II, I: 59–67. The traditional Jewish hymn *Adon Olam* contains the line: "After all things have ended, He, awe-inspiring, alone shall reign: He who was, is, and will be in glory."

19. Ibid., II, I: 70.

20. Ibid.

21. Ibid., II, I: 78.

22. Ibid., II, I: 78ff., 98.

23. Ibid., II, I: 97.

24. Ibid., II, I: 81ff.

25. Ibid., II, I: 99.

26. Ibid., II, I: 98. Hegel's Job has a remarkable resemblance to Kierkegaard's Abraham who in the very act of absolute resignation has faith that all will be restored to him, a resemblance all the more remarkable since it is most unlikely that Hegelian influence, obvious elsewhere in Kierkegaard's thought, helped shape his image of Abraham. That two Christian dialectical thinkers trying to understand Judaism arrived at similar conclusions is a fact worthy of close examination. On different images of Job, see notes 33 and 147.

27. For the relation between "feeling," "representation" and "cult" in religious existence, see RD, pp. 120–124.

28. *PhRel.*, II, I: 94.

29. Ibid., II, I: 96ff., 100 (Italics added.)

30. Ibid., II, I: 97.

31. See, in this chapter, "Hegel's Account of Judaism."

32. See *I and Thou* (New York: Scribner, 1958); *Kingdom of God* (New York: Harper and Row, 1967).

33. See Martin Buber, *At The Turning* (New York: Farrar, Straus and Young, 1952), p. 61: "Job . . . charges that the 'cruel' (30:21) God has 'removed his right' from him (27:2) and thus that the judge of the earth acts against justice. And he receives an answer from God. But what God says to him does not answer the charge; *it does not even touch upon it*. The true answer that Job receives is God's appearance only. . . ." (Italics added.) See also note 147.

34. See, in this chapter, "Athens and Jerusalem."

35. *PhRel.*, II, I: 82.

36. Ibid., II, I: 59, 62, 82. See RD, pp. 129–33, 134, 189n.

37. *Sifra* 89b. Cited in Loewe-Montefiore, *A Rabbinic Anthology* (London: MacMillan, 1938), p. 172. Since rabbinic sources are not easily accessible to philosophical scholars we shall, wherever possible, give references to this excellent anthology. (Hereafter cited as *RA*.)

Notes

38. Of the countless passages the following is especially apt: "Love and fear God; tremble and rejoice when you perform the commandments." (*Abot d'Rabbi Nathan*, 61:67, *RA*, p. 379.)

39. *Bab. Talmud, Tractate Menahot*, 29b (*RA*, p. 217).

40. The fact that the Torah was given in the desert is used by the rabbis to give Midrashic proof that it is "free to all the inhabitants of the world;" that "everyone who desires it may come and accept it;" that no tribe may say to the others "I am better than you;" and that "if a man does not make himself free to all as the desert, he is not worthy to receive the Torah." (A selection from the many relevant passages is assembled in *RA*, pp. 166ff.)

41. *PhRel.*, II, I: p. 96.

42. Ibid., II, I: pp. 95ff.

43. Hegel, *Early Theological Writings*, pp. 158ff., 203. Hegel here states that "the ordinary Jew," unwilling to let go of his God but faced with the "grim reality" of the loss of the Jewish state, "fled" from this reality by means of the Messianic hope. This view of Jewish Messianism as escapism may be an important clue (one that, after the Nazi holocaust and the rise of the first Jewish state in two thousand years, no Jewish thinker may take lightly) to Hegel's subsequent neglect of Jewish Messianism. But what might Hegel have to say about the state of Christian Messianism in the contemporary world? And, in view of the epoch-making events in contemporary Jewish history just referred to, could Hegel today still write: "The scattered remnants of the Jews have not abandoned the idea of the Jewish state, but they have reverted, not to the banners of their own courage, but only to the standards of an ineffective Messianic hope" (p. 159)? See, in this chapter, "Left-wing Hegelianism and 'the Jewish Problem'" and "Judaism and Hegelianism: A Contemporary Encounter."

44. For the complex reasons for our alternating use of the terms "Greek" and "Greek-Roman," see *RD*, especially pp. 133–138, 157–158, 166–171.

45. In Hegel's view, a philosophical standpoint vis-à-vis religion must be superior as well as merely external to religion unless the reality of religion is to escape its comprehension, not to speak of its judgment. In the present context, however, we must let the philosophical claim to such superiority unfold gradually, lest the crucial issues in the encounter aimed at are not confronted but rather prejudged from the start.

46. See Fackenheim, "Actuality of the Rational." Whether the possibility of *all* things in empirical history is in fact banal, or merely held to be so by Hegel's philosophy, is a question we must suspend until the end. Not until then can we ask how Hegel copes, not with the nonspiritual, but with absolute anti-Spirit. Does evil remain banal when it is absolute?

47. For corroboration, see *RD*, pp. 133–138, 157–158, 166–171.

48. *PhG*, II: 528.

49. See *RD*, p. 165 for a statement, and pp. 165–184 for a sketch of Hegel's demonstration, of this central (and most controversial) thesis of his three volume *History of Philosophy*.

50. The Hegelian schools, left as well as right (see, in this chapter, "Left-wing Hegelianism and 'the Jewish Problem.'"), created the legend of a Hegel *simply* siding with Athens. We have dealt with this prejudice (or deliberate distortion) in *RD* (especially pp. 157–158) and will here confine ourselves to citing a single passage:

> Divinity, self-determined as Holiness, is a higher truth than a merely beautiful Subjectivity . . . , where the absolute content is still particular . . . , a rela-

Notes

tion analogous to that between animal and man. Animals have particular characteristics; the characteristic of universality is human. . . . Self-determined Subjectivity is wisdom and holiness. [To be sure], as regards content the Greek gods are ethical powers; [but] they are not holy, for they are still particular and limited. (*PhRel.* II, I: 57).

51. See *RD*, especially pp. 158, 171n, 179n, 184–192. That this view is here maintained only on Hegelian assumptions is obvious, and concepts of a "Jewish philosophy" outside these assumptions transcend the limits of the present discourse. As will be seen, within his crucial assumption—that philosophy is a rise in thought to identity with God—Hegel is consistent both in the denial of a philosophy within Judaism itself and in his view that Spinozism is Judaism transfigured into "free" modern thought. This does not exclude the possibility that, on different assumptions, Spinozism is the anti-Jewish modern philosophy par excellence.

52. Very likely it is not accidental that the phrase "Greek god," found in Lasson's critical edition, is omitted in the original edition, in the compilation of which Bruno Bauer had a share. (See *RD*, pp. 157–158). On Bauer's proclassical and anti-Jewish bias, see, in this chapter, "Left-wing Hegelianism and 'the Jewish Problem.' "

53. See Fackenheim, "Actuality of the Rational."

54. Elias Bickerman, "The Maccabees" in *From Esra To the Last of the Maccabees* (New York: Schocken, 1962), p. 94. We are immensely indebted to Bickerman's brief but brilliant and authoritative work, which makes on purely historical grounds the exact point we make on philosophical grounds—a rare confirmation that a speculative concern with history may have a firm foundation in historical fact.

55. The following citations are all from Bickerman's work, respectively pp. 102, 103, 108–109, 97, 126, 100, 121, 156, 162–164.

56. On this point, see further *RD*, pp. 133–138.

57. See further *RD*, pp. 138–159, 193–222.

58. See also *RD*, pp. 171–175, 158–159, 216–217.

59. *Lectures on the History of Philosophy*, trans. E. S. Haldane and F. H. Simson (London: Kegan Paul, Trench, Trübner, 1895), vol. III, pp. 52–53.

60. Hegel is therefore consistent in asserting that, while the Jewish people has world-historical significance throughout the Christian Middle Ages, this lies not in its own testimony and self-understanding, but rather in a "fate" for which it was "held in readiness" by "Spirit and its world." (*PhR* § 358) See further, below in the present section.

61. The rabbinic response to this event is dealt with masterfully by N. N. Glatzer, *Untersuchungen zur Geschichtslehre der Tannaiten* (Berlin: Schocken, 1933), especially pp. 5, 106. See also Emil L. Fackenheim, *God's Presence in History* (New York: New York University Press, 1970), pp. 26ff.

62. While it will emerge that by any serious standard the restoration of a Jewish state after two thousand years is an epoch-making event, we may here simply note that no "Zionist"—"religious" or "secularist"—identifies that event with the Messianic days.

63. *Bab. Talmud, Tractate Menahot*, 29b (*RA*, p. 217). For the rabbinic concept of "oral Torah," the reader may conveniently consult the representative collection in *RA*, ch. 5.

64. See, in this chapter, "Hegel's Account of Judaism," and ch. 2, "The Parting of Ways between Kant and Judaism."

Notes

65. For an exposition of Rabbi Akiba's Midrash concerning the divine exile, see Fackenheim, *God's Presence in History*, pp. 28ff.

66. All these elements are explicitly contained in Rabbi Akiba's Midrash.

67. *PhR* § 358.

68. We use the term "bourgeois" for convenience's sake only, and with hesitation, since in Hegel's thought the "secular" aspect of the modern world transcends bourgeois limitations. In "Left-wing Hegelianism and 'the Jewish Problem' " this hesitation will vanish.

69. On Hegel's relation to his immediate predecessors on this point, see *RD*, pp. 225–233.

70. At stake here is Hegel's vitally important and relentless critique of romanticism—a Protestant temptation to this day. Hegel himself never connects this critique with his view of Judaism. However, that Christianity in its romantic form is furthest removed from Judaism is argued persuasively by Leo Baeck, "Romantic Religion," in *Judaism and Christianity* (New York: Meridian and Jewish Publication Society, 1958), pp. 189–292. See also, for example, Schleiermacher's scandalous treatment of Judaism in his *The Christian Faith*, trans. H. R. MacIntosh and J. S. Stewart (Edinburgh: Clarke, 1928), pp. 37, 43ff., 60ff. In his *On Religion*, trans. J. Oman (New York: Harper Torchbooks, 1958), Schleiermacher, though professing to be "charmed" by the "beautiful, childlike character of Judaism," nevertheless flatly declares that it is "long since dead"—after having urged his readers to "remove anything political and moral" from this religion and to "regard only its strictly religious elements" (pp. 238ff.). One need hardly add that Schleiermacher defines these "elements" in his own romantic terms, and that he makes a sweeping judgment on Judaism quite undisturbed by the fact of his total ignorance of postbiblical Judaism. An intriguing fact (which, however, does not exonerate Schleiermacher) is his intimacy with Jews—and Jewesses!—who shared his views on Judaism and were equally ignorant of it. Infatuation with what Hegel calls the romantic "beautiful souls" on the part of Jews themselves (and consequent Jewish self-hatred) is a sorry chapter in Jewish history, and, to judge by current types of Jewish beautiful souls, it is not yet ended. That chapter includes such people as Henrietta Herz, Dorothea Schlegel, Rahel Varnhagen and, in our time, Simone Weil. Hannah Arendt's *Rahel Varnhagen* (London: East & West Library, 1957), a sympathetic study of a Jewess in conflict, quotes her as writing: "the Jew must be extirpated from us; that is the sacred [*sic!*] truth, and it must be done even if life were uprooted in the process" (p. 105).

71. Hegel writes:

> We see that thought moves to begin with [i.e., in the Middle Ages] within Christianity, accepting it as absolute presupposition. Later, when the wings of thought have grown strong [i.e., in the modern world], philosophy rises to the sun like a young eagle, a bird of prey which strikes religion down. But it is the last development of speculative thought to do justice to faith and make peace with religion.

[*Vorlesungen über die Geschichte der Philosophie*, ed. J. Hoffmeister (Leipzig: Meiner 1944) pp. 190ff.)]

72. This is developed at length in *RD*, ch. 6, where the interpretation here merely asserted is corroborated, albeit without specific reference to the "justice" done by Hegel to Judaism. The reader will bear in mind that the passage cited in note 71 explicitly refers to Christianity only.

73. We have argued in *RD* that this term is vitally important for the overall understanding of Hegel's entire thought, pp. 98, 112, 256n.

Notes

74. For left-wing Hegelian trivializations, see, in this chapter, "Left-wing Hegelianism and 'the Jewish Problem.' "

75. If a demonstration of this kind is possible, it is because Hegel's "implicitly actual" modern religious-secular union is and remains creative diversity. Secular self-activity never ceases to confront contingent fact, while for Protestant faith Good Friday and Easter never overcome the contingent form of receptivity characteristic of all religious faith. The philosophical *recognition* of their union does not therefore replace this diversity with a new form of postsecular, post-religious life, but rather *reinstates* that diversity. See *RD*, ch. 6, especially pp. 220ff.

76. *PhR* § 270; also § 209. Under direct Hegelian inspiration some of his students led the fight for the admission of Jewish students to fraternities, fanatically opposed by most fraternities and especially by those who took their inspiration from the supposedly "liberal" but in fact viciously antisemitic philosopher Fries. See Shlomo Avineri, "Hegel's Views on Jewish Emancipation," *Jewish Social Studies*, 25, 1963, pp. 145–151.

77. We have argued elsewhere that Hegel would not be a Hegelian today. See "Would Hegel Today Be a Hegelian?" (*Dialogue*, 9, 1970, pp. 222–226), an article that should be read together with the rejoinder by James Doull (Ibid., pp. 226–235). See also the section in this chapter, "Judaism and Hegelianism: A Contemporary Encounter."

78. From an address by Eduard Gans published by Salman Rubaschoff, "Erstlinge der Entjudung: Drei Reden von Eduard Gans im Kulturverein," *Der Jüdische Wille*, I (1918), p. 198. Quoted in Michael A. Meyer, *The Origins of the Modern Jew* (Detroit: Wayne State University Press, 1967), p. 167. Meyer's excellent study should be consulted for this whole subject.

79. Ibid.

80. Rubaschoff, "Erstlinge der Entjudung," p. 32.

81. Meyer, *Origins of the Modern Jew*, p. 164. This formulation is by one of the 7, Joel Abraham List.

82. Rubaschoff, "Erstlinge der Entjudung," p. 33.

83. For Zunz, see Luitpold Wallach's thorough *Liberty and Letters: The Thought of Leopold Zunz* (London: East and West Library, 1959). The famous expression "decent burial" was coined by the great scholar Moritz Steinschneider.

84. Rubaschoff, "Erstlinge der Entjudung," p. 33.

85. Ibid., pp. 112–113. Quoted by Meyer, *Origins of the Modern Jew*, p. 168.

86. See especially Gershom Scholem, "Germans and Jews" in *The Jewish Expression*, J. Goldin, ed. (New York: Bantam, 1970). pp. 465–483.

87. Rubaschoff, "Erstlinge der Entjudung," p. 34.

88. Hirsch's *Religionsphilosophie der Juden* appeared in 1841, Hess's *Rom und Jerusalem* in 1862. On Hirsch, see Emil L. Fackenheim, "Samuel Hirsch and Hegel," in *Studies in Nineteenth Century Jewish Intellectual History*, ed. A. Altmann (Cambridge, Mass.: Harvard University Press, 1964), pp. 171–201. This study argues that at least in one crucial point Hirsch would not or could not surrender the otherness of the Jewish God.

89. *Rome and Jerusalem* (New York: Bloch, 1945), p. 43.

90. For an excellent biography of Geiger and a selection from his writings representative of his thought, see Max Wiener, *Abraham Geiger and Liberal Judaism* (Philadelphia: Jewish Publication Society, 1962).

91. Samson Raphael Hirsch (who was a voluminous writer) summed up his own thought in his *Nineteen Letters* (New York: Feldheim, 1959).

Notes

92. Max Wiener, *Jüdische Religion im Zeitalter der Emanzipation* (Berlin: Philo, 1933), pp. 72–73, writes as follows:

He goes so far as to spiritualize the ancient national existence of Israel, its independent statehood, denied in no other quarter, when he declares that these were never the meaning and purpose of Israel's peoplehood, but always mere means to her "spiritual vocation." He projects Heine's dictum of the Torah as the "portable" fatherland of the Jews back into the national, heroic age. . . .

93. At this point it should expressly be stated that the following treatment of these thinkers, and especially that of Rosenzweig, is confined to their significance as responses to Hegelianism. Indeed, since existentialism has yet to face *Jewish* existentialism (see below ch. 5), their thought, considered in its own right, transcends the scope not only of the present chapter but of this entire book.

94. *Ethik des reinen Willens*, 2nd ed. (Berlin: Cassirer, 1907), p. 407. See Emil L. Fackenheim, "Hermann Cohen—After Fifty Years" (Memorial lecture no. 12, Leo Baeck Institute, New York, 1969), for a brief attempt to locate this breakthrough on Cohen's part in his philosophical system.

95. Cohen softens but does not abandon this stand when he establishes a close link between the spirit of Judaism and that of Protestantism. According to a well-known anecdote Cohen was asked by a Marburg colleague whether he would attend a Luther festival and replied: "If I did not attend, who should?" (Cohen's image of Luther as an apostle of modern freedom is close to that of Hegel.) When Cohen died in Berlin, the local philosophers ignored the funeral of the thinker who, virtually alone, had resurrected nineteenth-century German philosophy.

96. Leo Strauss, "Preface to the English Edition of *Spinoza's Critique of Religion*," reprinted in *The Jewish Expression*, J. Goldin, ed. (New York: Bantam, 1970), p. 360.

97. *Hegel und der Staat* (Munich & Berlin: Oldenbourg, 1920). The book was written before World War I. In the preface, written in 1920, Rosenzweig confesses that in 1919 he was able only to complete it and could no longer have begun it. "I do not know whence one can still derive the courage today of writing German history." (p. XII)

98. Whereas Kant's God retains an aspect of otherness, this is not true of Cohen's God-Idea, except possibly for his posthumous *Religion der Vernunft aus den Quellen des Judentums*. See Fackenheim, "Herman Cohen—After Fifty Years."

99. *Jüdische Schriften*, ed. B. Strauss (Berlin: Schwetschke, 1924), vol. I, p. 8. See Fackenheim, "Herman Cohen—After Fifty Years," p. 10.

100. The *Star of Redemption* is now available in English (New York: Holt, Rinehart & Winston, 1970). Relevant passages sufficient for our present purpose are found in N. N. Glatzer, *Franz Rosenzweig: His Life and Thought* (New York: Schocken, 1953; paperback ed., 1961). See part II, § 1 of that work for Rosenzweig's "new thinking," and part II § 5 for his views on Judaism and Christianity.

101. That here, too, the disciple surpasses the teacher is evident from his views on Zionism, which, inadequate though they are in hindsight, at any rate do not dispose of this phenomenon in terms of bloodless and unreal categories. (See Glatzer, *Franz Rosenzweig*, part II, § 6, 3.) Cohen's philosophy of Judaism is shattered by the epoch-making events in contemporary Jewish history; that of Rosenzweig is merely required to absorb the overwhelming fact that, having been for two millennia merely of history, the Jewish people is suddenly, once again, in history, with consequences unforeseeable for the destiny of the people and the faith alike.

Notes

102. See, in this chapter, "Judaism and Hegelianism: A Contemporary Encounter."

103. See the end of *PhRel,* and *RD,* pp. 233ff.

104. The reservations with which we have used this term drop in this section, in which it assumes its one-dimensional left-wing Hegelian meaning.

105. This term, appearing from Feuerbach on, replaces Hegel's "Spirit."

106. The allusion is, of course, to Marx's famous ninth thesis on Feuerbach.

107. The best general account of these and other left-wing Hegelians is Karl Löwith, *From Hegel to Nietzsche* (New York: Holt, Rinehart & Winston, 1964). A representative selection from their writings, otherwise hard to come by, is *Die Hegelsche Linke,* Karl Löwith, ed. (Stuttgart: Frommann, 1962).

108. The translation is ours, but this passage from Marx's *Critique of Hegel's Philosophy of Right* has frequently been anthologized. (See for example, *Marx and Engels on Religion,* [New York: Schocken, 1964], pp. 41ff.; *Karl Marx: Early Writings,* trans. T. B. Bottomore [New York: McGraw-Hill, 1964], pp. 43ff.; *Writings of the Young Marx on Philosophy and Society,* ed. L. D. Easton and K. D. Guddat [New York: Anchor 1967], pp. 249ff.) Lest it be thought that here is not yet the "true" or "mature" Marx we add the concluding sentences of the whole essay:

> Always seeking fundamentals, Germany can only make a fundamental revolution. The emancipation of the Germans is the emancipation of mankind. *The head of the emancipation is philosophy, its heart is the proletariat. Philosophy cannot be actualized without the transformation* (Aufhebung) *of the proletariat; the proletariat cannot be transformed without the actualization of philosophy.*
>
> When all the inner conditions are fulfilled, the day of the German resurrection will be announced by the French rooster. (Italics added.)

109. *Die Hegelsche Linke,* p. 46.

110. *From Hegel to Nietzsche,* p. 86.

111. *Die Hegelsche Linke,* p. 111.

112. Ibid., p. 228.

113. *The Essence of Christianity* (New York: Harper Torchbooks, 1957), p. XXXVIII. This fundamental thesis is expanded throughout the work; see for example, pp. 14, 18, 46, 54. That Feuerbach "transforms" Protestant Christianity, and yet means to encompass in this transformation *every* religion, is evident even to the most casual reader. Sweeping assertions such as "the real God of any religion is the so-called Mediator, because He alone is the immediate object of religion" (p. 74) serve to show that Judaism—than which no religion rejects a mediator more emphatically—must be a "riddle" to Feuerbach as to Hegel. It will be seen, however, that unlike Hegel, Feuerbach makes no attempt to do "justice" to Judaism.

114. *From Hegel to Nietzsche,* pp. 349–350.

115. Shlomo Avineri, *The Social and Political Thought of Karl Marx* (Cambridge University Press 1969), p. 202; also p. 35. A single additional passage may suffice to give substance to Avineri's characterization.

> The perfected Christian state is not the so-called *Christian* state which acknowledges Christianity as its basis, as the state religion, and thus adopts an exclusive attitude towards other religions; it is, rather, the *atheistic* state, the democratic state, the state which relegates religion among the other elements of civil society. (*Early Writings,* p. 16.)

116. *The Essence of Christianity,* pp. 112, 113, 114, 115, 32, 118, 119.

117. For another interpretation see Nathan Rotenstreich, "The Bruno Bauer

Notes

Controversy," *Leo Baeck Institute Yearbook*, vol. IV (London: East and West Library 1959), pp. 25ff. Rotenstreich derives Feuerbach's image of Judaism from Mendelssohn's conception of Judaism as a religion of law, so reinterpreted as to fit into his own atheism. Our disagreement with Rotenstreich derives more from a desire to take Feuerbach on his own terms philosophically seriously than from available evidence. In the nature of the case, *any* philosophical understanding of *all* the left-wing images of Judaism is largely speculative.

118. Hegel expressly states that Judaism is "fanaticism" but not "egoism" (*PhRel.*, II, I, p. 100).

119. Ibid., p. 298.

120. Ibid., p. 299.

121. Reprinted in English translation as an introductory essay to *The Essence of Christianity*.

122. Ibid., pp. X, XIX.

123. *The Jewish Problem*, trans. Helen Lederer (Cincinnati: Hebrew Union College, 1958). See also Bauer's "Die Fähigkeit der heutigen Juden und Christen, frei zu werden" *Feldzüge der reinen Kritik* (Frankfurt: Suhrkamp, 1968), pp. 175–195.

124. *The Jewish Problem*, p. 85.

125. Ibid., p. 124.

126. Beyond belief is at least the fact that serious thinkers at the time took Bauer seriously. See Rotenstreich, "The Bruno Bauer Controversy." Even this, alas, is no longer beyond belief in an age in which the works of Hitler and Alfred Rosenberg have been taken seriously by reputable German academicians.

127. See Fackenheim, "On the Actuality of the Rational."

128. *Feldzüge*, pp. 178, 179.

129. *The Jewish Problem*, pp. 39, 41.

130. *Feldzüge*, pp. 178, 182, 183, 181.

131. *The Jewish Problem*, pp. 18ff.

132. Rotenstreich's essay, "The Bruno Bauer Controversy" gives both Jewish and Christian reactions.

133. *The Jewish Problem*, pp. 32, 20.

134. The main relevant texts are his two lengthy and influential reviews of Bauer's two treatises (*Early Writings*, Bottomore translation pp. 1–40), together with short sections in *The Holy Family*, coauthored with Engels (Moscow: Foreign Languages Publishing House 1956). Since we shall here consider Marx purely as a dialectical thinker, we shall leave unconsidered whether Marx *as a person* was or was not antisemitic. Any serious student of this latter question must disregard both cold war propaganda (see Karl Marx, *A World Without Jews*, ed. Dagobert Runes [New York: Wisdom Library, 1959]) *and* the view that "to designate Marx as an anti-Semite is nothing but cold war propaganda" (Erich Fromm in Karl Marx: *Early Writings*, p. V). Instead he must examine the evidence, as is done, for example, by Edmund Silberner in "Was Marx an Anti-Semite?" *Historia Judaica*, vol. XI, 1949, pp. 3–52, and Shlomo Avineri, "Marx and Jewish Emancipation," *Journal of the History of Ideas* (1964), pp. 445–450.

135. For example, *Early Writings*, p. 8:

Bauer asks the Jews: have you from your standpoint the right to demand *political emancipation?* We ask the reverse question: from the standpoint of *political* emancipation, can the Jew be required to abolish Judaism ... ?

Marx goes on to affirm:

It is only in the free states of North America, or at least in some of them,

Notes

that the Jewish question loses its *theological* significance and becomes a truly *secular* question.

136. Avineri, "Marx and Jewish Emancipation," p. 449.

137. *Early Writings*, pp. 34ff.

138. In Bauer's view Jewish nationality, "chimerical" *now* (*The Jewish Problem*, p. 45), *always has been so* because of the "positivity" of the Mosaic law, since "this law is in itself chimerical and incapable of forming the core of a real national life" (*The Jewish Problem*, pp. 26, 29–33). Moreover, whatever reality it may have had has long been rendered anachronistic by Christianity:

> The Jewish people was a nation which was not really a nation, the people of the chimera, inconsistent only in that it wanted to exist as a real nation. Christianity abolished this inconsistency, this deceptive illusion of national existence. [*The Jewish Problem*, p. 50.]

Marx rejects Bauer's crypto-theological presuppositions. Yet he asserts that *in the present* "the *chimerical* nationality of the Jew is the nationality of the trader and, above all, the financier" (*Early Writings*, p. 38), an assertion virtually indistinguishable from Bauer's (in *The Jewish Problem*, p. 6):

> ... like the gods of Epicure who live in the interstellar spaces and are freed from specific labors, so the Jews have struck roots outside the corporate interests in the gaps and crevices of society, and have caught the victims of ... civil society.

Moreover, since, like Bauer, he considers Judaism to be "practical egoism" it follows that not only present but also past Jewish nationality is "chimerical," bound up as it is with this egoism. Thus the only difference between Bauer and Marx concerns the future. Unlike Bauer's doctrine, that of Marx might conceivably be so altered as to allow for *future genuine* Jewish nationalists. However, Marxist Jewish nationalists must honestly face the fact that the writings of their master give less succor to them than to their enemies. See notes 141 and 150.

139. *The Jewish Problem*, p. 89. In response to Jewish attacks on Eisenmenger, Bauer asks why no Jew has written a corresponding critique of Christianity—an *Entdecktes Christentum*. The obvious answer—that any such Jewish work in nineteenth-century Germany would have produced an antisemitic explosion—does not occur to him.

140. *Early Writings*, p. 38.

141. See note 138. Any serious Jewish effort to give the revival of the Jewish nation Marxist foundations must cope with the facts that Marx, no abstract liberal internationalist, assigns concrete reality to nations such as France and Germany in the postcapitalist future; that he denies the Jewish nation any such future on the grounds of its "chimerical" past; and that *no* dialectical thinker can affirm *any* future for a nation if its past is *simply* "chimerical."

142. For an English version of the poem "Princess Sabbath" see *The Poetry and Prose of Heinrich Heine*, Aaron Kramer et al., trans. (New York: Citadel Press, 1948), pp. 263–267. The translation here given is ours.

143. According to Talmudic teaching the biblical commandment to "remember" the Sabbath is twofold, involving mental recollection and anticipation during the week, and reliving on the Sabbath itself.

144. See Avineri, *The Social and Political Thought of Karl Marx*, p. 142.

145. Marx's own paradigm of the future liberated Man—the proletariat—has had to be expanded in our own time so as to include many liberation movements. Of these, one—Zionism—"*represented the only intentionally downwardly mobile social movement ever experienced in the history of immigration.*" (Shlomo Avineri, "The Palestinians and Israel," *Commentary*, June 1970, p. 35; the italics

[251]

Notes

are the author's.) Only a fusion of "secular" self-activity and "religious" Messianic hope—of the "everyday" and the "Sabbath" Jew—could have produced such a development. For a sample of Marxist ideologizing responses to these facts, see note 150.

146. *Das Prinzip Hoffnung* (Frankfurt: Suhrkamp, 1959), for example, pp. 1412ff., 1456ff., 1464ff.

147. Bloch's image of Job contrasts totally with that of Hegel. He attacks the church when it makes of Job the prototype of all who "practise praiseworthy submission" to God, and replaces this image with a Job who is an *absolute* rebel. He does not hesitate to eliminate on purely a priori grounds the end of the book where God "blessed Job more than hitherto." (*Atheismus im Christentum,* [Frankfurt: Suhrkamp, 1968], pp. 159ff.) See note 33 for an image of Job that is not only authentically Jewish but also approaches the text without a priori commitments.

148. *Das Prinzip Hoffnung,* pp. 1456–1457.

149. Ibid., p. 1413.

150. To disabuse the reader of the opinion that the nasty disposals have disappeared one might quote an enormous amount of Soviet and Arab propaganda. To stick instead to a presumably serious philosophical work, in his *Marx's Theory of Alienation* (London: Merin Press, 1970), I. Meszaros (1) asserts a "Judeo-Christion alienation" from God, oblivious to the fact that in Judaism, unlike Christianity, reconciliation with God (*T'shuvah*) is possible without a vicarious divine self-sacrifice (p. 28); (2) contrasts a merely "particularistic Jewish" with a "universalistic" Christian prohibition of usury, failing to mention that Christians —not "capitalists"—first forced Jews to do the dirty business of usury on their behalf (pp. 29–30); (3) identifies the "spirit of Judaism" with that of capitalism— with the new twist that one must, of course (but does not and presumably cannot always) distinguish between Judaism as "an empirical reality"—i.e., actual Jews— and Judaism as a universal principle, and that the failure to do so "could [sic!] lead to . . . scape-hunting anti-Semitism" (p. 30); and (4) maintains that by virtue of their "narrow particularism" Jews have no universal talents except for philosophy, and even this only when, like Spinoza and Marx, they explicitly turn against that narrowness (pp. 71–72):

> Only those Jewish philosophers could achieve the comprehensiveness and degree of universality that characterize the system of both Spinoza and Marx who were able to grasp the issue of Jewish emancipation in its paradoxical duality, as inextricably intertwined with the historical development of mankind. Many others, from Moses Hess to Martin Buber, because of the particularistic character of their perspective or, in other words, because of their inability to emancipate themselves from "Jewish narrowness," formulated their views in terms of second-rate, provincialistic utopias.

Since Chinese and Cubans may legitimately remain Chinese and Cubans (p. 274), despite the fact that the liberation movements of both nations have yet to produce a thinker of the stature of Martin Buber, the above assertions can only mean that even in an age of rebirth unequalled anywhere, Jewish nationality, alone of all nationalities, is and remains "chimerical," an assertion that is in fact repeated throughout the book. The reader who wonders what, except slavish adherence to Marx and even Bauer, could justify this double standard is asked to substitute in the following statement, "Israel" for "Cuba," "Russian military threats" for "American imperialism," and "American" for "Soviet help":

> Admittedly, in Cuba's survival in face of the massive naked power of American imperialism, Soviet help, both military and economic, played an enor-

[252]

Notes

mously important role. *But no country can survive on outside help alone.* [p. 274, italics added.] Meszaros's book was awarded the Isaac Deutscher Memorial Prize for 1970.

151. See the introduction to this chapter.

152. See note 8.

153. *PhG*, I, p. 5.

154. We here resume the argument suspended at the end of "Jewish Existence in the Bourgeois-Protestant World."

155. This is the main burden of the argument of *RD*, ch. 6.

156. See *RD*, pp. 168ff.

157. The title of a memoir by Alexander Donat (New York: Holt, Rinehart & Winston, 1965), which, more terrifyingly than any other work known to this writer, conveys the fact that the Nazi murder camp had acquired a self-perpetuating dynamic power that, except for the Nazi defeat, might have conquered the world. It still may.

158. Among these we might list a linguistic moral philosophy, which, with dubious humility, confines its analysis of moral reasoning to those abiding by the rules of the "game"; a Kantian ethics that is undisturbed by the fact that Adolf Eichmann acted from duty rather than inclination, and an existentialism that, though holding fast to the scandal of human uniqueness, manages to overlook the uniqueness of Auschwitz. See ch. 5, especially "Heidegger."

159. So far as we know, there exists as yet no Protestant counterpart to Gordon C. Zahn's Catholic *German Catholics and Hitler's Wars* (London & New York: Sheed, 1963). Since in any case there is a growing myth that no good German Christian ever was a Nazi it is apt to quote the eminent Protestant theologian-philosopher Emanuel Hirsch:

> Leadership involves the free . . . confessing commitment of the led to the leader. . . . That leader and *Volk* find and understand each other is a free gift of God. . . . We must . . . relate the image of the Christian which the Gospels bid us form to the image of the German which is about to be realized in the new German order. . . . [With the performance of this "fruitfully paradoxical task"] faith may perform a service for the national-socialist spirit which could become an act of gratitude for all the possibilities of Christian proclamation and new Christian thinking granted it by the new hour. (*Die gegenwärtige geistige Lage im Spiegel philosophischer und theologischer Besinnung* [Göttingen: Vanderhoeck & Ruprecht, 1934], pp. 64, 143.)

160. For a fragment of an investigation, see ch. 4.

161. For our views on the doctrines of Dietrich Bonhoeffer and his followers here referred to, see "On the Self-Exposure of Faith to the Modern-Secular World," *Quest For Past and Future* (Bloomington: Indiana University Press, 1968; Beacon, 1970), ch. 18.

162. The allusion is, of course, once again to Marx's ninth thesis on Feuerbach.

163. Here, as in *RD*, p. 162, we quote from *Werke* (2nd ed., Berlin: Duncker & Humblot, 1840–1847), vol. 12, p. 147. Lasson's *PhRel* makes the same point in a much more involved way.

164. We quote, again as in *RD* (p. 190), from *Werke*, vol. XII, pp. 222ff.; XIII, pp. 117ff.

165. *Werke*, vol. XIII, p. 337, *RD*, p. 189.

166. For this characterization by Karl Barth, see, in this chapter, "Left-wing Hegelianism and 'the Jewish Problem.' "

167. *I and Thou* (New York: Scribner, 1958), p. 96.

Notes

168. It should be stressed, however, that when Buber, like Hegel, uses the expression "antinomy" (ibid.), both thinkers, as might be expected, take a conscious departure from Kant and are thus at least indirectly related.

169. Precisely this doctrine makes *I and Thou* Buber's first mature work—the work in which, according to a remark by him to the present writer, he started thinking. In the light of this, it would be improper to understand Buber as rejecting Hegel's "one double activity" only epistemologically, and not ontologically as well, in passages such as: "Certainly in my answering I am given over into the power of His Grace, but I cannot measure Heaven's share in it" (*Between Man and Man* [Boston: Beacon, 1955], p. 69).

170. The following several pages reproduce with some slight alterations a segment of a paper entitled "Demythologizing and Remythologizing in Jewish Experience: Reflections Inspired by Hegel's Philosophy," which was read at the 1971 meeting of the American Catholic Philosophical Association and is published in the *Proceedings* of that association, vol. XLV, *Myth and Philosophy* (Washington: The Catholic University, 1971), pp. 16–27.

171. *Midrash Rabbah*, Song of Songs, V, 16, no. 3, trans. M. Simon (London: Soncino Press, 1961), pp. 252ff. (*RA*, p. 60).

172. *Sifre on Deuteronomy*, Berakhah 346, 144a (*RA*, p. 35).

173. *Midrash Rabbah*, Psalms, commenting on Ps. 123:1 (*RA*, p. 34).

174. We have made some fragmentary attempts to deal with this crisis on several occasions, most fully thus far in *God's Presence in History*. The attempts made in the present book are limited by the respective contexts of the philosophies with which a Jewish encounter is carried out.

175. See Strauss, "Preface to the English Edition of *Spinoza's Critique of Religion*," p. 347.

176. See chs. 1 and 5.

177. *Early Theological Writings* (Chicago: University of Chicago Press, 1948), p. 159.

178. Louis Ginzberg, *The Legends of the Jews* (Philadelphia: Jewish Publication Society, 1964), vol. II, p. 373.

Chapter 4

IDOLATRY AS A MODERN POSSIBILITY

1. The other two sins are murder and incest.

2. "Whosoever acknowledges idols repudiates the whole Torah, but whoever repudiates idolatry is as though he accepted the whole Torah" (*Sifre*, Deut. Re'eh No. 54).

3. This is in application of the rabbinic admonition to "build a fence around the Torah" (*Pirke Abot* I, 1).

4. The traditional *Aleynu* prayer anticipates a Messianic future "when Thou wilt remove idols from the earth, and the non-gods shall be wholly destroyed." The corresponding passage in the modern liberal *Union Prayer Book* still is: ". . . when superstition shall no longer enslave the mind, nor idolatry blind the eye. . . ."

5. *Mekilta de-Rabbi Ishmael*, Jacob Z. Lauterbach, ed. and trans. (Philadelphia: Jewish Publication Society, 1949), vol. II, pp. 237ff.

6. For Hegel this characteristic of the Christian God has become fully actual only in the modern world, and is anticipated in the ancient world only by the philosophies of Plato and Aristotle.

7. The coupling of Hegel and Toynbee is by no means to suggest that they are thinkers of comparable rank but much rather to exemplify the extremes of profundity and shallowness. Hegel's universalism is an unequalled synthesis nourished by a desire to do justice to every historical phenomenon. Toynbee's universalism is a mere watery syncretism, nourished by the platitude that men may rise on the stepping stones of their dead "particularistic" selves to higher, more "universal" things. It is thus not surprising that Toynbee not only fails to show the slightest historical understanding for the biblical war on idolatry but can actually assert that "the most notorious historical example of . . . idolization [*sic!*] of an ephemeral self" is the biblical belief in the chosenness of Israel. (*A Study of History*, abridgment of vols. I–VI by D. C. Somervell, [New York and London: Oxford Press, 1947], p. 310).

8. Ibid., p. 244. See also Moses Maimonides, *Guide for the Perplexed*, I, 36: "In examining the Torah and the prophets, you will not find expressions such as 'jealousy' . . . applied to God except in reference to idolatry."

9. See for example, Maimonides, *Mishneh Torah*, Book I, IV, 1.

10. See for example, *Midrash Genesis Rabba*, Noah, XXXIV, 8.

11. *Babylonian Talmud, Tractate Shabbat*. 105b.

12. See Plato's *Timaeus*.

13. *Grosser Katechismus*, commentary on the first commandment.

14. The negation is obviously a slip. In view of the following, one is almost tempted to regard it as Freudian.

15. *Church Dogmatics*, II, 1, T. H. Parker et al., trans. (Edinburgh: Clark, 1957), p. 431.

16. Ibid., IV, 1, C. W. Bromiley, trans. (Edinburgh: Clark, 1956), p. 703.

17. Ibid., p. 433.

18. *Against the Stream* (London: S.C.M. Press 1954), p. 115.

19. *Systematic Theology*, I (Chicago: University of Chicago Press, 1951), p. 13.

20. Ibid., p. 128.

21. As will emerge in our subsequent exposition, "The Process of Demythol-

ogizing," this dilemma is not wholly fair to Tillich, which is why we put it in the form of an open question. The context of the Apollo passage shows that Tillich is himself aware of the dilemma. It also suggests, however, that he can escape from it only by means of a quasi-Hegelian turn that defines ancient idolatrous religion as a partial truth whose idolatry lies only in its claim to comprehensiveness, and defines nonidolatrous truth in terms of comprehensiveness. Within such a framework there can be no such thing as absolute idolatry, and one might well ask Tillich (as, incidentally, Hegel himself) whether he would grant to Baal and Moloch what all of us would like to grant to Apollo. We have, of course, dealt with Hegel in ch. 3. See, in ch. 5, "Heidegger."

22. If any sweeping judgment may be made about all present forms of "radical" theology (a subject transcending the scope of this book), it is that their self-styled modernity makes them far more obtuse to modern idolatry than either Barth or Tillich.

23. *Judaism and Modern Man* (New York: Farrar, Straus and Young, 1951), p. 75.

24. *God in Search of Man* (New York: Farrar, Straus and Cudahy, 1955), p. 119.

25. It will be remembered that these questions have been dealt with (albeit within limited contexts) in all the previous chapters of this book.

26. See ch. 3, note 159.

27. See Emil L. Fackenheim, *The Religious Dimension in Hegel's Thought*, (Bloomington: Indiana University Press, 1968), chs. 5 and 6.

28. A proverb that was much quoted in Germany in the 1930s is to the effect that the soup is not as hot on the table as on the stove. Among the statements reflecting inability to take the leap from "theory" to execution one must surely reckon Heidegger's "The *Führer* himself and he alone is German reality and its law, today and henceforth." (Written in 1933, quoted in Maurice Friedman, ed., *The Worlds of Existentialism* [New York: Random House, 1964], p. 530.)

29. The distinction between Nazism and Italian fascism is admirably developed in Hannah Arendt, *The Origins of Totalitarianism* (New York: Meridian, 1958). Further, in contrast with Soviet communism, Nazism could never have survived either a turn to a policy of coexistence or a repudiation of the cult of personality.

30. Quoted by Herbert Luethy in "Der Führer," *The Commentary Reader* (New York: Atheneum, 1966), p. 64 (italics added).

31. See Martin Heidegger's shocking statement cited in n. 28 and discussed in ch. 5, "Heidegger."

32. We refer, of course, to the title of the notorious book by the Nazi Alfred Rosenberg, second in the Nazi canon only to *Mein Kampf*.

33. For a criticism of some of these theologians, see "On the Self-Exposure of Faith to the Modern-Secular World," *Quest for Past and Future* (Bloomington: Indiana University Press, 1968, ch. 18; Boston: Beacon, 1970).

34. By Hubert Selby Jr., (New York: Grove Press, 1965).

35. *Babylonian Talmud, Yoma* 9b. The passage cites, in addition to idolatry, harlotry and murder among the causes of the destruction of the first Temple.

Chapter 5

EXISTENTIALIST FINALE—AND BEGINNING

1. According to such qualified critics as Leo Strauss and Karl Löwith, Franz Rosenzweig's *Star of Redemption* is the philosophical equal of Martin Heidegger's *Being and Time*. Yet Löwith is forced to report:

If Heidegger ever had a "contemporary" who deserved the name in a more than temporal sense, it was this German Jew whose major works, published six years before *Being and Time*, were not even remotely known to Heidegger or his pupils. The similarity in origin between the "new thought" of Heidegger and that of Rosenzweig, although it did not become common knowledge, was apparent to Rosenzweig. ("M. Heidegger and F. Rosenzweig: A Postscript of *Being and Time*," *Nature, History and Existentialism* [Evanston: Northwestern University Press, 1966], p. 52.)

Despite advanced age, Martin Buber did not shrink from the task of a detailed critique of Heidegger and Sartre (*Eclipse of God* [New York: Harper Torchbooks, 1957], pp. 63–78; also *Nachlese* [Heidelberg: Lambert Schneider, 1965], pp. 136–138). Yet neither thinker has troubled to reply or, so far as one can tell, even to take notice.

Unlike Rosenzweig, Buber has been widely influential in and even beyond the existentialist movement. But not much attention is necessary for the discovery that precisely to the degree to which his thought has been influential has it also been emasculated, wittingly or unwittingly, of its Jewish content.

2. Reported by Harold Rosenberg, "Does the Jew Exist? Sartre's Morality Play about Anti-Semitism," ed. A. A. Cohen, *Arguments and Doctrines* (New York: Harper & Row, 1970), p. 6.

3. *Anti-Semite and Jew* (New York: Schocken, 1948), p. 71. The French edition of the work appeared in 1946 (italics added).

4. Ibid., pp. 10, 17, 18, 21ff.

5. Ibid., p. 49.

6. Ibid., pp. 54, 40ff., 54. The general Sartrean doctrines referred to, are, of course, developed at length in *Being and Nothingness* (New York: Philosophical Library, 1956). Since our present goal is confined to *testing* their applicability to Jewish existence no purpose is served by specific textual references. For an existentialist position that is obliquely critical of Sartre's unhistorical individualism, see Emil L. Fackenheim, *Metaphysics and Historicity* (Milwaukee: Marquette University Press, 1961).

7. Ibid., pp. 73, 72, 57, 58.

8. This distinction will be denied by current ideologies that do not hesitate to blur or deny the difference between physical and "cultural" genocide. It is borne out, however, if we reflect that for the racist the good Negro "keeps his place" whereas for the antisemite there is no place for a Jew to keep. A further distinction may be made in passing. Once, for the white settler of North America, "the only good Indian was a dead Indian." And once, for the Christian antisemite, the only good Jew was a dead Jew or a Christian. (I owe the last-named formulation to the Christian theologian Coert Rylaarsdam.) At the same time, the white settler wished to rob the Indian of his land while the antisemite was not satisfied with robbing the Jew of his money. And when the adjective "Christian" disappeared only the dead Jew remained.

Notes

It will become evident that Sartre's inability to make these distinctions has its origins in his divorce of present existence from the historical past.

9. Elie Wiesel has discovered that some critics have contrasted a "universal vision" with a merely Jewish one in the poetry of Nelly Sachs, and comments: Her greatness lies in her Jewishness, and this makes it belong to all mankind. It is perhaps only natural that there are those who try to remove her, if not to estrange her, from us. But this will never happen. She has many melodies left to sing. . . . What disturbs me is that strangers have stolen them. ("Conversation with Nelly Sachs," *Jewish Heritage* [Spring 1968], p. 33.) What current "democrat" would dare to steal the work of James Baldwin from black Americans? Sartre, unable to make this distinction for the reason cited in the previous note, in the end himself in effect advocates the dissolution of Jewish identity, while at the same time saying not a word about dissolving French identity. For this "exceptionalism" in his thought, see Rosenberg, "Does the Jew Exist?" p. 8.

10. While Sartre's widely reprinted *Existentialism* (New York: Philosophical Library, 1947; sometimes published under the original title *Existentialism is a Humanism*) does no justice to the subtlety of Sartre's thought, it expresses the foregoing conceptions with admirable clarity.

11. For my own concept of historical situation, see Fackenheim, *Metaphysics and Historicity*, especially pp. 48–55.

12. The Catholic historian Malcolm Hay ends his chapter on the Dreyfus affair as follows:

The whole world was watching the drama of Israel, which was also the drama of France, the battle of a mere handful of upright men who withstood a population demented by hate. These gallant few were able in the end to awaken the national conscience and to save their country from a fate which, forty years later, befell the proud Germans—when the devils went into them also, but were not cast out, so that the whole herd ran down the slopes, and perished. (*Europe and the Jews* [Boston: Beacon, 1961], p. 212.)

Where is Sartre's clarion call for an army of upright men to complete the work these gallant few had begun? *Anti-Semite and Jew* ends with the observation that one cannot wait for a future revolution to solve the "Jewish question" (p. 151) and with the call for a league against antisemitism formed by Gentiles rather than Jews (p. 152)—an honorable, but in view of what has preceded, a puny and anticlimactic end. See also, in this chapter, "Conclusion."

13. Sartre, *Anti-Semite and Jew*, p. 136.

14. Ibid., pp. 66–67, 85.

15. In the popularized version of *Existentialism*, Sartre's atheism is given the formulation that any God would be the Creator of the human essence, whereas man's fundamental freedom is the possibility and necessity to create his own essence (pp. 15ff). This version accurately simplifies the doctrine of *Being and Nothingness*. (See for example, pp. 281, 290, 423, 566.) This Sartrean either/or falls far below the level achieved by the dialectic of Hegel and his left-wing followers, discussed earlier in this volume. Only occasionally does a religious dialectic appear in Sartre's thought, such as when a character in *The Devil and the Good Lord* confesses: "I killed God because He divided me from mankind, and now I see that His death has isolated me even more surely" [(New York: Vintage, 1960). p. 147].

From the point of view of Judaism, we have nothing to add to the critique of Sartre's atheism offered in Buber's *Eclipse of God* (New York: Harper Torchbooks, 1957), pp. 65ff., except that we shall leave undecided the correctness of

Notes

William Shearson's ingenious thesis that Sartre's ontology is theologically neutral, his atheism being an "ontic" commitment on his part. (*The Notion of Encounter in Existential Metaphysics* [Unpublished doctoral dissertation, University of Toronto, 1970], pp. 130ff.)

16. *New Outlook*, May 1967, pp. 14ff.

17. Ibid., pp. 18, 17. The passage concerning French and Jewish history deserves to be quoted in full:

> You will surely say that we in France have a tradition too, perhaps not going back three thousand years, but more than two thousand years. Only, there is a difference. Because we have not been the target of persecution, because we have not been expelled from our country, because we have had to fight often enough, but not to keep France whole, to keep its frontiers, to preserve a political way of life, our relations with our tradition are rather weak. Take Vercingetorix, for instance. Vercingetorix is for us somebody about whom we are told in school, and that is all. And when I hear young Jews, even when they have not been born in Israel, speak passionately about the Jewish revolts against the Romans, then I understand that there is something different, that there is really a will to preserve the historical tradition in its deepest sense. Then I understand that in many Jews—I do not say, in every Jew, but in many of the Jews I have met—there is a depth which is historical, and at the same time there is a traditional depth which involves basic contradictions.
>
> Therefore it seems to me—and that is where I want to end—that if the new Israeli, the new Israeli Jew, can develop in peace and can take these contradictions, make them his own and overcome them in action, then he will be—he is already, but he certainly will be one of the richest men that can be found in history. On this last note, and with the hope that this peace will continue, I should like to end. . . .

18. Ibid., pp. 19ff. The four reasons listed by Sartre are: (1) that a "fifth column full of hate" would cause Israel to "explode from within"; (2) that after 20 years, land once owned by Palestinians was otherwise developed, and that returning refugees would "not be satisfied with the land they will be given" instead; (3) that being more fertile, Arabs would soon outnumber Jews; (4) that a country expecting to take in more Jews could not economically absorb an additional 1,200,000 Arabs as well. Sartre here raises more objections than many Israelis. Some might list only the first.

19. "Sartre Looks at the Middle East Again," *Imperialism and the Middle East* (London: Ad Hoc Committee for Peace in the Middle East, n.d.), p. 12. See also note 12.

20. Ibid., p. 13.

21. Ibid.

22. Ibid.

23. Ibid., p. 15. Sartre asserts this to be "the argument of all the Arabs," but does not dissociate himself from it. He goes on to concede that this "argument could equally, *in some way*, be turned against them," but fails both to turn it against them and to indicate the "way" in which this could be done (italics added).

24. Expounding the later Sartre, Wilfred Desan still writes in 1965: ". . . the Jew becomes a Jew only because he is considered as such by the non-Jew. Indeed, all character cannot exist in and for itself, but only for-the-Other" (*The Marxism of Jean Paul Sartre* [New York: Doubleday Anchor, 1966], p. 168).

25. See above, note 15.

26. *Sein und Zeit* (Halle: Niemeyer, 1926, and subsequent unchanged editions); *Being and Time*, trans., John Macquarrie and Edward Robinson (New York:

Notes

Harper & Row, 1962). For the sake of convenience, we shall quote this work by paragraphs only.

27. See Fackenheim, *Metaphysics and Historicity*, pp. 55ff. and especially "The Historicity and Transcendence of Philosophic Truth," *Proceedings of the Seventh Inter-American Congress of Philosophy* (Quebec: Laval, 1967), pp. 77–92. The last-named essay is wholly geared to the subject "Heidegger and historicism."

28. In 1954 the present writer affirmed that "the analysis of the human condition constitutes the necessary prolegomenon for all modern Jewish, and, indeed, all modern theology." (Fackenheim, *Quest for Past and Future*, [Bloomington: Indiana University Press, 1968; Boston: Beacon, 1970], p. 101.) It will soon appear that he now repudiates that earlier affirmation.

29. Among the authors stressing that resemblance are Karl Löwith, Otto Pöggeler, and Hans Jonas. Particularly instructive is Pöggeler's account of Heidegger's early lectures on the phenomenology of religion and on St. Augustine and Neoplatonism (*Der Denkweg Martin Heideggers* [Pfullingen: Neske, 1963], pp. 36ff). Richard Kroner may have been extreme when, in a private discussion with the present writer many years ago, he said that he preferred to have his "human condition" straightforwardly and without scholasticism, that is, from Kierkegaard rather than Heidegger.

30. In the foregoing two paragraphs we abstract from all technical (terminological and other) subtleties, partly because we do not here require them, partly because Heidegger himself requires them only for the ontological goal of *Being and Time*, which has not yet emerged.

31. See "The Historicity and Transcendence of Philosophic Truth," especially p. 88.

32. See Heidegger, *Being and Time*, § 53.

33. Ibid., § 63, § 41, § 53. For a technical discussion of the Heideggerian circle, see Fackenheim, "The Historicity and Transcendence of Philosophic Truth," pp. 87ff.

34. The predecessors include Kant and Hegel. At least Hegel gives Stoicism its dialectical due. (See Emil L. Fackenheim, *Religious Dimension in Hegel's Thought* [Bloomington: Indiana University Press, 1968; Boston, Beacon, 1970], pp. 43ff., 60, 143, 149, 168ff.) Does Heidegger give Stoicism its due? In "M. Heidegger and F. Rosenzweig: A Postscript of *Being and Time*" (pp. 66–67), Karl Löwith writes:

> To make up one's mind depends on the actual possibilities of the historical situations. Hence, Heidegger refuses to be positive or even authoritative as to existential liabilities. The resolve shall constantly be kept open to the whole being *"in posse"* which includes the potential taking back of certain decisions. The resolve thus does not come to any conclusion; it is a constant attitude, formal, like the categorical imperative, and through its formality open to any material determination, provided that it is radical. Suicide, however, does not even remain an open possibility; it is explicitly dismissed, for it would terminate once and for all the possibility of a constant anticipation of a final reality.

However, that the immediate termination just referred to is in fact unauthentic is a thesis that the Stoic may well reject, as *itself* ultimately resting on a *particular* decision on Heidegger's part that is merely "ontic."

35. In "M. Heidegger and F. Rosenzweig" (p. 76), Löwith concludes his comparison between *Being and Time* and Rosenzweig's *Star of Redemption* with this observation:

> Heidegger inadvertently deserves credit for the fact that his radical temporalization of truth and existence renewed and brought attention to a question

Notes

that his Jewish contemporary raised, the question concerning eternal being—the eternal God or the world that always exists without beginning and without end. See also note 48.

36. Heidegger, *Being and Time*, § 74.

37. In "The Commune in *Being and Time*" (*Dialogue*, 1971, pp. 708–726), an essay in pursuit of a different objective, my colleague Professor Graeme Nicholson has arrived independently at the conclusion that the *Volk* is an alien and unjustified intruder into *Being and Time*.

38. William Richardson, "Heidegger and God—and Professor Jonas," *Thought* (Spring 1965), p. 39. This essay is a response to Hans Jonas, "Heidegger and Theology," *The Phenomenon of Life* (New York: Harper & Row, 1966), pp. 235–261. Among other sources that should be consulted are Guido Schneeberger, *Nachlese zu Heidegger* (published privately in Bern, 1961 [the organization of the material here offered, though not the material itself, has been subject to legitimate criticism]); Francois Fedier, "A Propos de Heidegger: Une Lecture Dénoncée," *Critique* (Juillet 1967), pp. 672–686; John D. Caputo, "Heidegger's Original Ethics," *The New Scholasticism* (Winter 1971), pp. 127–38; Martin Buber, *Eclipse of God*, p. 70ff. A brief selection from the relevant material may conveniently be found in Maurice Friedman, *The Worlds of Existentialism* (New York: Random House, 1964), pp. 527ff.

39. Schneeberger, *Nachlese zu Heidegger*, p. 136; Friedman, *The Worlds of Existentialism*, p. 530. On this statement, see also Jonas, *The Phenomenon of Life*, pp. 247ff. and Buber, *Eclipse of God*, p. 77.

40. Jonas, *The Phenomenon of Life*, p. 247.

41. Caputo, "Heidegger's Original Ethics," p. 138.

42. We have been careful to select a statement, not from the *Rektoratsrede* delivered in May 1933, but rather from a manifesto issued in November of that year. The intervening months had given Heidegger much opportunity for observing events and having second thoughts.

43. See, in ch. 3, "Athens and Jerusalem."

44. Jonas, "Heidegger and Theology." This lecture was originally delivered in April 1964 at a consultation on hermeneutics convened by the Graduate School of Drew University.

45. Ibid., pp. 248, 256, 258. Jonas said to his Christian listeners: "I hope you agree with me that there are demons" (p. 254). Whether their responses bore out this hope is not known to this writer.

46. Jonas is right when he insists that it has a "blasphemous ring" to Jewish and Christian ears alike to "hear man hailed as the shepherd of being when he has just so dismally failed to be his brother's keeper." He is wrong, however, when, taking over the traditional Christian dichotomy between "*homo sub lege*" and "*homo sub gratia*," he implicitly denies what is now conceded by some Christian theologians themselves—that there is Grace *in* the Torah (pp. 258, 261).

47. "Andenken," *Erläuterung zu Hölderlins Dichtung* (Frankfurt: Klostermann, 1951), p. 108. We are using Buber's translation.

48. Buber, *Eclipse of God*, p. 73. Pöggeler, in addition to giving detailed references to Heidegger's earlier selective attention to St. Paul, St. Augustine, Luther, and other Christian figures (see note 28), also observes that "the whole Jewish-Christian tradition has no longer an original claim for [the later] Heidegger" (p. 192). Yet, though himself citing the criticism of Buber's that we have just cited, his criticism of the later Heidegger culminates only in the demand

Notes

that, if Heidegger's quest for the Divine is to be truly open, it must be "open as well to the Christian possibility of faith" (p. 194). A *Jewish* possibility of faith Pöggeler fails to consider.

49. Leo Strauss, "Preface to the English Edition of *Spinoza's Critique of Religion*," *The Jewish Expression*, Judah Goldin, ed. (New York: Bantam, 1970), p. 357. Strauss also refers the reader to Heidegger's *Nietzsche* (Pfullingen: Neske, 1961), II, p. 320, a passage instructive to cite:

> Negatively, the liberation toward the new freedom is a disentanglement from the security of salvation which rests on faith in revelation and is Christian-ecclesiastical. Within this latter, the truth of salvation is not confined to the believing relation to God but at the same time decides about what-is. The meaning of philosophy within this limitation is to be the handmaiden of theology. The order of what-is is the creation of the Creator-God, which through the Redeemer-God has again been raised and brought back from the Fall into the supersensual realm. The liberation from this truth-as-securing-of-salvation, however, since it places man into free insecurity and dares the venture of self-choosing, must move toward a freedom which just because of this produces the securing of man and determines security in a new way.

This passage, unlike that cited earlier, abandons any pretense that Jewish as well as Christian faith comes under consideration in Heidegger's later thought. Hence his "thinking" can only be viewed as an *exclusively post-Christian* thinking, and any *Jewish* thinking about "security," "insecurity," and a "liberation" from past forms of philosophy must begin with a genuinely Jewish account of all pertinent matters. (The passage clearly both interprets Nietzsche's thought and gives Heidegger's own.)

For Buber's own view of prophetic insecurity, consider also this statement: "The false prophets make their subconscious a god, whereas for the true prophets their subconscious is subdued by the God of truth. . . ." (*The Prophetic Faith* [New York: Macmillan, 1949], p. 179.) The context makes it clear that the true prophet can have no *absolute* certainty that he *is* true.

50. See Deut. 13:2: "If there appears among you a prophet or dream-diviner and gives you a sign or portent, saying, 'Let us follow and worship another god'—whom you have not experienced—and the sign or portent that he named to you comes true: do not heed the words of that prophet or that dream-diviner. For the Lord your God is testing you. . . ."

51. This distinction, supported below and in the texts cited in note 49, is overlooked in Strauss' otherwise arresting criticism of Buber.

52. Martin Heidegger, "Hölderlin and the Essence of Poetry," *Existence and Being* (London: Vision Press, 1949), p. 304.

53. Genesis 2:19. Citing rabbinic sources, the medieval Jewish commentator Rashi *ad loc.* explicitly connects this human naming of all things with a God who has created them and handed them over for human domination.

54. Heidegger, "Hölderlin and the Essence of Poetry," pp. 305, 307, 311, 313.

55. "Überwindung der Metaphysik," *Vorträge und Aufsätze* (Pfullingen: Neske, 1967), I, pp. 84–85.

56. The essay under discussion is said by Heidegger to consist of "notes toward the surpassing of metaphysics composed between 1936 and 1946" (p. 119). We make allowances for the possibility, normally considered irresponsible, that Heidegger failed to reconsider the passage under discussion before first publishing it in 1951.

57. *Gelassenheit* (Pfullingen: Neske, 1959), p. 17.

Notes

58. Ibid., p. 19. The image of England as the country of soul-less merchants is standard part of vulgar Teutonic ideology, long antedating Nazism. In this connection it is necessary to cite also the following assertions made in *Einführung in die Metaphysik* (Tübingen: Niemeyer, 1953): America and Russia are, "metaphysically considered," the same "frenzy of a boundless technology and a soil-less organization of human mediocrity," whereas Germans are "the metaphysical people" *par excellence* (pp. 28–29); the quest for Being is connected with the fate of Europe, the fate of the whole globe is decided in Europe, and the German *Dasein* is the center of Europe (p. 32); and, finally, there is an "inner truth and greatness" in the Nazi movement (p. 152). The book consists of lectures given in 1935, but the preface written in 1953 states that "repetitions have been cut, errors removed, the inexact has been clarified."

When the book appeared in Germany a public furor resulted about the last-named assertion, with Heidegger himself taking the rare step of issuing a terse statement. (See Paul Hühnerfeld, *In Sachen Heidegger* [Hamburg: Hoffmann & Campe, 1959], pp. 104ff.) However, the statement speaks for itself. The other two statements should be compared with Hegel's guess that the World Spirit might emigrate from Germany and Europe to America. Hegel's outlook is open. Heidegger merely updates ideological aberrations that have plagued the German mind ever since the Napoleonic wars, and certainly since the death of Hegel.

59. See Heidegger, "Hölderlin and the Essence of Poetry." See also ch. 5, "Protestant Concepts of Idolatry."

60. Manès Sperber, . . . *Than a Tear in the Sea* (New York: Bergen Belsen Memorial Press, 1967), pp. xiii–xv. The essay was written in March 1964.

61. Ibid., p. xiv.

62. Sartre states in 1946 "the Jew of today is in full war," but despite this admission, made after the collapse of the Third Reich, does not then or ever after reach the radical conclusion that this "war" can come to an end only with either the total end of antisemitism or with its total impotence.

63. See for example, his preface to Frantz Fanon, *The Wretched of the Earth* (New York: Grove Press, 1968), pp. 7–31.

64. Sperber, *Than a Tear in the Sea*, p. xv.

65. Löwith's essay "M. Heidegger and F. Rosenzweig" makes the foregoing points clearly and is in fact required reading, particularly for theologians. Rosenzweig himself was prophetic when he wrote in 1923 that European culture was threatened with imminent collapse, that it could be saved only with the help of "super-European, superhuman powers" one of which was Judaism, and that if these powers were bound to be secularized again and again in the process of being Europeanized, their power forever again to re-enter this process confirmed their "eternity" (*Briefe* [Berlin: Schocken, 1935], p. 476).

66. Martin Buber, *Die Stunde und die Erkenntnis* (Berlin: Schocken, 1936), p. 13.

67. In his essay "Heidegger and God—and Professor Jonas" Richardson reports the following anecdote:

> Two years ago at a reception, someone who had read my book made reference to the chapter on the Epilogue to *What is Metaphysics?* that begins (banally enough) by saying: "1943 was a prolific year." The gentleman said: "I remember 1943 well, Father. I was just talking with some of your friends about it, regaling them with amusing stories—they laughed and laughed. You know in 1943 I was in one of the concentration camps. It was a very prolific year indeed."

In the "Epilogue" referred to by Richardson, Heidegger admittedly deals deeply

[263]

with what he considers *the* basic philosophical question since the Greeks—"the wonder of wonders—*that* something *is*." He might have been saved from moral vacuity had contemporary events induced him to turn to a question hardly less basic to the Greeks (not to speak of the Jews)—"whence cometh evil?"

68. In a frequently reprinted open letter to Gandhi, most conveniently accessible in Will Herberg, ed., *The Writings of Martin Buber* (New York: Meridian, 1956), pp. 281ff. Buber's Zionism, of course, antedates that letter by several decades.

69. It would be an instructive exercise to try to rewrite § 74 of *Being and Time* so as to do "ontic" justice to authentic Jewish community in our time.

70. Elie Wiesel, *One Generation After* (New York: Random House, 1970), pp. 3–9.

71. See ch. 3, "Judaism and Hegelianism: A Contemporary Encounter," for our views on what is there termed a contemporary, post-Hegelian Hegelianism. A comparison between that section and the present section will leave the reader in no doubt as to the writer's view (it may be added, after many years of holding otherwise) that Hegelianism far exceeds existentialism not only in intrinsic profundity but also in contemporary fruitfulness, including such as is displayed in an encounter with Judaism.

72. Abraham J. Heschel, *Israel: An Echo of Eternity* (New York: Farrar, Straus & Giroux, 1969), pp. 5ff.

INDEX

Index

believers and unbelievers, 17, 23, 24, 25, 26, 66
believing openness, 25
Belzec, 225
Ben Zakkai, Rabbi Yohanan, 177
Bergen-Belsen, 77
Berlin, 126
betrayal, 10
Bevin, Ernest, 224
beyond good and evil, 191
bias, anti-judaic, 22; Protestant, 28
Bible, Christian, 64; Jewish, 64, 173, 179–180, 182, 185, 188; *see also* Torah
Bickerman, Elias, 106
blacks, 197, 204, 205, 209, 211, 212
blik, 10, 18; religion as, 17; universally possible, 18
Bloch, Ernest, 135, 151, 152, 165
Buber, Martin, 96, 131, 160–161, 198, 202, 212, 218, 220–221, 222, 226
Buchenwald, 77
Bullock, Allan, 193

Canaan, 152, 176
capacity, universal human, 38
capitalism, 145
catastrophe, 165
categorical imperative, 60, 67, 68
causes, "Supernatural," 13
challenge, pristine, 45
"chamber serfs," 114
change, political, 95, 99, 118
charisma, 192
choice, eschatological, 10; freedom of, 46
Christ, 26, 113, 143, 182; as Truth and Love, 74
Christianity, 3, 11, 15, 19, 21, 23, 89, 97, 98, 110–111, 116, 119, 127, 135–150 *passim*, 183, 213, 216; as absolute religion, 161; anti-, pre-, and post-, 138, 148, 149, 150; antinomy, 161, 163; and consensus, 15; contemporary, 219; criticism of, 148; defense of, 17; eschatological expectation, 20; freedom, 143; intolerance, 145; liberal, 18; and martyrdom, 73–74; as misfortune, 143; Nazi, 157; orthodox, 18; otherworldly, 23; perfection of Jewish egoism, 147; religionless, 158; as religion of religions, 17; religious self-understanding, 122; representational, 160; Trinitarian, 112
church, 114; German-Christian, 157, 181
circle, ontic-ontological, 214, 225
circumcision, 140
city state, 104

civilization, critical self-consciousness of, 4
Cohen, Hermann, 131–132, 133
commandments, 43, 47, 49, 50, 177; God-given, 52; man's appropriation, 51; as moral, 59; performed for God's sake, 62; teleological suspension, 56
commitment, 112
communication, 65
community, 217; human, 66; Jewish, 75, 207, 208
composition, divine-human, 124
comprehension, Hegel's philosophical, 125
comprehensiveness, all-mediating, 83
condition, human, 204, 213
confidence, absolute, 165; of Jews, 96, 164–165; Messianic, 165
conflict, religious, 142
confrontation, 95–101
conquest, right of, 137
conscience, 45
consciousness, religious, 34; Divine in, 92
consensus, 15
consent, 73
content, 55, 56
contingency, 154–155
contrast, 95; Greek-Jewish, 103
covenant, Christian, 164; Jewish, 9, 10, 29, 66, 67, 75, 97, 99, 105, 118, 125, 128, 132, 153, 162, 165, 168; with a jealous God, 197–198
creatio ex nihilo, 92, 195
Creation, 87
creativity, religious, 130; spiritual, 45
crisis, 156, 166
criticism, 142; impartial philosophical, 23; Jewish evasion of empiricist, 11
crucial experiment, 20
Crusades, 21, 114
cult, Christian, 112; Jewish, 94
culture, 128; European, 127; German, 84; Greek, 106; Western, 107

data, 13; empirically ultimate, 132; miraculous and revelatory, 14
David, 99
Day of Atonement, 29
death, 72, 74, 77, 173, 214, 224; Jewish, 168
"death by a thousand qualifications," 10, 16
decay, contemporary spiritual, 134
decision, 206
Deism and deists, 90, 91, 138
Deity, alien, 41; nonexistent, 140; private relation with, 64; tribal, 93

Index

Index

falsification, 16–22

falsity, 26

fascism, 158; *see also* Nazis (m)

Fate, 93

fear, 94; and willing, 50

Fear and Trembling, 34

feeling(s), 13, 23, 24

Feuerbach, Ludwig, 135–153 *passim*, 160, 185, 190

Fichte, Johann, 123, 190; and moral self, 191

fidelity, 106

flight, 155, 156, 168; unauthentic, 204, 207

fragmentation, contemporary spiritual, 156, 157

France and the French, 131, 203–213 *passim*

freedom, 98, 102, 113, 114, 121, 125, 163, 187; European, 131; Greco-Roman, 105; heteronomous, 46; human, 46, 160, 161, 162; modern philosophical, 122; modern secular-Protestant, 123; unconditional, 46; Western, 105

French Revolution, 4, 121

Freud and Freudians, 27, 186, 195, 196; reductionism, 28

frivolousness, 93

Führer, 187, 192, 193, 194, 195, 217, 223

future, absolute, 156; contingent, 154–155

Gans, Eduard, 127, 128

Geiger, Abraham, 129–130

Genesis, 222

genius, "free" Jewish, 129

genocide, 223

Gentiles, 38, 57, 97, 178, 225

Germanism, 86

Germanness, 191

Germany and Germans, 84, 126, 131, 135, 136, 157, 193, 217

ghetto, 106

Giver, divine, 47–50

God, absolute duty toward, 63; against God, 22; alien, 193; anthropomorphic, 112; a priori conception of, 59; biblical, 188; dead, 192; destruction of, 135; dialogue with Abraham, 65, 66; direct awareness of, 25; in distinction to man, 88, 119; dying and living in love of, 72; empirically manifest, 11; existence, 21, 25; of Exodus, 151; expulsion, 180; falling away from, 118; as Father and King, 97; fear of, 50–51, 91, 125; into flesh, 113; and future, 23; "glorified in Himself," 164; as god, 107; hatred of idolatry, 179; honor to,

92; humility before, 49; as immanent, 104, 112; immediate or absolute relation with, 35; infinite, 92; jealous, 176–179; of the Jews, 89, 93, 97, 107, 109, 125; of Judaism, 140; Judeo-Christian image of, 68; of Judeo-Christian tradition, 219; of Israel, 176, 177, 183, 189; infinite, 190; love of, 36, 55, 62; loving, 16, 21, 23, 51; of Moses, 82, 100, 113, 121, 123; and mercy, 19, 20, 178, 179; and one's neighbor, 48–49; and pain, 19; particularistic, 151; relation to individual, 36; and sacrifice, 34–35; self-alienation from, 182; of Sinai, 152; of Spinoza, 125; sporadic manifestations, 92; state of, 108, 116, 117; and suffering, 19; tempting of, 75; as transcendent and immanent, 111, 120; as tribal deity, 129; true, 198; turning to, 29; unheeding, 27; voice of, 10, 29; in the world, 94; worldless, 104, 105, 111

God-idea, 82, 132

God-hypothesis, 10, 14–15, 16, 190

gods, false and true, 85, 119, 179, 180, 198, 220, 226, 227; metaphorical, 197, 198

Good, 159

Goodness, 92

Grace, divine, 69, 97, 118, 159, 160, 161, 162, 163

Graetz, Heinrich, 127, 128

Greece and Greeks, 5, 64, 68, 92, 93, 102, 179; and beauty, 103; historicity, 104

Grundidee, 98–125 *passim*, 164

Guide for the Perplexed, 81

gulf, between God and man, 47

Hadrian, 70, 75, 117, 177

Hananiah, 76

Ḥanukah, 109

hatred, 68

Hegel and Hegelianism, 43, 81–169 *passim*, 177, 184, 190, 196, 201, 208, 228; account of Judaism, 89–95; challenge of, 128; conclusions concerning, 152–153; contemporary crisis, 166; historicity, 100; and Judaism, 88, 153–169; judgment, 102–103; left-wing, 124, 134–168; philosophical comprehension, 125; philosophical integrity, 85; philosphy refuted by history, 110; philosophy as "science," 122; self-understanding, 132, 133, 137; system, 99–100, 101, 134; thought-experiment, 159, 160; transformation in, 134–135, 137

Index

Index

Index

Luther and Lutheranism, 136, 138, 147, 148, 180–181, 182, 183, 184, 213
Lykurgos, 81, 82, 94, 102

Maccabee, Judah, 109
Maccabee, Mattathias, 108, 109
Maccabees, 97, 106–110, 113, 115
magic, 14, 15
Maidenek, 77, 225
Maimonides, Moses, 58, 59, 69, 72, 75, 81
man, 137; authentic, 204; in distinction to God, 89, 119; as man, 50, 205; as person, 68; religious, 42–43; Sartrean, 206; virtuous, 50
Manicheanism, 204
martyrdom, 66, 119; Jewish, 20, 73, 75–76; for mankind, 61; religious, 73; see also *Kiddush Hashem*
Marx and Marxism, 4–5, 85, 87, 131–153 *passim*, 183, 185, 190, 191, 195, 196; ignorance of Judaism, 150; nontheological, 145, 147
massacres, 164
mass-delusion, 14
materialism, 147
Mayence (Mainz) (Germ.), 72, 74, 75
means, 60
mediation, 84; divine-human, 93, 123–124; universal, 158
Mein Kampf, 192
Mendelssohn, Moses, 89
merit, 66
mercy, 56; in judgment, 67
Mesha, 54, 56
Messiah and Messianism, 9, 21, 29, 105, 125, 130, 131, 132, 133, 137, 152, 165, 169
Messianic age, 20–33, 82, 87, 88, 167, 169
Micah, 49, 56, 64, 69
Middle Ages, 13, 86, 89, 111, 112, 114, 119, 120, 206
Midrashim, 5, 15, 33, 34, 53–76 *passim*, 95, 115, 119, 162, 163, 164, 165, 168–169, 173, 176
militancy, Jewish, 207
miracles, 14, 15
Mishael, 76
misunderstanding, 28
Moab, 54, 56
mobs, 72, 75, 115
Mohammedanism, 183
Moloch, 189
money, 146
monotheism, 34, 93, 174
moral imperative, 225
morality, a priori standard of rational, 59; core of Jewish, 49; creative, 41; foundations, 39; three-term, 53

moral law, authorship, 42–43; autonomous, 40; as bridge, 47–50; conformity with, 35; and external sanction, 48; God-given, 41–43; intrinsic value, 70; obedience to, 48; prior to love, 52; rational as well as revealed, 68; revealed, 37–53; written, 38
moral theology, 48, 56, 59; Kantian, 40–43
Moses and Mosaism, 14, 81–82, 103, 107, 113, 118, 122, 152, 164, 169, 218; obscurantism, 82
Mt. Carmel, 9, 10, 15, 22
Mt. Moriah, 33, 53, 54, 57
murder, 57, 58, 63, 68, 69, 75, 157, 195
mystery, 227, 229
mysticism, 208

naming, 222
National Socialism, 182
naturalism, 196
nature, worship, 139
Nazis(m), 5, 21, 72, 75, 77, 133, 157, 164, 168, 192, 207, 215, 216, 222, 223, 226; goals, 193; and Heidegger, 217, 218; idolatry, 175, 181, 187, 193, 194; revelation of, 158
Nebuchadnezzar, 76, 117
negativity, absolute, 120, 126
Negroes, *see* blacks
neighbor, 48–49; love of, 36
neo-orthodoxy, 141, 157, 158
neo-Kantianism, 133
neo-Lutheranism, 192
Neoplatonism, 104, 122, 134, 156
Nero, 61, 182
neuroses, 195
New Moon, 107
New Testament, 22, 98, 112, 113
Niebuhr, Reinhold, 198
Nietzsche, Friedrich, 182, 185, 190, 191, 195, 196, 218
Noah and Noahidic covenant, 36, 38, 58, 97
nonunion, divine-human, 90–91, 111, 123
nothingness, 16
Notion, 159–160, 161, 162, 165, 168
nuclear war, 21

obedience, 40
obligation, 40
obscurantism, 82
Ockham, William of, 13
Of Miracles, 14
Old Testament, 15, 177, 181–182
ontology, 214
Other, 201

Index

Index

system, "universal," 132

ta'ame mitzvut, 96
Talmud, 95, 97, 115, 118, 140, 141, 157, 173, 176
technology, 14, 156
Temple, 107, 116, 197
temporality, human, 213
terror, 121
testimony, Jewish, 167
Teutonism, 191
Thales, 92, 179
theism and theists, 14; "Judaic-Christian," 19
theologians, 13
theological morality, 48, 56, 59
theology, 219; American, 195
thinkers, Jewish religious, 174; medieval Jewish, 68, 82, 132; modern Jewish, 176; Protestant, 180–184
thought, 89, 122, 159–160; as abstracting from existence, 201; all-mediating, 83, 85; liberation of Jewish, 202; modern, 37, 155, modern Jewish, 4; nonobjectifying, 219; philosophical, 161, 228; subjective-objective, 90; theological, 112
threat, 155–157
Tillich, Paul, 181, 182–184, 189
toleration, 108
Torah, 35, 53, 57, 63, 67, 69, 70, 81, 97, 117, 118, 130, 173, 176; assimilation to Hellenism, 109; bridge between God and man, 47–50; in exile, 118–119; interpretation, 109; living by, 51; oral, 96; positivity, 96; restoration, 108
totalitarianism, 193, 195
Toynbee, Arnold, 82–83, 177
tradition, Jewish, 212
transcendence, 111
transformation, 134–135, 137, 139, 154; atheistic left-wing, 152; radical, 164
transmythologization, 160
tribalism, relapse into, 158
triumphalism, American, 195–196
Truth, 82, 110, 112, 122, 124, 142, 159; all-comprehensive, 83; anachronistic, 84; Davidic star of, 226; religious, 90, 91, 95, 138
turning, 69, 218
twentieth century, 175; myth of, 193
tyranny, philosophical, 161

ultimacy, true, 183
unclarity, methodological, 185
Understanding, 156, 157

unfreedom, 98, 125; Jewish, 97, 99, 103, 143
unhappiness, 104–105
union, divine-human, 90–91, 103, 111, 123; finite-infinite, 103; secular-religious, 123; of union and nonunion, 91
United States, 211
universal, the, 63
universalism, 4, 83, 177; of prophets, 98
universality, 39–40
"University Discussion," 19
Unmensch, 136
unmoved and unmoving, 105
untruth, medieval, 119–120
USSR, 147, 211, 228

Verein für die Kultur und Wissenschaft der Juden, 126–127
verification, 12–15; eschatological empirical, 19
virtue, 50
voice, divine, or false, 10, 29, 33, 36, 57, 58; empirical, 69; immediate, 34–35; of Sinai, 167
Volk, 187, 193, 194, 216, 217

wager, 21
Wailing Wall, 229
war, 222, 223
Warsaw Ghetto, 224, 225
Weltanschauung, religious and nonreligious, 17
West, 101, 104, 111, 144, 216; empirical, 195
will, divine, 47, 51, 55; human, 55; subject of the law, 39
wisdom, 10, 11; power of, 91; of world, 102
Wisdom, John, 10
Wissenschaft des Judentums, 127
withdrawal, 24, 25
Word, 162, 169
world, absolutely posited finite, 91; bourgeois-Protestant, 120; Christian, 89; divinely posited, 92; as finite, 92; flight from, 122, 134; God in, 94; godless, 111; Greco-Roman, 88, 89; Greeks at home in, 102; "inversion" of, 113; Jewish response to, 126; modern, 100, 122, 123, 124, 126, 129, 135, 137, 153, 155, 158, 166; secular-Protestant, 82, 88, 100; transfigured, 23; "ultimate," 135; wisdom of, 102
world-historical comprehension of Hegel, 125
world-historical viewpoint, 154, 157, 158

Index

World Soul, 179

World Spirit, 117, 156

World War, 131

Worms (Germ.), 71, 72, 74, 75

worship, alien forms, 97; false, 180; of finite objects, 179, 185–186; idolatrous, 186, 187; metaphorical, 197

"Yisroel-Man," 130

Yohanan, Rabbi, 162

Yom Kippur, *see* Day of Atonement

Zion, 226

Zionism, 90, 129, 133, 167, 207, 211, 212, 224

Zunz, Leopold, 127

4